The Best of

TORONTO

Editor
Jim Burns

Contributing Editors
Byron Ayanoglu, Anne Z. Cooke, Peter Crossley,
Kathleen Sloan, Deborah Sroloff, Steve Veale, Cynthia Wine

Associate Editor
Catherine Jordan

Chief Restaurant Critic
Edward Guiliano

Additional editorial assistance
Mary Adachi

Page Makeup
Kevin MacDowell

Operations
Alain Gayot

Directed by
André Gayot

Prentice Hall
Travel

New York ▪ London ▪ Toronto ▪ Sydney ▪ Tokyo ▪ Singapore

Other Gault Millau Guides Available
from Prentice Hall

The Best of Chicago
The Best of Florida
The Best of France
The Best of Hawaii
The Best of Hong Kong
The Best of Italy
The Best of London
The Best of Los Angeles
The Best of New England
The Best of New Orleans
The Best of New York
The Best of Paris
The Best of San Francisco
The Best of Thailand
The Best of Washington, D.C.

Published by Prentice Hall
A division of Simon & Schuster Inc.
15 Columbus Circle
New York, NY 10023

Copyright © 1991
by Gault Millau, Inc.

All rights reserved
including the right of reproduction
in whole or in part in any form

PRENTICE HALL TRAVEL and colophons
are registered trademarks of Simon & Schuster Inc.

Please address all comments or advertising queries
regarding *The Best of Toronto* to:
Mr. Alain Gayot, Vice President
Gault Millau, Inc.
P.O. Box 361144
Los Angeles, CA 90036

Library of Congress Cataloging-in-Publication Data
The Best of Toronto / editor, Jim Burns; contributing editors, Byron Ayanoglu . . . [et al.]; associate editor, Catherine Jordan.
   p.   cm.
Includes index.
ISBN 0-13-085341-0: U.S.$17.00
  1. Toronto (Ont.)–Description–Guide-books. I. Burns, Jim, 1952- .
II. Ayanoglu, Byron. III. Jordan, Catherine.
F1059.5.T683B47 1991
917.13'541044–dc20   91-10292

Printed in the United States of America

CONTENTS

INTRODUCTION 1

RESTAURANTS 5
In these candid, penetrating, often amusing reviews, you'll learn about Toronto's amazing variety of restaurants. We'll take you around the city, sampling its food from the high and mighty temples of gastronomy to the gutsy neighborhood places where ethnic cuisine reigns.

QUICK BITES 91
The simple pleasures, visited by experts for your delectation. Reviews of cafés, delis, diners, noodle shops, burger joints, sandwich shops and more.

HOTELS 103
A hotel guide to suit every taste and budget. Where to live like a king or queen. Where to get the most for your money, or the best service.

NIGHTLIFE 129
A tour of the city's most stimulating and exciting nightspots, with tried-and-true advice about what goes on in Toronto after dark.

SHOPS 147
A listing of where to buy the best Toronto has to offer, from antique armoires and Victorian jewelry to designer boutiques and an electic assortment of bookshops.

SIGHTS 173
Touring with Gault Millau means discovering the special, secret places that even many Torontonians don't know about. Unusual finds, fascinating tours and detailed reviews of the classic sights and sites.

ARTS 189
Looking at the museums, the galleries and the cultural events that make Toronto special.

OUT OF TORONTO 201
Around and about the city, with excursions to Stratford, Cottage Country, Niagara Falls and Niagara-on-the-Lake.

BASICS 231
Everything you need to know about getting around like a native. Includes helpful phone numbers and a calendar of noteworthy events.

MAPS 241
Finding your way around Toronto and its environs, including detailed maps of downtown and the Toronto Transit Commission system.

INDEX 249

INTRODUCTION

TORONTO THE GREAT

Toronto's history can be charted through various comments and quotes over the years (albeit loosely): in 1792, John Graves Simcoe, the city's first governor general, carped that "the city's site was better calculated for a frog pond or beaver meadow than for the residence of human beings."

This earliest description of Canada's largest metropolitan center was found in a 1792 entry in Simcoe's diaries. We can forgive the statesman—who was sent by Britain's King George III to establish law and order in this colony—his bitter remarks quite easily when we imagine him leaving the luxuries of London for the unruly wilderness of the New World. The picture had brightened considerably a half century later, when author Charles Dickens duly noted that ". . . the town itself is full of life and motion, bustle, business and improvement."

Certainly, these comments are a far cry from the accolades heaped on the city today, aptly summed up by actor Peter Ustinov's quip that "Toronto is New York run by the Swiss." Torontonians favor the very succinct summation by contemporary writer Anthony Astrachan: "A city that works."

And that it does. At about three million inhabitants, this is now the largest city in Canada, the financial and business center, the cultural and artistic core, the publishing and literary base, the wining and dining playground. For most Americans who see the daily decay of their urban centers, Toronto is the stuff of their dreams—safe, clean, modern, friendly, well-managed—the Disneyland of North American cities. Today's inhabitants, by the way, pronounce the city name as "Trawna" dropping all the *o*'s and the final *t*. You can always tell a newcomer or visitor if they verbalize the name in correct phonetic English.

Some time during the mid-twentieth century, the epithet "the Good" was added to the city name. This was a backhanded compliment to the dull and boring lifestyle led by the genteel citizenry of former Hogtown (Toronto's name in an earlier incarnation); for though it had grown, it was still a small-minded provincial town. As W.C. Fields is said to have drawled once, "I went to Toronto last Sunday. It was closed."

The base for the Toronto transformation came after World War II when Canada opened its borders to European and Asian immigration. These New Canadians changed the face of the city seemingly overnight: new cultures, new languages and new religions broadened the scope and understanding of the staid Establishment. Principally, the city achieved its minor renaissance through one of the age-old primal necessities—food.

INTRODUCTION

Suddenly the standard Torontonian dish of roast beef and potatoes was replaced with Italian spaghetti, Chinese noodles, Jewish latkes, Greek souvlaki, Japanese sushi, Hungarian goulash, Jamaican jerked pork, German schnitzel, Thai saté. The tight WASP collar was loosened as Toronto embraced multiculturalism through exotic foods from round the globe.

More than 70 ethnic groups now live in metropolitan Toronto. A city of neighborhoods and neighbors, in recent years the cultural mix might leave you spinning. For instance, a stroll along College Street will find a recently arrived Polish "New Canadian" grilling some hearty kielbasa, while his Thai neighbor whips up those perfect sweet-hot noodles; across the way is the favorite shop of local Russian Jews, which serves the best bagels in town; down the block a West Indian bakery offers a spicy beef roti.

Don't think of Toronto as the proverbial melting pot for these diverse ethnic backgrounds; it's more like a multicultural mulligan stew with a colorful yet stylish blending of the globe's culinary and cultural offerings. The wave of cultural immigration during the 1950s and 1960s prepared Toronto the Good for the coming changes in style and thinking that would help the city evolve into Toronto the Great. The initial shock to the city fathers came in 1965 when the startling design of the new city hall—two huge arched twin towers by Finnish architect Viljo Revell—took shape beside the old, stately city hall. When this modern structure was completed, and the city failed to self-destruct by fire and brimstone (as predicted by doomsaying adversaries), people began to realize, "Hey, maybe we can loosen our belts a little! Perhaps we don't have to be dull and boring to be respectable!"

The city began a campaign, with a spirit bordering on vengeance, to throw off the shackles of a solid, staid past and charge breakneck into the future. Bank towers of bold gold design flaunted traditions of conservative gray; bigger became better; the city's nightlife exploded; attitudes changed overnight and, best of all, the flow to the suburbs reversed itself as young working families moved back into the city core to become part of a vibrant downtown scene of bars and restaurants, nightlife and nightclubs, theater, ballet, opera and movies.

The city came into its own during the 1970s, bursting into the international limelight as one of the great lively urban centers; a city that had always been there, newly transformed and recently discovered. Quite literally, a visitor to Toronto in the 1960s would fail to recognize the Toronto of the 1990s, both in style and in spirit.

The not-so-surprising consequence of all this sudden expansion and new-found popularity is that Torontonians pay the price, which is exactly that: the Price. Everyone wants to live in Toronto, to do business in the city, to visit. And this is reflected in the soaring costs of everything. This has become a most expensive city, but mainly for its inhabitants; it has not yet affected the expense-account businessperson or the visiting tourist family. The Canadian dollar, which fluctuates daily, is approximately 10 percent less than its American counterpart.

Also predictably, the traffic in the city and surrounding highways has practically doubled what it was in the mid-1980s. If you drive into Toronto, it's best to take a

INTRODUCTION

cab, enjoy the sightseeing en route, and let someone else worry about traffic problems.

Though the city may be paying that inevitable price for popularity, these are problems that plague the inhabitant, not the tourist. The visitor to Toronto can just savor all the amenities—the first-class hotels, the fine dining, the funky eateries, sidewalk cafés, the nightlife and trendy bars, dozens of theater performances, the National Ballet and Canadian Opera Company, the sports teams, museums, art galleries and exclusive Bloor Street shopping. A tourist can enjoy sunning on the miles of beaches, walking through any of the many acres of green parkland scattered throughout the city or just strolling at 2 a.m.—safely—along the well-lit, densely populated Yonge Street on a warm summer evening.

Toronto has many faces, and if you long to take in the theater of life that plays constantly in this great urban center, a collection of neighborhoods and neighbors, the players will gladly welcome you to the cultural mélange that is Toronto the Great.

A DISCLAIMER

Readers are advised to remember that prices and conditions change over the course of time. The restaurants, hotels, shops and other establishments reviewed in this book have been reviewed over a period of time, and the reviews reflect the personal experiences of the reviewers. The reviewers and publishers cannot be held responsible for the experiences of the reader related to the establishments reviewed. Readers are invited to write the publisher with ideas, comments and suggestions for future editions.

RESTAURANTS

INTRODUCTION	6
ABOUT THE REVIEWS	7
TOQUE TALLY	9
BY CUISINE	11
RESTAURANTS	14

INTRODUCTION

ETHNICALLY YOURS

How many ethnic cuisines would you expect to find in a cosmopolitan city? In the case of Toronto, the question is akin to asking a visitor to Nebuchadnezzar's fabled Babylon how many wonders he would expect to find inside that magnificent city's walls. Just as the ancient center of the Babylonian empire once contained two of the Seven Wonders of the World among its treasures, so, too, the ethnic diversity of this Canadian city makes it a modern wonder. Toronto may well be the new culinary Babylon, with all its riches and its splendor.

Torontonians, of course, already know this all too well. They are in the habit of gobbling up authentic, first-generation ethnic cuisine from every corner of the globe, and continuing the feast with second- and third-generation ethnic-Canadian assimilations. The relatively open-door immigration policies, added to the magnetic appeal of Canada's largest English-speaking city, have injected Toronto with a remarkable culinary diversity, which lends to its gastronomic identity. We don't mean to suggest that modern Toronto, with its more than four thousand restaurants, doesn't have its share of colorful and clean fast-food joints, or stately hotel dining rooms, or cutting-edge "new" restaurants. It does, but, in the main, they are not the city's great strength.

Merely look at the rich ethnic display: Caribbean, Chinese, Ethiopian, German, Greek, Hungarian, Indian, Indonesian, Japanese, Jewish, Laotian, Mexican, Middle Eastern, Peruvian, Polish, Russian, Thai, Vietnamese . . . there's a list even Nebuchadnezzar could have loved.

The wave of Vietnamese immigrants who arrived in the 1970s and 1980s with their rich and refined cuisine announced a wonderful influx of undercapitalized, overachieving restaurants. Now explosions of Hong Kong dollars, triggered by the impending return of this rich island of capitalism to mainland China, burst over Toronto and its old-time Chinese neighborhoods. Investing in Canadian real estate development appears to be the kind of gamble expatriate Hong Kong financiers find attractive, and the city has some of the slickest new Chinese restaurants this side of Kowloon.

Before the Asians came, there were the Eastern Europeans, the Portuguese and the Greeks, among many others. As they were yesterday, so they remain today as well. To see (and taste) for yourself, take a stroll down the Danforth and stop in at a taverna for some taramosalata, garlic-infused lamb and a jug of retsina. Or, venture to Cabbagetown for cilantro-soaked East Indian idli or deeply spiced lentil stew. The Kensington Market area is home to some inspired Jamaican "jerk" joints that serve up goat curry and fried plantains; while you're in the neighborhood, you can discover a

Vietnamese dish of succulent shrimps served on sugar cane, or a Laotian preparation of whole grilled pompano in a tamarind sauce. And, of course, Little Italy has its fair share of—guess what—checkered tablecloths, pungent red sauces and *fiaschi*.

So take some time while making your culinary explorations and visitations in Toronto, and don't be afraid to explore new territory. How splendid are the culinary wonders of our modern times!

André Gayot

ABOUT THE REVIEWS

RANKINGS & TOQUES

Restaurants are ranked in the same manner that French students are graded, on a scale of one to twenty. The rankings reflect *only* the quality of the food; the decor, service, wine list and atmosphere are explicitly commented on within each review. Restaurants that are ranked 13/20 and above are distinguished with toques (chef's hats), according to the table below:

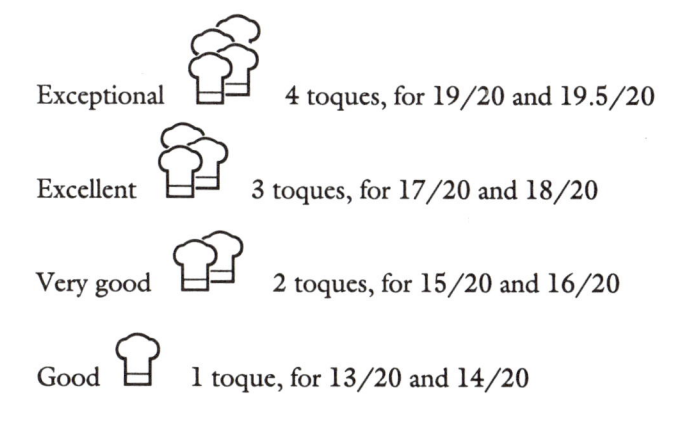

Exceptional — 4 toques, for 19/20 and 19.5/20

Excellent — 3 toques, for 17/20 and 18/20

Very good — 2 toques, for 15/20 and 16/20

Good — 1 toque, for 13/20 and 14/20

Keep in mind that we are comparing Toronto's restaurants to the best in the world, and that these ranks are *relative*. A 13/20 (one toque) is not a very good ranking for a highly reputed (and very expensive) restaurant, but it is quite complimentary for a small place without much culinary pretension.

RESTAURANTS About the Reviews

THE LAW OF THE MARKET

What decides the rating of a restaurant? Among the most telling signs of a restaurant's culinary status is the quality of its produce. It requires a great deal of commitment and money to stock the finest grades and cuts of meat and the finest quality of fish. There is tuna, for example, and there's *tuna*. Ask any sushi chef. One extra-virgin olive oil is not the same, by far, as the next. Ditto for chocolates, pastas, spices and one thousand other ingredients. Quality restaurants also attune themselves to seasonal produce, whether it be local berries or truffles from Italy. Freshness is all important, and a telling indication of quality.

What else do we look for? If sauces have a homogeneity to them, you know that the kitchen is taking shortcuts. The bread on the table is also a tip-off to the level and commitment to quality in a restaurant. Similarly, the house wine can speak volumes about the culinary attitude and level of an establishment. Wine is food, and wine lists and offerings can be revelatory. A list doesn't have to be long or expensive to show a commitment to quality.

Finally, among the very finest restaurants, creativity and influence can be determining factors. These qualities, however, are relatively unimportant for simply good restaurants, where the quality and consistency of what appears on the plates is of paramount importance. A restaurant that serves grilled chicken well is to be admired more than a restaurant that attempts some failed marriage of chicken and exotic produce, or some complicated chicken preparation that requires a larger and more talented kitchen brigade than is on hand. Don't be taken in by attempted fireworks that are really feeble sideshows.

PRICES & CREDIT CARDS

Unless otherwise noted, the price given at the end of each review is in Canadian dollars, and is for a complete dinner for two, including an appetizer and a main course and dessert per person, along with tax, tip and a bottle of wine. As it is hard to estimate the cost of wine; we assume a modest bottle at a modest restaurant and a good wine (Can$18 to Can$27 a bottle) at a more serious place. Lovers of the great Burgundies, Bordeaux or Champagnes will find their tabs higher than our estimates; conversely, those who eat lightly, sharing appetizers and desserts, will spend less.

Credit cards are abbreviated as follows:

AE: American Express and/or Optima
D: Discover
DC: Diners Club and/or Carte Blanche
ER: enRoute
MC: MasterCard
V: VISA

TOQUE TALLY

15/20

Lotus

14/20

Berkeley Café
Centro Grill and Wine Bar
China Blues
La Fenice
Langdon Hall (*Cambridge*)
N44°
Orso
Peter's Chung King Restaurant
Il Posto
Pronto Ristorante
Truffles

13/20

Avocado Club
Le Bistingo
Bistro Bernard
Bistro 990
Browne's Bistro
Cuisine of India
Flowers for My Daughter (*Kleinburg*)
Holt Renfrew Café
Indian Rice Factory
Jade Garden
Lee Garden Restaurant
Liberty Café
Madras Express Café
Massimo Rosticceria
Nami Japanese Restaurant
Ouzeri
Le Paradis
Pearl Court Restaurant
Prego della Piazza
Queen of Sheba
Rodney's Oyster House
The Roof Restaurant, Park Plaza
Scaramouche Restaurant/Pasta Bar & Grill
Senator Steak House
Sisi Trattoria
Southern Accent
Tall Poppies
Tapas Bar
Thai Magic
Thai Shan Inn
Tipplers Restaurant
Trapper's Restaurant

12/20

Arax Armenian Restaurant
Auberge Gavroche/L'Entrecôte
Barolo Ristorante
Bigliardi's Steak, Veal and Seafood Restaurant
Café La Gaffe
Celestino's
C'est What
Chiaro's

RESTAURANTS Toque Tally

The Church Restaurant (*Stratford*)
Epicure Café
Filet of Sole
Foodworks
Future Bakery
Grano
La Grenouille
Hard Rock Café
Japanese Restaurant Ematei
Joso's
Kahee Restaurant
Lobster Trap
Mariko Japanese Restaurant
Metropolis
Mobay Caribbean Cuisine
Natalie's House
The Old Prune (*Stratford*)
Peter Pan
Rivoli Café & Club
The Rosedale Diner
Samovar Barmalay Restaurant
Sanssouci
Santa Fe
Le Sélect Bistro
Senator Diner
Shopsy's
Simcoe North
Trata Psaro Taverna
Trattoria Giancarlo
United Bakers Dairy Restaurant
Vanipha Fine Cuisine
Vietnam Village
Yamase
Zydeco

11/20

Bamboo Club
Bangkok Garden
Bindi Ristorante
Bloor Street Diner
The Boulevard Café

Café Victoria
Carman's
Charmers
Cibo
Daily Planet
The Doctor's House and Livery (*Kleinburg*)
Iguana
Jennie's
My Cahn
Peppinello
Le Petit Gaston
The Prince of Wales Hotel Restaurant (*Niagara-on-the-Lake*)
Queen Mother Café
The Real Jerk
Rundles (*Stratford*)
Sai Woo

10/20

Athenian Garden Restaurant
Auberge du Pommier
The Buttery Theatre Restaurant (*Niagara-on-the-Lake*)
Halfway House Dining Room (*Kleinburg*)
Hsin Kuang
Hughie's
Mad Apples Restaurant
Mövenpick
The Oban Inn Restaurant (*Niagara-on-the-Lake*)
The Pillar and Post Inn Restaurant (*Niagara-on-the-Lake*)
Queen's Inn at Stratford (*Stratford*)
Roberto's
Savunth Restaurant
Skylon Tower (*Niagara Falls*)
The Waterlot Restaurant (*Stratford*)

RESTAURANTS By Cuisine

9/20

Bemelman's
Fran's Restaurant
Last Temptation
Pimblett's
Table Rock Restaurant (*Niagara Falls*)
Tortilla Flats

> *Restaurant prices are for a complete three-course meal for two, with an appetizer, main course and dessert per person, including tax, tip and a bottle of wine.*

BY CUISINE

AMERICAN

Bloor Street Diner
Foodworks
Fran's Restaurant
Hard Rock Café
Hughie's
Jennie's
Last Temptation
Mad Apples
Senator Diner
Table Rock Restaurant (*Niagara Falls*)
Tortilla Flats

CAJUN/CREOLE

Southern Accent
Zydeco

CALIFORNIAN

Café la Gaffe
Centro Grill and Wine Bar
Charmers
Daily Planet
Holt Renfrew Café

CANADIAN

Halfway House Dining Room (*Kleinburg*)
Metropolis
Natalie's House
Trapper's Restaurant

CARIBBEAN

Bamboo Club
Mobay Caribbean Cuisine
The Real Jerk

CHINESE

Hsin Kuang
Jade Garden
Kahee Restaurant
Lee Garden Restaurant
Pearl Court Restaurant
Peter's Chung King Restaurant
Sai Woo

CONTINENTAL

Café Victoria

RESTAURANTS By Cuisine

Chiaro's
The Church Restaurant (*Stratford*)
The Doctor's House and Livery (*Kleinburg*)
Mövenpick
The Old Prune (*Stratford*)
The Pillar and Post Inn Restaurant (*Niagara-on-the-Lake*)
The Prince of Wales Hotel Restaurant (*Niagara-on-the-Lake*)
Queen's Inn at Stratford (*Stratford*)
Rundles (*Stratford*)
Sanssouci
Skylon Tower (*Niagara Falls*)
The Waterlot Restaurant (*Stratford*)

ECLECTIC

C'est What
China Blues
Rivoli Café & Club

ENGLISH

The Buttery Theatre Restaurant (*Niagara-on-the-Lake*)
Langdon Hall (*Cambridge*)
The Oban Inn Restaurant (*Niagara-on-the-Lake*)
Pimblett's

ETHIOPIAN

Queen of Sherba

FRENCH

Auberge Gavroche/L'Entrecôte
Auberge de Pommier
Le Bistingo
Bistro 990
Browne's Bistro
La Grenouille
Le Paradis
Le Petit Gaston
Queen's Inn at Stratford
The Roof Restaurant, Park Plaza
Le Sélect Bistro
Tipplers

GERMAN

Bistro Bernard

GREEK

Athenian Garden Restaurant
Ouzeri
Trata Psaro Taverna

HUNGARIAN

Future Bakery

INDIAN

Cuisine of India
Indian Rice Factory
Madras Express Café
Savunth Restaurant

INDONESIAN

Bamboo Club

INTERNATIONAL

Bemelman's
Holt Renfrew Café
Peter Pan
Queen Mother Café
Simcoe North
Truffles

ITALIAN

Barolo Ristorante
Bindi Ristorante
Celestino's
Centro Grill and Wine Bar

RESTAURANTS By Cuisine

Cibo
Epicure Café
La Fenice
Grano
Joso's
Massimo Rosticceria
Orso
Peppinello
Il Posto
Prego della Piazza
Pronto Ristorante
Roberto's
Sisi Trattoria
Trattoria Giancarlo

JAPANESE

Japanese Restaurant Ematei
Mariko Japanese Restaurant
Nami Japanese Restaurant
Yamase

JEWISH

Samovar Barmalay Restaurant
Shopsy's
United Bakers Dairy Restaurant

LAOTIAN

Vanipha Cuisine

MEDITERRANEAN

Flowers for my Daughter
(Kleinburg)
The Rosedale Diner

MEXICAN

Charmers
Iguana
Tortilla Flats

MIDDLE EASTERN

Arax Armenian Restaurant
Last Temptation

PACIFIC RIM

Avocado Club
Berkeley Café
Liberty Café
Lotus
N44°
Scaramouche Restaurant/Pasta Bar
& Grill
Tall Poppies

PERUVIAN

The Bouvelard Café

POLISH

United Bakers Dairy Restaurant

RUSSIAN

Samovar Barmalay Restaurant

SEAFOOD

Filet of Sole
Jennie's
Joso's
Lobster Trap
Mad Apples
Rodney's Oyster House
Scaramouche Restaurant/Pasta Bar
& Grill
Trata Psaro Taverna

SOUTHWESTERN

Santa Fe
Tall Poppies

RESTAURANTS

SPANISH

Tapas Bar

STEAKHOUSE

Bigliardi's Steak, Veal and Steakhouse Restaurant
Carman's
Senator Steak House

SUSHI

Yamase

SWISS

Bistro Bernard
Mövenpick

THAI

Bangkok Garden
Rivoli Café & Club
Thai Magic
Thai Shan Inn
Vanipha Cuisine

VIETNAMESE

My Cahn
Vietnamese Village

> We're always interested to hear about your discoveries, and to receive your comments on ours. Please feel free to write to us, and do state clearly exactly what you liked or disliked.

RESTAURANTS

Arax Armenian Restaurant

1979 Lawrence Ave. East, Scarborough
• 288-1485
MIDDLE EASTERN

12/20

No one ever doubted that Arax had the best Middle Eastern food in Toronto, customers just worried about the war zone they would have to eat it in. At its first location, the family was feuding: arguments would take place in the kitchen and the waiter would take it out on the customers in the dining room. At the new location, the atmosphere has changed for the better and the food, thankfully, hasn't changed at all. Dips such as hummus and baba ghanouj are thick with garlicky flavor. The kitchen combines eggplant with onions, tomatoes and garlic for a superb ratatouille; or, it's sliced very thin, coated in tempura-style batter and quickly fried. Customers sometimes phone ahead on weekends to make sure they get their share of this popular dish. Armenian meat pie is a round, unleavened dough, sprinkled with meat and spices, then rolled up and eaten with the hands. Steak tartare is made with cracked pepper then served either with hot pepper or with pine nuts and oil. Two can eat amply for about Can$50 without wine. Service is congenial. Isn't it nice when families can work things out?
Open Mon.-Fri. 11 a.m.-10 p.m., Sat. 4 p.m.-11 p.m. Cards: MC, V.

Athenian Garden Restaurant

526 Danforth Ave., Danforth
• 465-4001
GREEK

10/20

There's very little to recommend Athenian Garden outside of its patio and its lamb. Naturally, then, the best time to visit is in the summer, when both patio and lamb are at their best. Situated in the epicenter of "the Danforth," the main street of a hundred thousand Greek-Canadians, it has a large, curbside patio, where one can eat and drink (from a well-stocked cellar of Greek vintages, plus, of course, ouzo), while watching the Greeks promenade and socialize. On a summer's evening, after a whole day of humid, Midwestern heat, the exodus onto the avenue is massive, and the resulting street theater is priceless.

Now, the lamb. Fresh local produce is skewered on a spit, and slow-charred, turning over a bed of real charcoal. The only thing missing from a total image of Greece is a cypress-ringed Aegean cove. The meat, though cooked through without a trace of pink in it, is tender and moist. The crackling is the dreamy stuff on which addictions thrive. It is served in obscenely large portions that are so filling, that it's advisable to fast a day before going. Unfortunately, most of the rest that comes out of this utilitarian kitchen is substandard. Burned calamari, obliterated spinach (in the spinach pie), fishy taramosalata, even terrible potatoes and rice used to garnish the lamb. The one serviceable alternative to lamb is the grilled whole fish, which comes in two varieties (one of which is snapper, so fresh that it succeeds in tasting good despite its long stay on the flames). Fish or lamb dinner for two, with wine, Can$65.

Open Tues.-Fri. noon-1 a.m., Sat. noon-1:30 a.m., Sun. noon-1:30 a.m. Cards: AE, MC, V.

Auberge Gavroche/ L'Entrecôte

90 Avenue Rd., Bloor-Yorkville
• 920-0956
FRENCH

12/20

Attitude, an all-important component in any restaurant, used to be a wee bit of a problem at Auberge Gavroche. Long regarded as one of *the* spots for authentic French fare, servers at this lovely old house in the correct part of town, with its French-inn facade of forest green and terrace, supplied haughty hints. Happily, this has passed with time, and while a few fairly reputable chefs have also come and gone, the interpretations of Didier Leroy, coupled with the new staff's gentler, kinder attitude, make this a gratifying place to be.

Inside, warm bisque-colored walls and pale-green shutters on the bay windows continue the French auberge experience, with tastefully appointed wine prints hung throughout the room. Upstairs, L'Entrecôte caters to the steak-frites crowd in a convivial prix-fixe bistro setting. Service comes smiling, attentive and, well, downright happy. Auberge Gavroche's deceptively simple-sounding menu of classic and nouvelle preparations—appetizers, meat and fish—changes frequently, and courses are presented on different plates, which are chosen by some maven of china style to harmonize with the food. There

RESTAURANTS

were a few mishaps at a recent meal, but Leroy's classic French training and his marvelous, careful touch on the dishes that work suggest that in time, both Leroy and his menu will blossom. For the meantime, a flavorful scallop soufflé with tomato butter sounded encouraging, but emerged as more of a tepid mousse than a soufflé, wrapped, as it was, in wide green zucchini ribbons and encircled with dangerously underdone potato rounds. The wishy-washy bouillon-based soup of root vegetables and oyster mushrooms needed help—and heat. Happily things improved somewhat with a finely presented silky-pink foie gras. Also on the plus side of the scorecard, we enjoyed an ultrafresh red-snapper filet, which came simply pan-fried, resting atop a nest of interwoven leek-and-scallion strands with beurre blanc. Sliced white turnip disks danced around the edge. Later, a rack of lamb roasted to a deep pink inside arrived in a Stonehenge formation. The quality of the meat excelled. The lamb concealed a tasty but soggy circle of Rösti potatoes and a demi-glace infused with basil. Lengths of scallion and sculpted zucchini assisted the final effort. Desserts are few but fine: a Cointreau-spiked soufflé tastes eggy and hot; crème brûlée, while not stellar, came properly thick, sweet, burnt on top. We look forward to watching (and tasting) the growth of this chef's talent. Dinner for two with wine is possible for Can$120, but Can$150 is more like it. *Open Mon. 5:30-midnight, Tues.-Fri. noon-2:30 p.m. & 5:30 p.m.-12:30 p.m., Sat. 5:30 p.m.-1 a.m. Cards: AE, MC, V.*

Auberge du Pommier

4150 Yonge St., Toronto North
• 222-2220
FRENCH

10/20

The restaurant, salvaged from two picturesque old houses, has three fireplaces, a wooden-beamed ceiling, gorgeous wide tables. But that's not all: the plates match the menus; the menus match the flowers; the flowers match the upholstered banquettes.

Look at the menu and you'll find pure poetry. For appetizers, there are a light mousse of smoked trout, poppy-seed pastry and crabmeat remoulade, asparagus-walnut vinaigrette and on and on into the entrées. Alas, if only the chef were as good as the interior decorator and the menu writer in this lovely and comfortable north Toronto restaurant. Still, you can survive if you keep it simple.

Sautéed venison medallions arrive nicely tender and flattered by a cranberry compote and a gentle jus that the menu announces is flavored with juniper, even if the taste shows little evidence of it. Crispy duck might be glazed with honey and garlic, then served with a balsamic vinegar dressing.

For starters, there will be a variation on a pasta with tomato sauce, Parmesan and bacon that won't taste as bright as it could, but that will satisfy and fill. The plates always appear gorgeous in their puddles of sauce, splats of color and spirals of sliced meat and vegetables. Fast forward to dessert, where marquise of chocolate looks sybaritic and tastes puritanical. Don't dare to miss the wonderful-tasting sugared peel that will garnish some of the desserts.

Service may be pokey, but the staff is extremely cordial and kind. The wine list is substantial with many good French and Italian bottles in the Can$40-to-Can$80 range. The Auberge is always full of dressed-up people who look like they think they're out for a special meal. If eye food is what you need, you may feel the same. Dinner with wine for two costs Can$150. *Open Mon.-Fri. 11:30 a.m.-2:30 p.m. & 5:30 p.m.-10:30 p.m., Sat. 5:30 p.m.-10:30 p.m. All major cards.*

Avocado Club

165 John St.,
Downtown
• 598-4656
PACIFIC RIM

Up until recently, the Avocado Club was known as Beaujolais, a *très* upscale, nouvelle Pacific Rim restaurant. But the owners saw which way the economic winds were blowing, and decided to change direction with them: they transmuted Beaujolais into the Avocado Club, still serving a Pacific Rim cuisine, but more casual, with lower prices. And while the menu is even more eclectic than it previously was, it's also more accessible—a menu that encourages the diner to taste a little of this and a little of that, without doing major damage to his or her bank account.

On the second floor of a rather cavernous-looking building, the Avocado Club has a lively buzz, and some of the peppiest, friendliest staff in Toronto. It's the perfect dining spot for this SoHo-style neighborhood, and attracts a refreshingly mixed crowd of hipsters, yuppies and post-baby boomers. Thanks to carpeted floors and upholstered banquettes, the noise level is manageable; the spot doesn't sacrifice comfort for the sake of coolness. Colorful murals painted on the walls and stenciled moldings add a touch of whimsy to this vibrant room.

The menu is a real mixed bag, with the accent on Southwestern and Asian dishes. When your moniker is the Avocado Club, you'd better pony up a good guacamole, and the kitchen does just that. Unfortunately, the tortilla chips were a little stale. But the mixed saté plate with a spicy peanut sauce was quite good, as was the shell pasta with a hot-hot eggplant sauce, and the earthy/briny soba noodle salad with gingered sushi. A nice touch here is that several of the dishes can be ordered in either appetizer or main course portions. Also good was the roast half chicken—garlicky and moist with a crispy skin, infused with herbs and basted with a citrus sauce—served with real mashed potatoes and a fragrant thyme gravy; the grilled swordfish with tropical fruit salsa was well cooked.

For dessert, the black rice pudding sounded and looked a lot more exotic than it actually tasted, but the angel-food cake with praline icing delivered more than just good looks. We also

RESTAURANTS

enjoyed a delicate orange crème caramel. In fact, the ambition of some of the food here extends its reach, but you can eat quite well, besides, the place is so much fun, it's almost craven to kvetch about a lack of culinary perfection. Dinner for two, with wine, will run about Can$60.
Open Mon.-Fri. noon-2 p.m. & 6 p.m.-10 p.m., Sat. 6 p.m.-10 p.m. Cards: AE, MC, V.

The Bamboo Club
312 Queen St. West, Downtown
• 593-5771
CARIBBEAN/INDONESIAN

11/20

Funky, unpretentious and fun, The Bamboo Club really feels like an island watering hole in the middle of the great northeast, which is no easy feat. A lively, overgrown courtyard dining area, weather permitting, is the place to sit. The service is almost giddily friendly, definitely of the "don't worry, be happy" school.

The food comes plentiful, cheap and well prepared. The gado-gado salad, comprised of shredded cabbage, cucumbers, bean sprouts and tofu with a spicy peanut dressing, is hot yet refreshingly good, as are the satés (marinated chicken, pork or both), the puffy Malaysian shrimp chips, the shrimp rolls and the wonton dough stuffed fat with vermicelli, shrimp, black mushrooms, ginger and bamboo shoots.

The house favors Thai-style spicy noodles. You can order them mild, medium-hot or "yow!" (as the menu has it). It's a tangle of noodles, chicken, shrimp, tofu and egg, dusted with chopped, roasted peanuts. Also flavorful are the stir-fried green tiger shrimp, flavored with tamarind and joined by fresh veggies and cashews, and the steamed mussels perfumed with butter, lemon, garlic, and a hint of cilantro. Naturally, the desserts carry a whiff of the trade winds with them: a yummy, artery-clogging coconut-cream pie, a puckery Key lime pie and a dense, fruity banana cake. This is happy food, and the tariff will reinforce that glee: two can dine like potentates for about Can$35, with drinks.
Open Mon.-Sat. noon-4 p.m. & 5 p.m.-11 p.m. Cards: AE, MC, V.

Bangkok Garden
18 Elm St., Downtown
• 977-6748
THAI

11/20

Journalist Sherry Brydson lived in Thailand for ten years and returned to Toronto to open this spiffy emporium in an old building that was once a home for wayward women. The original residents wouldn't recognize the place. Consider this restaurant when you hunger for flamboyance: waiters run about in costume, a rushing waterfall attempts to re-create those in Lanna Thai, plates are grandly decorated and presented with a flourish. Though the spicing of many dishes regrettably is restrained, some, spicy by nature, are authentic. As well, ingredients come fresh and carefully assembled. One dish, the Royal Barge, floats to your table with thin slices of grilled beef tossed with shallots, mint and toasted chilies; "Drunkard's Fish" de-

RESTAURANTS

livers a knockout punch of fish flesh smoothed with curry paste and fresh chilies. Noodle dishes satisfy, though remain on the timid side. The magical Asian way with noodles is better demonstrated in the downstairs lunch bar, The Brass Flamingo. It operates on the principle of a salad bar; using noodles as the base, you top them with meat, chicken or vegetables, then fill the bowl with rich broth and spice it with any variety of chilies, peanuts and tiny vegetable dices. Dinner at Bangkok Garden will cost Can$100 for two. A simple lunch for two at the Brass Flamingo costs about Can$20.
Open Mon.-Fri. 11:30 a.m.-2:30 p.m. & 5 p.m.-10:30 p.m., Sat. 5 p.m.-10:30 p.m. Cards: AE, ER, MC, V.

Barolo Ristorante
193 Carlton St., Cabbagetown
• 961-4747
ITALIAN

12/20

Despite its claim to be serving a "grand" version of Italian nouvelle cuisine, what Barolo Ristorante actually dishes out has nothing to do with grand or nouvelle: this is hearty food with very little pretense. The kitchen delivers reliable fare—even fabulous from time to time—and its plates show up as delightful canvases of color.

One signature dish, scallops Barolo, brings marinated, lightly cooked scallops annointed with roasted-fennel-seed butter. Scallops also shine in combination with tiger shrimp, presented on a bed of kale for a main course. Pastas are fresh and occasionally inspirational. Note, however, that owner Michael Pagliari's interest in accomodating individual tastes in pasta and wine can send the menu off track in places. You might ask him, for example, to leave out the ill-advised baby shrimp in the otherwise beautifully balanced dish of fettuccine with sun-dried tomatoes, eggplant and chili paste. Or forgo the pasta altogether and have the eggplant roasted with raisins and pine nuts. True to its name, Barolo offers a wine list with a good selection of Italians at varying price ranges. The most fun can be had with some of the richer wines; ask for a vintage Barolo or Amorone. You can also order one of the bottles you see tucked into the corners and crevices in the walls, and Pagliari himself will usually present your choice with a flourish and a brief history. Desserts, from the tiramisu to the gelatos, resemble Miró paintings, with their trademark dots, splashes and streaks. We prefer to skip these and finish the rest of our wine with the good cheese plate. One last plus: it's in a neighborhood where there's still room to park on the street. A three-course dinner for two will cost Can$100.
Open Mon.-Fri. noon-3 p.m. & 5 p.m.-11 p.m., Sat. 5 p.m.-11 p.m. Cards: AE, MC, V.

RESTAURANTS

Bemelmans
83 Bloor St. West,
Bloor-Yorkville
• 960-0306
INTERNATIONAL

9/20

We had high expectations for Bemelmans because it lies on the tony stretch of Bloor Street West that reminds us of Madison Avenue, and we love the Madeleine books of Ludwig Bemelmans. Unfortunately, while the place looks wonderfully like a vintage 1930s brasserie, complete with tiny octagonal tiles on the floor, wooden booths and an outdoor patio, the food isn't up to the decor.

This isn't to say that everything fails. The huge hunks of pumpernickel and rye breads brought to the marble-topped tables are quite good, as is the bruschetta, toasted bread slices; also, chopped tomatoes, olive oil, basil and garlic arrive on focaccia, a nice touch. But the Caesar salad can only be described as so-so, and last time we ordered the gazpacho verde, though it was very fresh, it was overwhipped to a froth and tasted sweet. The onion soup also suffered from that peculiar sweetness.

Bemelmans ought to keep its focus on even simpler dishes. The burgers are good, as is the tuna niçoise. But why mess with *faux*-Southern dishes such as the Louisiana barbecue veal burger with a cloying pecan barbecue sauce, or the New Orleans seafood gumbo? And there also failed forays into the Caribbean, with the Jamaican jerk chicken breast and leg of lamb in a goofy "Caribbean" sauce.

The rather lackluster desserts sound better than they are: chocolate-Cognac truffle cake, Grand Marnier chocolate brownie with vanilla ice cream, peach pie. Although Bemelmans has a reputation as a high-stepping joint, it suffers from a lack of focus, a staff that offers erratic service, and just plain mediocre food. It's too bad that such a good-looking restaurant in this neighborhood doesn't deliver what it could. A meal for two, with wine, will run about Can$65.

Open Mon.-Thurs. 11:30 a.m.-1 a.m., Fri.-Sat. 11 a.m.-3 a.m., Sun. 11 a.m.-11 p.m. Cards: AE, MC, V.

Berkeley Café
141 Berkeley St.,
Cabbagetown
• 594-6663
PACIFIC RIM

14

The Berkeley Café, a little converted house tucked away on a side street off Queen Street East lies in a neighborhood "in transition," as they say in real estate lingo, meaning it's populated by architects, budding design firms, galleries and assorted street types. Delightful food comes from its minuscule kitchen. The owner-chefs, Camilo Costales (a Filipino) and Andrew Chase, claim to be heavily influenced by renowned chef Ken Hom, but the food here betrays more complex, eclectic roots. There are Filipino/Chinese/Vietnamese/Indonesian and even Mediterranean cues at work here; in fact, the food compares favorably to that at Bruce Cost's San Francisco restaurant, Monsoon. It may not have quite the ambition or polish, but it definitely stands on the same general level.

We especially enjoyed the fat grilled shrimp in a hot ginger-

RESTAURANTS

lime-chili chutney, the green chutney chunky with scallions and ground peanuts; all the flavors fairly burst off the plate. The salad of mixed greens laced with big bites of Gorgonzola and studded with walnuts in an almost ethereally light dressing was above average, as was the grilled chicken, Vietnamese-style, with bok choy and fluffy, almost nutlike white rice. The Thai vegetarian curry served with more of that wonderful rice brought a heady, deep bowl of hunks of vegetables bathed in a well-spiced curry sauce, tinged with lemon grass, a dish satisfying to both the body and soul. For dessert, the multitextural purple sticky rice with coconut crème anglaise and fresh mango; the dense, muddy flourless chocolate cake; and the creamy, dreamy ginger crème caramel constitute a fine bouquet of desserts, with different ice creams or sorbets homemade daily. Ours was a superbly fresh pear ice, and they'll assemble a dessert plate for two, allowing you to taste all these sweet treasures.

The wine list is compact, but well-chosen, with a single U.S. house (Guenoc Sauvignon Blanc). You can opt without regret for a refreshingly different iced chrysanthemum tea. Dinner for two, with wine, will run about Can$60.

Open Mon.-Fri. 11:30 a.m.-11 p.m., Sat.-Sun. 4 p.m.-11 p.m. Cards: MC, V.

Bigliardi's Steak, Veal and Seafood Restaurant
463 Church St., Downtown
• 922-9594
STEAKHOUSE

12/20

Bigliardi's opened about two decades ago, and it has hardly changed since: the dark wood, low lights and cushy chairs make you feel as if you'd gone out for a smoke and returned to find the same steakhouse you left in the seventies. Chances are the people beside you at the next table are having escargots bourguignon for starters and crème-de-menthe parfaits for dessert. Here's what's so great about this old-fashioned restaurant: the steak. You order meat and what you get is a simple, sublime cut of meat, beautifully cooked, with only a baked potato for company. No crunchy green stuff to distract you. Bigliardi's has the best prime rib in the city. It is served off the bone, alone on a wooden board, sitting like a sacrifice at the altar. When it arrives at your table, all talk about cholesterol levels and oat-bran diets comes to a grinding halt. Steak tartare is not as spicy as some, but it still has zing. Lamb chops seem endlessly thick, and burst with so much flavor, you'll want to nibble every last bit off the bones. Pepper steak is wonderfully tender, with a peppercorn-cream sauce that nicely balances the peppery bite and soothing cream. To try almost anything else is to be reminded why steakhouses have gone out of fashion: shrimp cocktail hangs limply, cheesecake sports a shiny red top that may or may not have started life as a cherry. With the desserts, as with nearly all of the other asides, the lesson is: save yourself for the steak. There's an adequate wine list, but better

RESTAURANTS

Bindi Ristorante
3241 Yonge St., Toronto
• 487-2881
ITALIAN

11/20

is to be found if you ask your waiter. Dinner for two will cost about Can$120.
Open Mon.-Sat. 5 p.m.-1 a.m. All major cards.

Not exactly a walk on the wild side, this North Toronto restaurant is more like a trustworthy friend: people come here for its reliable, well turned out Italian dishes and its casual, comfortable atmosphere. Risotto ai calamari tastes less creamy than the best risottos should be, but a hint of hotness from a few cheeky peppers livens it up, and a good amount of squid and shrimp fattens it up. Manzo alla boscaiola is a few thickly sliced and tenderly cooked pieces of beef tenderloin, each with a nugget of ground mushrooms, hazelnuts and spinach. The restaurant's suburban location may explain such heavy steakhouse dishes as snails cooked in cream with garlic, basil and Gorgonzola, all served in a gratin dish with large, soft slices of polenta. For dessert, chocolate Bindi, a pleasure bomb the size of a giant's thumbnail, made with a mixture of pure chocolate, pure butter and ground nuts, will make your heart sing and your ears ring. The assassin who devised it should be congratulated. Service is as efficient as the restaurant's popularity will allow and on busy weekend nights, crowding may mean a wait or a rushed meal. Dinner for two costs about Can$90.
Open Mon.-Fri. noon-2:30 p.m. & 5 p.m.-11 p.m., Sat. 5 p.m.-11 p.m. Cards: AE, ER, MC, V.

Le Bistingo
349 Queen St. West, Downtown
• 598-3490
FRENCH

In 1990, this restaurant downscaled from trendy French to recession brasserie and the happy result is a menu and ambience that are each lively and interesting. The warm, comfortable room mixes terra-cotta color with black-and-white photographs of artists and writers. The crowd will be an amalgam of local celebrities from the nearby TV station, the business population from funky Queen Street West and a few downscaling suburbanites. The menu is short, the prices are what the owners call "soft" that means, not too hard to take. No menu entrée is over Can$13 (specials are higher); wine prices are also kept down. And though appetizers and desserts still hover between Can$5.50 and Can$8.75, two may still have dinner and not break the dreaded Can$100 three-digit ceiling.

Shellfish comes tender and gently cooked in sauces that are light but alive with peppery flavor. The creamy broth that fills the bottom of the big bowl under the tenderly steamed mussels has an intense pepper and onion flavor. Open ravioli, of shrimp and scallops tossed with a julienne of vegetables, gives a good look at what the kitchen can do; consider the dish a "must." The concoction is laid between two flaps of black lasagne. Sauce

RESTAURANTS

on each of these seafood dishes invites you to clean the plate with some of the good bread. Chef Claude Bouillet still gets to strut his stuff in the daily specials, conversationally presented on a separate piece of paper, thusly: "Tonight, I would begin with the fish soup, followed by the tenderloins of rabbit and a bottle of Cabernet Sauvignon Geyser Peak '87 (Can$26). The profiterole au chocolat makes a perfect ending." Go for the main courses, which may be accompanied by perfect roast potato wedges and buttery steamed spinach. Avoid the profiterole and have instead the superb hot apple tart with Calvados ice cream that must be ordered at the start of the meal. Service may be harried, but it is thorough.
Open Mon.-Sat. noon-2:30 p.m. & 5:30 p.m.-11 p.m. Mon-Sat. Cards: AE, MC, V.

Bistro Bernard
6 St. Joseph St.,
Downtown
• 926-1900
SWISS/GERMAN

This small bistro is the gastronomic equivalent of a soothing afternoon at the Wiesbaden Spa. In other words, Bistro Bernard will never set the world on fire, but you can escape to this gentle haven for good, reliable food, and leave feeling somehow more serene. It sits in a row of renovated townhouses downtown. Downstairs, the more casual floor, you can spread out in wide booths and cushy banquettes (a relief from those tiny seats apparently designed only for little-boy bums). Upstairs, two small, understated rooms are linked by a bar. Wherever you sit, feel safe in ordering the steak tartare, with a fresh, satiny-smooth sauce. Tender veal is bathed in a cream sauce; Rösti potatoes come properly crisp. Look for any other dumplings offered, such as the spaetzle or the capuns, which are made with spinach, boiled and then sautéed until their delicate edges curl with crunch. Desserts, standard cheesecake and mousse, make a very satisfying finish. Take note of such seasonal surprises as white asparagus in the spring or a kirsch-rich cheese fondue in midwinter. Dinner for two with wine will be about Can$90. There is a small list of Swiss wines.
Open Mon.-Fri. 11 a.m.- 2:30 p.m. & 5:30 p.m.-10:30 p.m., Sat. 5:30 p.m.-10:30 p.m. Cards: AE, MC, V.

Bistro 990
990 Bay St.,
Toronto
• 921-9990
FRENCH

Bistro 990 looks like a French countryside farmhouse you'd drool over in the latest issue of *Maison et Jardin*. The lighting casts an almost honeyed glow on diners at the Bistro 990. Ceilings are low yet vaulted, with Lascaux-style drawings on the wall and Gallic music playing. There's a cozy, intimate bar in the front of the restaurant, subtly separated from the main room. Fresh flowers fill huge earthen jars, and a friendly crowd animates the place; the service is absolutely professional yet unobtrusive.

RESTAURANTS

Homemade, rough wheat bread, studded with green olives, tasted marvelous at a recent dinner. We could have made a meal of it, but then we would have missed the divine, hot leek-and-Roquefort tart, a savory melt contained by a lighter-than-air crust and served with a cool little salad of gently dressed watercress; a supernal tomato-and-basil soup, which tasted of just-picked, flavorful tomatoes, and had a smooth consistency. Other worthy first courses extend to the crisp confit of duck with a salad of haricots verts, and the galantine of rabbit with morels and sweet and sour figs.

Main courses do not disappoint, either. The grilled filet of salmon was made delicious by its light bath of capers, scallions and yogurt, served with tiny, purple Peruvian potatoes and a mélange of acorn squash, baby carrots, peppers and bright green, crisp sugar snap peas. The kitchen did a fine job with the seared New York sirloin steak with fresh horseradish and basil jus, which came heaped with thin, crisp pommes frites.

Desserts are definitely worth saving some room for: the galette of apples, a lightly sugared dream of razor-thin sheets of apple in a meltingly good crust and garnished with fresh, red currants, the "lasagne," a chocolate-lover's fantasy of layers of white- and dark-chocolate mousse; the crème brûlée, ice creams and sorbets are also worth a whirl. Dinner for two, with wine, is about Can$80.

Open Mon.-Wed. noon-11 p.m., Thurs.-Sat. noon-midnight, Sun. 11:30 a.m.-11 p.m. Cards: AE, MC, V.

Bloor Street Diner
50 Bloor St. West,
Bloor-Yorkville
• 928-3105
AMERICAN

11/20

This high-tech, neon-tubed café attracts an upwardly mobile crowd that appreciates late hours, good service and tasty food. The menu carries something for everyone, although the slinky staff obviously doesn't gorge on the fat, juicy burgers here and still manage to keep their figures. There are pastas, quiches, and fish-and-chips on the menu, as well as ratatouille and salads. In fact, the menu is quite extensive, so no matter what you're in the mood for, you're bound to find something approximating it. We like the Buffalo-style chicken wings, and the greasy yet fabulous deep-fried mozzarella slices served with a jalapeño dip. The roomy booths are quite comfortable, and the music is kept to a tolerable level; you won't get blasted out of here. The Bloor Street Diner really feels more like a restaurant than a diner; people like to linger here. Dinner for two, with drinks, is about Can$40.

Open daily 11 a.m.-3 a.m. Cards: AE, MC, V.

RESTAURANTS

The Boulevard Café
161 Harbord St., Toronto
• 961 7676
PERUVIAN

11/20

In Peru, they love their anticuchos: highly spiced kebabs of ox or calf hearts. No hearts here at The Boulevard Café, but the fare is still sizzlingly good; the anticuchos are marinated and charbroiled kebabs of sea bass, shrimp, beef tenderloin or chicken. People come to this popular neighborhood restaurant for its counter-culture atmosphere, its pleasant patio and a few tasty dishes at decent prices. A blackboard menu lists specials such as chile-hot lamb chupe (stew), yogurt-marinated grilled chicken or albondigas Peruvian-style, made with potatoes and spicy chicken or beef. If either the tamal verde (a tasty mixture of cornmeal and chicken in a coriander-scented green sauce) or the zesty bean dish doesn't come with your meal, order one of them as an aside. At lunchtime, a menu of generous salads includes a Peruvian standard—assorted steamed vegetables served cold with a spicy cheese sauce. The Boulevard is noted for its Key lime pie, though we find the filling a bit shallow. This restaurant fills up quickly, especially on warm summer evenings and weekends, so try to go during nonpeak hours. Dinner for two with wine will be about Can$65.
Open daily 11 a.m.- 4 p.m. & 5:30- 10:30 p.m. Cards: MC, V.

Browne's Bistro
4 Woodlawn Ave., Toronto
• 924-8132
FRENCH

(13)

Peter and Beverly Burge ran a French cooking school for years, and opened this small bistro to put into practice everything they had been teaching their students. The result is a place Torontonians go for solid, reliable food at honest prices, which is why it remains one of the city's most popular upscale bistros. Located nearby the Waspy Rosedale neighborhood, the decor is fittingly classy and understated, with tables and chairs of rosewood and clean white walls.

At Browne's, dishes come and dishes go, but those that stay are deservedly demanded: there is a cult of those who love the goat-cheese pizza, and others who equally cannot pass by its doors without wandering in for the signature lamb sausage seasoned modestly with thyme, rosemary and garlic and accompanied by mashed potatoes and brown gravy. Grilled liver shows a little pink at its center, and is served with onions in a reduced red-wine-and-sage sauce. Bouillabaisse mixes the garlicky rouille right into the soup stock, rather than floating it on a crouton. The stock, further scented with Pernod and saffron, swims with a generous amount of fish and mussels, which is one of the reasons you'll see so many being ordered around you. Watch for the tasty roast rack of lamb scented with rosemary, and the grilled chicken and fish specials. Two of our favorite desserts are the hazelnut meringue—layers of crunchy meringue, sweet cream and puréed fruits that create a textural

RESTAURANTS

contrast made in heaven—and the rich chocolate cake with crème fraîche. Another appeal of Browne's is that you can come here to taste wines: a wide-ranging list, usually about three dozen selections, is offered by the glass. By the bottle, most wines are in the Can$20-to-Can$40 range, with a few more expensive picks for high fliers. Service is usually fine, though weekend crowding may mean that you will be coaxed from your table to make room for another party. A three-course dinner for two will reach Can$70.
Open Mon.-Fri. noon-2:30 p.m. & 6 p.m.-11 p.m., Sat. 6 p.m.-11 p.m. Cards: AE, MC, V.

Café La Gaffe

Baldwin St.,
Kensington Market
• 596-2397

51 Kensington Ave.,
Kensington Market
• 595-5337

CALIFORNIAN

12/20

If location is a factor in a restaurant's success, then Café La Gaffe has it made. Not content with its original venue in the bosom of Toronto's vibrant Kensington Market, it has replicated itself in an equally charming nearby storefront, right in the middle of the city's most tree-shaded, and most cosmopolitan roller coaster of civilized pleasures, Baldwin Street. La Gaffe, despite its self-derogatory name, is no joke. It represents a serious "from-the-heart" attempt to make people feel at home, while feeding them huge portions of top-quality ingredients in sometimes messy but always well-meaning recipes. The orientation of the cooking, which derives from the abundance of produce alongside a wide selection of international delicacies in the market surroundings of the first Gaffe, continues unabated in the second. Any one night, the blackboard will have chalked specials that have roots in other countries, and are adapted for the North American palate, mostly in the style of fresh-market, Californian concepts. You can find designer pizzas here, and giant bowls of soup that might be anything from black-bean to squash chowder. The homemade salsas, the goat cheese with walnut dusting, the various pestos, the corn bread, the wild-mushroom crêpe and the meal-size salads dressed with sautéed sea-scallops are all natural consequences of a cuisine that pleases best when it stays light and lively.

Unfortunately, La Gaffe is less successful when it tackles main courses. Attempts at chicken, grilled fish and flabby crabcakes fall flat when compared to the top half of the menu. They are especially unappealing beside the mountainous garnishes of starch and vegetables, which might make you reminisce about your student days, when a plate like this had to suffice for an entire day's nourishment. The modest wine list is as forgettable as the choice of beers is extensive. Gruff but sincere, the service matches the attitudes of most of the intellectual art-crowd regulars. If nothing else, this place provides an interesting peek

RESTAURANTS

at Toronto's café society. Dinner for two, with wine or beer, costs Can$60.
Baldwin St.: open Mon.-Thurs. noon-4 p.m. & 6 p.m.-10 p.m., Fri. noon-4 p.m. & 6 p.m.-11 p.m., Sat. 6 p.m.-11 p.m. Kensington Ave.: open same hours, plus Sun. 6 p.m.-9:30 p.m. Cards: MC, V.

Café Victoria
King Edward Hotel,
37 King St. East,
Downtown
• 863-9700
CONTINENTAL

11/20

The King Eddie is a grand old hotel, all posh elegance and crystal chandeliers. The service is professional, and courtly yet friendly, which makes one wonder what was going on in the hotel's Café Victoria the night we dined here. Our experience was more opera bouffe than grand opera; in fact, we felt as though we'd fallen through the rabbit hole, and landed in the making of *A Hard Day's Night*. The restaurant itself is lovely, if a little stuffy, but the staff goofed consistently, at least on our visit. When we queried our waiter as to one of the pastas on the menu, he sneered, "If you want pasta, go to an Italian restaurant—ours is terrible!"

As for the food, it won't be etched indelibly into your memory. The Caesar salad was all right, but nothing special; we obviously steered clear of the pastas (grilled salmon on rigatoni, fettuccine with Italian sausage and leeks), and the lobster bisque lacked character, limping along without much of its namesake. Main courses did not escape blandness, especially the dull poached salmon and the much-touted Tum-Tum Burger, a big, tasteless hunk of ground meat, smothered to no avail with overcooked mushrooms and onions. And shouldn't sole meunière be retired from menus for evermore? The lifeless pastries do not justify the calories. Dinner for two, with wine, is about Can$125.
Open Mon.-Fri. 6:30 a.m.-3 p.m. & 5 p.m.-11 p.m., Sat. 7:30 a.m.-11 p.m., Sun. 7:30 a.m.-10 a.m., 11 a.m.-3 p.m. & 5:30 p.m.-10:30 p.m.

Carman's
26 Alexander St.,
Downtown
• 924-8697
STEAKHOUSE

11/20

Even in these fat-phobic times, don't be surprised to see a roomful of people slicing zealously into Carman's gargantuan slabs of red meat. After all, aerobics and mineral water aside, everybody still enjoys a good, genuine steak. You can find quite a few of those here, in this overdecorated, dusky, dark-walled restaurant that's a Toronto institution and a long-loved hyperbole. Arthur Carman's personal philosophy and poetry overflows sentimentally onto several pages of the menu, which, like the steaks, is enormous. In case you miss his poems there, he'll personally recite them for you at the table, as only a Greek could

RESTAURANTS

do. People come anyway, for the tender, lovely steaks—especially the sirloins—for the garlic that infuses every item from bread to vegetables, and partly to smile about the overkill in both dinner and decor. Portions of the main course are huge, but before you even get to them, you must work through baskets of garlic bread and trays of feta, olives and dill pickles. Carman's is not the place for you if you consider ten ounces of red meat to be excessive. It has been estimated that the number of doggie bags leaving the restaurant exceeds Toronto's canine population by 62 percent. Go figure.

When ordering, take the term "steakhouse" literally, and avoid the seafood. The spareribs and the lambchops are both good bets. Treat the ubiquitous advertisment that lists Carman's as *The New York Times*'s choice as one of downtown Toronto's three best restaurants as an interesting historical memento. That was a long time ago. These days, a steak dinner for two, with wine, costs Can$100.

Open daily 5:30 p.m.- 11 p.m. Cards: MC, V.

Celestino's
1049 Eglinton Ave. West, York
• 789-1126
ITALIAN

12/20

The two Italian brothers who run this uptown eatery didn't plan originally on entering the eating business: the portly Celestino once trained for the priesthood, and his slender brother, Pino, began training as a doctor. Now Pino heals ailing souls with his heartwarming Italian cooking, and Celestino presides over a different kind of congregation, whose members arrive in long black limos, wearing sunglasses. To add to the effect, the walls are lined with photos of Celestino and Frank Sinatra. The otherwise austere appearance of this restaurant belies its hospitality and generous food.

They take very good care of you at Celestino's, if you know the drill. To use a menu marks you as a tourist. Toss it aside and ask Celestino or Pino what's up for dinner. You'll get a hint from the antipasti table at the entrance, which always carries lovely caramelized onions, marinated eggplant and artichokes, rice cakes and fagioli (beans). The kitchen keeps a good selection of fresh mushrooms and seafood, and you can have any of them done in any fashion. Ask for something light and you'll get spaghetti tossed with olive oil and garlic, followed by some simply grilled monkfish. Ask for a bit of spice, and you might get a pile of penne doused in a pungent tomato sauce. You can even go romantic: one night, risotto was flavored with rose petals and served with creamed spinach. It's best to build your meal around the antipasti and pastas; except for the occasional great grilled fish, the main courses aren't worth their prices. Inquire about the wine. There's always a special pick that

RESTAURANTS

Celestino would just love you to try. Tiramisu is best for dessert. Dinner for two, with wine, will be about Can$100.
Open Tues.-Sun. 6 p.m.-11 p.m. Cards: AE, MC, V.

Centro Grill and Wine Bar
2472 Yonge St.,
Toronto North
• 483 2211
ITALIAN/CALIFORNIAN

Franco Prevedello is the godfather of Toronto's Italian restaurants. There is hardly one among the top ten in which he hasn't played some part. This place is his masterwork to date: a cavernous glass-and-steel Milan-inspired space with a menu that borrows heavily from Californian cookery and an extensive wine list that misses little. From its opening day in 1987, Centro has been a spot to ogle and be ogled, a restaurant where customers dress up in tight leathers to eat what's on the plates and talk about who's at the tables.

For appetizers, they nibble at crispy little pizzas, a beautifully turned-out tuna carpaccio or any of several competent pastas, the occasional one goosed with chilies. Among the main courses, salmon is roasted and seasoned with Anaheim peppers and chervil, textured with cashews and served with salsa verde; a special of blackened sea scallops comes in a delicate tomato-fennel sauce. There's a thick veal chop you can slice into like a knife cuts through butter; after a grilling over mesquite, it's done up with leeks, green onions and mushrooms. The platters are prettily put together, with generous clusters of vegetables and the usual grainy asides. Similar theatrics go into the desserts, which are dolled up with coulis squirts and fresh-fruit clusters, though they rarely deliver on the pretty promises. The one exception: a heavenly rendering of tiramisu that receives a dusting of cocoa powder in the shape of a crossed knife and fork. Order it to believe it. Or, end simply with ice cream or fresh fruit.

It's rumored that waiters vie for a job at Centro because of the good tips from high flyers. Once there, they work with the team spirit and aggression of a hockey team. The wine list appropriately offers mostly California and Italian wines, most within the Can$30-to-Can$45 bracket, with a few in the splurge category.

Take a look at the pasta bar downstairs, wildly popular both as a singles spot and as a casual setting for decently priced meals. The menu carries the same small pizzas, pastas and grand desserts as upstairs, adding several sophisticated salads, pastas and trattoria-style main dishes. Several good wines are available by by the glass. Dinner for two upstairs will be about Can$120, downstairs, about Can$90 or more, depending on how freely the wine flows.
Open Mon.-Sat. 5 p.m.-11:30 p.m. Cards: AE, MC, V.

RESTAURANTS

C'est What
67 Front St. East,
Downtown
• 867-9499
ECLECTIC

12/20

Nuttily eclectic, C'est What is not for the inhibited, or those who pooh-pooh nonconformist behavior. If you're fond of party games, you can indulge in a round of Twister or Scrabble here; if you like music, they shoot whatever is new and offbeat on the sound system (both recorded and live), and if you like to dine in the later half of the evening, this is your kind of place.

Not only that, but the food's good. The menu reveals a mixed bag of American, Middle Eastern, Italian and Asian cuisines, with everything from satés to sandwiches (you can design them to your specifications), from lasagne to shepherd's pie. There are also beers on tap from more than a dozen microbreweries. One of our favorite dishes is the unholy mess of deep-fried yams and potatoes topped with sour cream and accompanied by a Greek salad—pure fun. And for dessert, Sex in a Pan is de rigeur (what would Senator Jesse Helms have to say about this?), a construction of cream cheese, chocolate mousse and whipped cream piled into a graham cracker crust. Quite the hangout for post-theater diners, as well as clubgoers and various other nightowls, C'est What is also worth a trip earlier in the evening, and for lunch as well. Dinner for two, with drinks, is about Can$50.

Open Mon.-Thurs. noon-3 a.m., Fri.-Sat. noon-5 a.m., Sun. 6 p.m.-1 a.m. Cards: AE, MC, V.

Charmers
1384 Bathurst St.,
Toronto
• 657-1225
CALIFORNIAN/MEXICAN

11/20

While Mexican restaurants do not abound in Toronto, an increasing number seem to be incorporating Mexican dishes on'to their menus. Charmers provides a good example of this: the food here mostly derives from the Californian/eclectic school, with some Thai and French dishes on the menu, but the best dishes are the Mexican ones. Charmers takes its name to heart; it is indeed a charming little café, with friendly service and well-prepared food. On the Spanish-speaking side of the menu, you'll find crispy, overflowing tostadas; delicious empanadas, stuffed with beef or chicken, and hotted up with a side of homemade salsa; and enchiladas served with a variety of fillings, textures, tastes and temperatures—filled with meat or seafood and crowned with sour cream and smooth guacamole—and beautifully presented. Also tasty is the garlicky-peppery chicken pueblo, marinated in tangy citrus juices. Seafood dishes are present as well, salads and soups (try the bean soup), pastas and even a Middle Eastern item, baba ghanouj, but stick to the Mexican dishes for a *buena comida*. Dinner for two, with drinks, runs about Can$45.

Open daily 11 a.m.-9:30 p.m. Cards: MC, V.

RESTAURANTS

Chiaro's
King Edward Hotel,
37 King St. East,
Downtown
• 863-9700
CONTINENTAL

12/20

Hotel dining rooms with their subsidized plushness and goofy parodies of formality are the last refuge for those seeking assurance that the occasion is indeed very special. Among such dining rooms in Toronto, the formal room at the King Eddy holds special significance: in its heyday the city's wealthy taught their children how cutlery should be used so not to embarrass the family. Today, though the food rarely soars, expect competence and an effusive presentation. At night, many of the dishes are prepared tableside on a glittering trolley: Champagne is sold by the glass; caviar comes by the gram and is offered up on tiny silver-pedestaled plates with all the trimmings.

Main meals, arriving on pretty plates, often have a Canadian bent. You might encounter the sweet, tiny shrimp from Matane, Quebec, served potted, or Prairie corn chowder, creamy with slices of vegetable and turkey. Baked East Coast salmon is tender and lovely. It doesn't need the lily gilding it receives in the form of a sesame crust and béarnaise, but the additions aren't offensive. The menu ventures into Asia with five-flavored Thai chicken with noodles and lemon grass. Advocates of a healthy heart will find alternative menus offering low-fat, low-salt meals. On one occasion, a first course was a large spinach salad with a light vinaigrette, followed by a thin slice of properly cooked venison annointed with a sweet-tart clear huskleberry sauce.

For dessert, stick to the mocha crème brûlée or the cheese plate; avoid the dessert trolley of French pastries that look like they have been subjected to an acrylic dip. The wine list is wide and grand, with pricey representations from the main countries. Ceremony accompanies any wine presentation. Dinner for two will be Can$160 or more.

Open Mon.-Fri. noon-3 p.m. & 6 p.m.-10:30 p.m., Sat. 6 p.m.-10:30 p.m. All major cards.

China Blues
125 King St. East,
Downtown
• 366-2556
ECLECTIC

(14)

Torontonians (ourselves included) have slavishly followed chef Greg Couillard as he has moved from one restaurant to another. That's because when his food is on, it's hard to find better. His platters are whimsical blasts of color, and he displays a remarkable ability to balance such wildly disparate flavor combinations as Caribbean-with-Chinese-with-Italian. Many of his dishes simmer with spice, their heat poulticed by sweetness. On occasion, the sweetness overwhelms, but for the most part, the balance is perfect and the dish soars. Take the polenta: light and custardy wedges of the stuff, filled with fresh corn, jalapeño peppers and spinach and laid out in a bright pool of salsa. It's one of the best dishes in any restaurant in Toronto. Chiang Mai Thighs (sounding more like a dare than a dish) are sautéed in galangal, ginger, lime leaf and lemon grass, then spiked with chili peppers, coconut, tamarind and a peanut sauce. The unusual "Jump Up" soup begins sort of like a thick, earnest minestrone, but goes astray from there—it incorporates okra, black-eyed peas and chicken, and receives a dousing in lemongrass, curry, ginger and cinnamon. The accessories in a Couillard creation demand equal attention with the main attraction, but rarely detract from it. For instance, rice pilaf is studded with currants and pine nuts. Or, you might run across an odd fruit, gleaned from one of Toronto's Chinese markets, maybe dragon's-eye lychees or lotus blossoms. Couillard plants paper umbrellas in the shrimp and tosses twisted sprigs of pasta into the pilaf, so the plate that's put in front of you might look like a send-up of a Singapore Sling. Desserts look swell, too—but, unlike the main courses, they can disappoint. If you must indulge, stay away from the heavy baked goods and order a dish of ice cream.

In addition to the dining room, in front is a casual *tapas* bar, where snack versions of the same food are ordered by the piece. Stick to the real dining area in the the back, a casual room with widely spaced tables. Service is friendly, but tends to be slow. The perfect accompaniment to this food is a good, cold brew—just choose from the wide selection of beer from local breweries. Dinner will run about Can$100 for two, with beers; two can spend easily half that in the bar.

Open Mon.-Fri. noon-2:30 p.m. & 6 p.m.-11 p.m., Sat. 6 p.m.-11 p.m. Cards: MC, V.

Cibo
1055 Yonge St., Downtown
• 921-2166
ITALIAN

11/20

Cibo is a small, crowded little restaurant, and if you dare venture in during peak dinner hours, be prepared to wait. The kitchen focuses on very fresh ingredients, putting a modern twist on classic Italian dishes, some of which can go awry (as in the rigatoni with hot, fresh fruit and scallions). Stay away from dishes with complicated berry sauces, or those with too many ingredients. This may remind you of the archbishop who allegedly complained to Mozart that one of his musical works had "too many notes." In the case of Cibo, though, overambitious flavor and texture combinations can produce true culinary dischord.) Salads are heavy on the radicchio, but taste good. So are the more peasant-inspired pastas, such as fettuccine with green pepper, sausage and tomato. The daily specials, chalked up on a blackboard, often include a couple of good, straightforward seafood preparations. Dinner for two, with wine, runs about Can$65.

Open Mon.-Sat. noon-3 p.m. & 6 p.m.-1 a.m., Sun. noon-3 p.m. & 6 p.m.-11 p.m. Cards: AE, MC, V.

RESTAURANTS

Cuisine of India

5222 Yonge St.,
North York
• 229-0377
INDIAN

13

North York has never been known in Toronto for its East Indian food—but it will be soon. This new restaurant's encyclopedia of flavors, which go into everything from its terrific tandoori roasted leg of lamb to its searing chicken vindaloo, has changed all that. The lamb is marinated in a collection of spices common to East Indian cookery—star anise, ginger and garlic—plus a less common touch of vinegar and a splash of rum. It comes sizzling to the table lathered in spices, steeped in flavor, the meat falling off the bone. Except for the lackluster tandoori chicken, other tandoori dishes from the glassed-in kitchen near the entrance must not be missed. One such dish, paneer soola, presents that tofulike Indian cheese in a marinade of yogurt, ginger, pomegranate-seed powder and mango powder, among other poetic flavorings. Curried dishes, blessedly light on ghee, achieve a sensitive balance of flavors: try the gobi dilpafand, cauliflower baked in a yogurt-and-poppy-seed sauce, or the bhagare baigan, strips of eggplant softly sauced with spiced coconut, cashews and peanuts, the result a pleasing contrast between silky sauce and crunchy nuts.

The range of regional cooking represented at Cuisine of India reflects the travels of owner/chef Shishir Sharma, originally from the Punjab. While working for an East Indian hotel chain, he traveled throughout India, later translating its regional cuisines for kitchens in Hong Kong, England and the United States. No dish is particularly spicy-hot, except the vindaloos, which have brought tears on occasion. The soft, warm naan and chapati breads from the tandoori ovens and the various rice dishes will take away the sting. A hearty dinner will be no more than Can$50 for two. Weekend brunches are blessedly cheap at about Can$20 for two.

Open Sun.-Thurs. 11:30 a.m.-2:30 p.m. & 5:30 p.m.-10 p.m., Fri.-Sat. 11:30 a.m.-2:30 p.m. & 5:30 p.m. Cards: AE, ER, MC, V.

Daily Planet

40 Eglinton Ave. East,
Toronto North
• 440-0030
CALIFORNIAN

11/20

Artsy and unpretentious, the Daily Planet offers better atmosphere than it does food, but you can eat pretty decently here if you stick to the basics on the varied menu. There's lots to choose from—just sit back and enjoy the scene, and don't fret too much over not having a peak culinary experience. Lots of snacks and light dishes fill the menu, as well as a host of salads, pizzas, pastas and chicken dishes. Nothing here will knock your socks off, but if you're uptown, and just want an easy meal in a lively boîte, the Daily Planet certainly fits that bill. Dinner for two, with wine, costs about Can$60.

Open Mon.-Sat. 11:30 a.m.-1 a.m., Sun. 11:30 a.m.-11 p.m. Cards: AE, MC, V.

L'Entrecôte

See Auberge Gavroche, page 15.

RESTAURANTS

Epicure Café

512 Queen St. West,
Downtown
• 363-8942
ITALIAN

12/20

The Epicure Café reminds us of those cozy little Italian restaurants in New York's Greenwich Village; after all, Queen Street West is the Village of Toronto. Intimate and friendly, the Epicure is a terrific place to relax and refuel after traversing this fascinating district. Take in the restaurant's contemporary yet comfortable ambience and menu, and begin with an order of bruschetta, toasted bread slices rubbed with garlic and served here with olives, and the salads are quite good. We like the tender, fresh tortellini in a mushroom-herb cream sauce, the surprisingly good cold poached salmon, and the zippy provençal-style chicken with crispy roast potatoes. The polenta with a Gorgonzola-tomato sauce works well, but we have steered clear of the fresh perch in a mango-coriander sauce for fear that the strange combination might not work. The coffee here is exceptional, as is the sour cherry tart offered for dessert. There's a small selection of inexpensive wines. And the price is right: dinner for two, with wine, will run about Can$60.
Open daily 11:30 a.m.-1 a.m. Cards: AE, MC, V.

La Fenice

319 King St. West,
Downtown
• 585-2377
ITALIAN

(14)

The streets near Toronto's new SkyDome boast a plethora of restaurants, and most have vied in vain for title of "the best." To our mind, La Fenice wins hands-down for its consistently excellent northern Italian food. For the food only, that is. Despite repeated efforts, the restaurant has never been able to overcome its crippling and cold decor: noises reverberate off bare plaster walls, heels click on ceramic floors and plates clank on marble tables. To exacerbate matters, food is conveyed on a metal trolley that clatters across the ceramic floor like an assault of some kind of deadly silverware militia.

But what it brings will take away all traces of annoyance: red peppers roasted to dark smokiness; octopuses dripping with a sublime marinade; boccancini wrapped with proscuitto and topped with herbed mayonnaise—the contrast between salty and soft jolts the senses like a sip of chilled wine in a hot tub. After the befores, there's spaghettini that shouts with rich, ripe tomatoes and fresh basil. The more glamorous pastas, such as agnolotti with Gorgonzola, pale against that dish's honest, direct flavors. There is hardly ever any red meat on the menu, better to let you sample the grilled fish. Choices vary with the market, but the whole grilled fish always has crisp skin and soft flesh. Zuppa di pesce beats all the others in town. Of the meat, medallions of veal sing with fresh rosemary; grilled chicken is simple and good. For dessert, the cappuccino-mousse cake or Swiss-chocolate-nut cake makes an ethereal finish. Dinner for two costs Can$110. A wine bar downstairs offers a lighter version of the menu, but in an atmosphere so frosty it makes

RESTAURANTS

upstairs seem cozy as a boudoir.
Open Mon.-Fri. noon-2:30 p.m. & 5:30 p.m.-11 p.m., Sat. 5:30 p.m.-11 p.m. All major cards.

Filet of Sole

11 Duncan St.,
Downtown
• 598-3256
SEAFOOD

12/20

Yes, it's loud, hectic, busy and famous for lines, waits and a phone that never seems to stop ringing. But the fish and other finned or shelled creatures come to the table very fresh at this warehouse-style eatery, where they are treated fairly and fairly priced to boot. Formerly a print shop, this high, wide checker-clothed space with massive windows sits smack dab in the middle of the theater district. Youthful servers negotiate around tables and each other, balancing massive trays loaded with top-heavy, generously portioned main courses. Lovers of seafood (a*fish*ionados?) dig into platters of glistening scampi, shrimp bubbling in butter, crab legs the length of which rivals dancers' in a Las Vegas show, steamed Canadian (only) lobster, or any one of dozens of daily combination specials. Don't forget the fresh fish: halibut, grouper, monkfish, bass, shark, kingfish, pompano, salmon, tuna—name it and it's probably here.

Here's a game plan. Order a bottle of wine from the restaurant's surprisingly intelligent and affordable wine list, or pick a beer, anything from Jamaica's Red Stripe to Ontario's local Sleeman's Ale. Next, study the menu, preferably at the affiliated Henry's Oyster Bar at the entrance. Believe us, make a reservation, it helps. Things we've enjoyed include spicy hot oysters Rockefeller; coconut-beer shrimp with Thai dipping sauce; and a fun platter of smoked fish, including filets of rainbow trout, black cod, haddock and salmon. Either chef's rice or baked or boiled spuds accompanies main courses, the rice nutty and buttered with bits of carrot and celery. Desserts taste fine, especially chocolate mousse cake and citrusy, puckery Key lime pie. Count on Can$70 for two with wine.
Open Mon.-Wed. 11:30 a.m.-2:30 p.m. & 5 p.m.-10:30 p.m., Thurs. 11:30 a.m.-2:30 p.m. & 5 p.m.-11 p.m., Fri.-Sat. 11:30 a.m.-2:30 p.m. & 5 p.m.-11:30 p.m., Sat. 5 p.m.-11:30 p.m., Sun. 5 p.m.-10 p.m. All major cards.

Foodworks

549 Bloor St. West,
The Annex
• 531-1195
AMERICAN

12/20

For a traditional burger with all the fixings, everything homemade and quintessentially fattening, Foodworks leads the large pack of contenders in Toronto. Permanently jammed with the endless parade of Bloor Street West's youthful walking traffic, and the almost-as-young Bloor Repertory Cinema habitués from across the street, this place's decoration symbolizes "burgeria" fashion. Bright and brash, it could be anyplace in the world. It's all in how the essentials of America's favorite sandwich are handled. Sides of beef hang in the window, aging before being ground daily. The egg-yellow buns are baked on the premises. Fries are cut from real spuds and then fried with the skin on; the cole slaw is shredded from fresh cabbages. The enormous salads offer earthy romaine lettuce instead of the pedestrian iceberg. Ribs, chicken and steak can be spotted on the menu, but one of the numerous styles of burger (for that matter, you can make up your own) is the only bet. A full license is here for the asking, but most of the clients make do with a soda or milkshake. A burger meal for two, with salad and beverages, costs no more than Can$30.

Open Mon.-Thurs. 10 a.m.-1 a.m., Fri.-Sat. 10 a.m.-3 a.m., Sun. 10 a.m.-1 a.m. All major cards.

Fran's Restaurant

20 College St., Downtown
• 923-9867

2275 Yonge St., Downtown
• 481-1112

21 St. Clair St., Downtown
• 925-6336
AMERICAN

9/20

One doesn't go to Fran's strictly for the food, any more than Humphrey Bogart's *Casablanca* character went to Casablanca to take the waters. The chain is a piece of Torontonian dining history, around for over 50 years and open 24 hours a day, every day. The College Street Fran's is fun, fast and cheap, serving gargantuan breakfasts all day: combos with German sausages, pancakes, eggs, home fries, toast and jam; corned-beef hash; and huge waffles with Fran's own brand of syrup. The burgers actually taste pretty good; the "Franburger" is made with freshly ground beef, *sans* preservatives. For the more adventurous, there's a steak-and-kidney pie, drab sole and mushrooms, fish-and-chips and lasagne, as well as a bargain turkey dinner (for kids and seniors only), and prosaic spaghetti and meatballs.

You can really go to town with the desserts here. Dive into the mile-high lemon-meringue pie, the dense carrot cake or one of the gut-busting sundaes, such as our favorite, the Brown Derby, built of a fudge brownie, mounds of vanilla ice cream, rivers of hot fudge and clouds of whipped cream. We also were fond of the rice-and-raisin pudding. You won't go broke here, either: dinner for two, with beverages, averages about Can$25.

Open daily 24 hours. Cards: AE, MC, V.

Future Bakery

483 Bloor St. West, Toronto
• 922-5875
HUNGARIAN

12/20

If you're a fan of Eastern European food, you'll love Future Bakery. Part cafeteria, part Bohemian café, you'll be well-fed at Future, and not much poorer than when you walked in. Contemporary in design, yet old-fashioned in feel and cuisine, you can either dine in the full-service patio, or help yourself at the steam-table counter; naturally, the latter is the more fun and funky of the two. You can dish up goodies like hearty borscht, which here is a thick, stewlike vegetable soup, wienerschnitzel, heavy yet agreeable mashed potatoes and toothsome potato varenekes. You can also go for the fair-to-middling cabbage rolls, but the salads, especially the cucumber-and-dill, offer a decent alternative (for those desirous of lighter fare, but then why come to a place like this for salad?).

In our book, Future Bakery is a hip place to dine in Toronto: the food's fine and filling, it opens early and closes late and you get good value for your money. Dinner for two, with beer, won't exceed Can$40.

Open daily 7 a.m.-3 a.m. No cards.

Grano

2035 Yonge St.,
Toronto North
• 440-1986
ITALIAN

12/20

Grano's "contrived-demolished" decor (bricks exposed under plaster, sheets of plastic over the windows last time we visited) and the frequent sense of chaos engendered by skittish service are tolerable because this is one of those rare, comfy places where everyone seems to feel at home. We come here when we're feeling jolly and sociable; like the other regulars who know the routine, we skim lightly over the printed menu—which lists one soup, one pasta and a hot meal per night—and head for the real offerings in the display case at the front. That's where you put together a piecemeal dinner of sunny, rich Italian appetizers. Working your way through the case is like raiding your refrigerator after a good party. There may be a spicy and satisfying ratatouille, a tasty rendition of sautéed cold sweetbreads or a dish of white rice and calamari flavored with squid ink. Soups can be exceptional: don't miss the egg-drop-and-spinach soup if they have it. Pastas sometimes suffer from timid seasoning but come in generous portions. Pizzas and calzones employ tender pastry and upmarket items such as sun-dried tomatoes. For dessert, pass up the zuccotto for the heavenly pear frangipane. Service tends to be hazardous, but communal tables let you get to know your neighbors while you wait.

Open Mon.-Thurs. 10 a.m.-10:30 p.m., Fri. 10 a.m.- 11 p.m., Sat. 9:30 a.m.-11 p.m. Cards: MC, V.

La Grenouille

2387 Yonge St.,
Toronto North
• 481-3093
FRENCH

12/20

What a sweet place this is! La Grenouille, basically a storefront in this burgeoning hip neighborhood of trendy boutiques and cafés, is a tiny, classic French bistro with a compact menu, and everything we tried here was good. On our last visit, one poor fellow was serving as maître d', waiter, reservation-taker and cashier. He handled all three jobs with great charm and aplomb.

He swiftly brought us a basket of soft crusty bread, which we instantly devoured. The classic soupe à l'oignon tasted rich and thick with caramelized onions, with a perfect glaze of Gruyère

RESTAURANTS

cheese blanketing it. Our simple salads were fresh and perfectly dressed; the oysters exuded a briny freshness, plump and tasty, and the baked endive with a gently biting chèvre cream was heavenly.

On to the main courses . . . La Grenouille serves a delicious version of steak frites, the meat simply grilled and glazed with a nice béarnaise, and the fries, thin, crisp and habit-forming. There's also a lovely filet of lamb in a peppercorn sauce, and the orange roughy was moist and flavorful.

Aside from the food, which we loved, we enjoyed the fact that one could really linger comfortably here over dessert (especially over the much-welcome cheese course) and coffee. Check out the limited yet well-priced selection of local and French wines. Dinner for two, with wine, is about Can$70.

Open Mon.-Thurs. 11:30 a.m.-2:30 p.m. & 5:30 p.m.-10:30 p.m., Fri. 11:30 a.m.-11 p.m., Sat. 6 p.m.-11 p.m. Cards: AE, MC, V.

Hard Rock Café
SkyDome,
300 Bremner Blvd.,
Harbourfront
• 341-2388
AMERICAN

12/20

A Hard Rock is a Hard Rock is a Hard Rock—except when it's located practically inside the awesome SkyDome. This is an Isaac Tigrett Hard Rock (he and original partner Peter Morton split up several years ago; each now runs their own, still-identical Hard Rocks), and it would be hard to imagine a more spectacular restaurant for sports and rock-and-roll fans. This Hard Rock is only a couple of years old, yet it's chockablock with rock memorabilia (reliquaries to such musical saints as Michael Jackson, Madonna, the Rolling Stones, Paul McCartney). The menu is typical Hard Rock fare: barbecued chicken, burgers, salads and sandwiches, and you can't complain about the quality of this simple food, which is better than it has to be, but the view is absolutely thrilling.

The restaurant is actually smack dab in the middle of the SkyDome complex, and has panoramic windows that put the stadium right up there in front of your table On game days, one can purchase tickets one hour in advance (they must be bought in person) for Can$18 to Can$20 for window seats. Before you start howling at the tariff, please note that you get a Can$15 discount off your meal check. During games, rock music is eschewed for the sound of the game, and you really do get a bird's-eye view of the proceedings on the field. This really has to rank as one of the top restaurant locations in the world. And dinner for two, with beverages, will only set you back about Can$40. You certainly get your money's worth on several counts.

Open daily 11 a.m.-1 a.m. Cards: AE, MC, V.

RESTAURANTS

Holt Renfrew Café

50 Bloor St. West,
Bloor-Yorkville
• 922-2333
CALIFORNIAN/
INTERNATIONAL

13

Holt Renfrew, the Bergdorf Goodman of Canada, oozes posh and ritz, so it's only befitting that the café of this emporium dedicated to the haute-est of fashion follow suit. Not only is it a wonderful place to stop while shopping here, it's also one of the best cafés in the neighborhood, worth a visit on its own merits. The room is situated right off the selling floor, yet one feels at a comfortable distance from the lure of Armani and Donna Karan. Done in cool beiges and pale pastels, there's a feeling of casual wealth here, and the menu offers a well-chosen bounty, as well. Ingredients are absolutely fresh and flavorful; not one dish disappointed us.

We enjoyed a wonderful Mexican chicken salad, spiced genteely, with firm black beans, corn and cilantro lightly piled atop mixed greens. The Caesar salad was perfection, speared with freshly baked Parmesan breadsticks rather than the usual, prosaic croutons. The baked goat cheese on croutons (so that's where they went!), served with field greens and golden caramelized onions makes for a wonderful lagniappe, as does the marinated beet salad studded with feta cheese and dill.

For heartier appetites, try the salmon-crabcakes, served with a small salad and tropical fruits taste fine, as do the spicy Thai noodles tossed with chicken, shrimp, coconut and ginger. Pastas, such as homemade rigatoni stuffed with a chicken-and-fennel mousse, are baked in a light cream sauce sprinkled with chives, a version of the famous "21" burger, topped with a glaze of opal-basil butter, and is served on grilled, rough Portuguese bread with onions, sliced tomato, horseradish, mustard and mayonnaise.

Leave some room for dessert—the pastries, especially a mixed berry crumble on our visit—are well worth it. You just may want to pass on trying anything on afterward, though. A meal for two, including beverages, is about Can$40.

Open Mon.-Wed. & Sat. 10 a.m.-5 p.m., Thurs.-Fri. 10 a.m.-8 p.m. Cards: AE, MC, V.

Hsin Kuang

287 King St. West,
Harbourfront
• 597-3838
CHINESE

10/20

Hsin Kuang, with its huge, opulent, old-fashioned Chinese dining emporium atmosphere, is reminiscent of Hong Kong. Sure, the elegance has gone a bit tatty, but it's an old local favorite. And while the food may not reach the heights of the Himalayas, Hsin Kuang is a lot of fun to be in. The specialty is seafood: several shark's-fin soup preparations are offered (very expensive, as ever); several abalone dishes, such as braised abalone with Hunan ham, Chinese mushrooms and vegetables; a host of shrimp dishes (the best we had were the salt baked shrimps with chili), and various squid, scallop and whole fish dishes. And it's always better to stick with what a restaurant does best. Hsin Kuang gives a tired nod to the tourist trade, with items such as boring, breaded fried shrimp and spring rolls, but you can also get tea-smoked chicken, braised grouper ("garoupa" on the menu) and various, semi-authentic casseroles, such as braised sliced beef with lily flowers and black fungus. Unfortunately, that dish isn't quite as exotic as it sounds, our order came looking and tasting more like a stripped-down beef stew.

Though Hsin Kuang really caters to *gwai loh* (foreigners), it does have a certain campy charm (if you like hostesses in the Hong Kong restaurant drag of skin-tight floor length skirts slit up to the North Pole), and it is quite lively in the evening. Dinner for two, with beverages, is about Can$50.
Open daily 11 a.m.-midnight. All major cards.

Hughie's
22 Front St. West,
Downtown
• 364-2242
AMERICAN

10/20

It makes perfect sense that Hughie's is owned by a fashion designer: the place looks as though it could be used as the set for *Cheers*. Serving up good, casual food, Hughie's, great for before or after the theater, is a very popular boîte among the local businesspeople. While never exactly boisterous, Hughie's is alive and humming with folks who go wild about the burgers here. And a good burger it is, with several variations: a Philly burger with sautéed onions, mushrooms and Swiss cheese; a diet burger, simply char-grilled; and even a lamb burger, made of 100 percent ground lamb, grilled and served on a bun with the usual condiments.

There are lots of finger foods here, such as nachos, potato skins and an impossibly gooey version of cheese-garlic bread, as well as some good salads (especially the huge Greek, and the Maui turkey salad with water chestnuts and curried mayonaisse). The fries, greaseless and crisp, can be had with gravy, chili, or just plain naked.

Though the pies are touted here, the kitchen doesn't keep its promise. The coconut-cream pie is pretty decent, as is the apple pie (goosed with currants) but such ambitious numbers as the frozen raspberry mousse pie or the sky-high lemon-lime mousse pie in a chocolate-cookie crust are a bit too-too. A meal for two, with beverages, is about Can$40.
Open Mon.-Tues. 11:30 a.m.-10:30 p.m., Wed.-Sat. 11:30 a.m.-midnight, Sun. 4:30 p.m.-9 p.m. All major cards.

Iguana

2050 Avenue Rd.,
Toronto North
• 488-5947
MEXICAN

11/20

Toronto has relatively few places where one can try the range of Mexican cookery: most are of the gluey-cheese-on-flaccid-nachos variety. This leaves the field to the few places like Iguana. The best of this north Toronto restaurant kitchen shows a knack for fresh fish and herbs. It's an attractive place, sparsely but carefully done with *faux* adobe walls and a few tasteful posters. In the back, the room opens onto a large kitchen, where you can watch family members at work. The bustle lends the room a comfy, hospitable ambience. What we go here for are the tapas, which are a bargain in terms of both taste and money. They change weekly, but watch for the fish: steamed clams with peppers and onion sauce or mixed shellfish and mollusks in a spicy, light sauce. Their presentation, arrayed on one platter and brightened with dollops of salsa, adds to their appeal. The advice for fish extends to the main courses. Pescado boca del rio (fish from the river's mouth) is a big bowl of a lyrical and hearty stew of grouper and shrimp, served with lots of homemade tortillas for dipping. Other fish bargains are the codfish with coriander, tomato and green olives for Can$10.95 or the red snapper in green tomato, coriander and a mild pepper sauce. Neither of the tortilla-based desserts tastes particularly special. Save your calories for the tapas and your budget for the fish.
Open Tues.-Sat. 6 p.m.-10:30 p.m. Cards: AE, MC, V.

Indian Rice Factory

414 Dupont St.,
Toronto
• 961-3472
INDIAN

13

Once upon a time this was just a humble little neighborhood spot, but word spread among tandoori-chicken fanatics, and now it's a humble little neighborhood spot always packed with Indian-food-lovers. All of the cooking is done by owner and expert chef Amar Patel, the only sister in a family of three restaurateurs who run Indian restaurants in Toronto. That hers is considered the best of the three must make for some family controversy. Though located in a rather grungy neighborhood, the restaurant is casual and comfortable, with the best seating at the round, clothed tables in the main room. There are no dishes to avoid, and some that absolutely can't be missed: chicken curry, cooked to tenderness in ginger, garlic and tomatoes; eggplant flavored with big slices of that same ginger, plus green pepper and coriander; and puri chole, a spicy chickpea curry full of texture and flavor, to be soaked up with good homemade bread. The Thali dinner, a generous sampling of vegetarian dishes, comes in the traditional divided metal plate. For fire-eaters, the chili pork will satisfy—the rich, chestnut-colored stew is full of big, lean chunks of meat and mean green peppers, all the more assaultive for the seeds left in them. Any

of the good breads will soothe a burning palate. So will the bill, which for two, won't exceed Can$40.
Open daily 11 a.m.-11 p.m. All major cards.

Jade Garden

222 Spadina Ave.,
3rd Floor
• 599-6000
CHINESE

13

You don't always know what you're eating at this gleaming dim-sum megacircus for one thousand, and that makes for adventure as well as generally good eating. Go to this restaurant in Spadina Avenue's new China Town center for Sunday brunch. You'll find yourself in a vast sea of 600 or more faces (550 of which seemingly belong to Chinese expatriates); just smile at the continually circulating waitresses who speak little or no English, and point to a wonder of tasty little dishes—plump dumplings stuffed with shredded pork and slivers of water chestnuts, elongated shrimp egg rolls, delicate har-gow, a vegetarian roll in tofu skin and a host of rice preparations, including a flattened square of rice noodles, lightly fried and slightly sweet. Among dozens of steamed-dumpling offerings, there are some usual preparations as well as the expected range of standards, from duck-mushroom to shrimp-peanut.

Take a bow, Jade Garden, for providing a morning of good fun and surprisingly good food at pleasingly low prices. (This is the restaurant version of Sears, Roebuck & Co., operating with low margins and reaping high profits based on large volume.) Like any of Hong Kong's traditional dim-sum palaces, this place puts on a good show, too. The huge room is warm and comfortable, with fields of wall-to-wall carpeting, green plants overhanging balconies and lots of big round tables with families and friends engaged in talking, pointing, munching, smiling and smoking. There is a more elaborate dinner menu and a full bar. Expect to pay about Can$36 for two, for a very filling brunch with a couple of cold beers.
Open daily 10 a.m.-4 p.m. & 5 p.m.-11 p.m. Cards: AE, MC, V.

Japanese Restaurant Ematei

30 St. Patrick St.,
Downtown
• 340-0472
JAPANESE

12/20

You'll miss this little place unless you look very carefully—it's small and undistinguished inside and out, tucked away on a side street without even a name in English to mark it. When you find it, you'll enter a new, clean, spare space, with a main room and three tatami rooms with wells under the tables. The traditional menu is very Japanese and very good. At a small sushi bar, you'll find the usual array of extremely fresh fish, prepared with the care and precision everyone has come to expect of Japanese restaurants. Notice, too, that the table is carefully furnished down to the last detail; plates carrying fresh cargo are a parade of prettiness; sashimi comes in deliberately lopsided cobalt-blue bowls; grilled eel is served in long slim plates that echo the shape

RESTAURANTS

of the fish. Most of the sushi selections can also be ordered grilled, as an entrée, and by all means sample one of these. Yellowtail, for instance, which makes terrific sushi, becomes even more succulent at the flame. Or, concentrate on the exceptional yosenabe, a sort of Japanese seafood hot-pot for two. The ingredients are arrayed raw: an extravagant spread of oysters, shrimp, clams, tilefish, octopus, squid, chicken, vegetables and rice noodles, all on one wide platter. Everything is cooked at the table in a rich fish-and-miso broth, to make a flavorful and playful feast. Ematei's version is expensive at Can$50 for two, but you won't need much more. A sushi feast for two, with saké, will total about Can$80. Ematei is a quiet place, the sort of modest restaurant that the community probably prefers to keep to itself. Ssssh—don't tell anyone we told you about it.

Open Mon.-Fri. 11:45 a.m.-2:30 p.m., Sat. 5:30 p.m.-10:30 p.m. All major cards.

Jennie's
360 Queen St. East, Downtown
• 861-1461
AMERICAN/SEAFOOD

11/20

It's not that the food isn't good at Jennie's—it's fresh, and competently prepared—but the atmosphere, at least on our last visit, left us a tad sullen. We'd call it dark deco (our lingering image retains a lot of shiny black surfaces). Jennie's is dressed in very slick neo-thirties garb, and came highly recommended to us by several different sources, but what we found was a restaurant with a rather desultory air to it (it was only about one-quarter full on a Saturday evening), and a staff with an indifferent-to-annoyed attitude.

When we arrived for dinner, we first asked to see a menu. We were directed to look at a blackboard hung near the open kitchen. The hostess then asked us, rather snippily, "Are you planning to stay for dinner?" When we replied that we wanted to see what was being served first, she harrumphed, and huffily walked away. Once seated, we found the food—fresh fish, pastas, stir-fries—to be pretty good Californian-Asian style cuisine. But where is the heart and soul that any restaurant needs to be successful? If you can make it to dessert, they're actually pretty tasty, including Key lime pie and chocolate-mousse cake. Although the wine list doesn't feature Canada's finest, there is a good international selection including some Australian and Chilean bottles. Dinner for two, with wine, is about Can$70.

Open Mon.-Fri. 11:30 a.m.-3 p.m. & 5:30 p.m.-10 p.m., Sat. 5:30 p.m.-11:30 p.m., Sun. noon-3 p.m. Cards: AE, MC, V.

RESTAURANTS

Joso's
202 Davenport (at Avenue Rd.), Toronto
• 925-1903
ITALIAN/SEAFOOD

12/20

No one should be sent to Joso's without being warned about owner Joso Spaglia's taste in art: The walls of this two-story converted (both morally and architecturally) Victorian house are covered with statuary and bold, Rubenesque paintings of nude females. Several Dalí prints anchor the other artwork, and the total effect is more whimsical than anything else. The place was born in the sixties as a coffee house (and a forum for the Yugoslavian singing duo of Joso and Malka), and evolved to become a respected fish restaurant by the late 1970s. It was then one of the few in town that served fish not gasping for breath through a blanket of cream sauce. Even now, few local eateries match Joso's touch. The menu centers around simple, grilled, very fresh fish and shellfish. The fare, displayed raw on a platter, comes with its flesh soft and moist, its skin crisp and charred. Souvlaki (the Greek shish kebab) is the only meat dish available, though many of the fish dishes match the heartiness of a good beefsteak. Spaghetti with chunks of octopus and its ink, hot and murky, fills a bowl with its strong, garlicky flavor. Risotto caragoi, a Venetian specialty, is a poisonously rich dish of shelled caragoi, or sea snails, in creamy, long-stirred rice. Joso's makes some of the best battered calamari in town, to be savored with the mandatory squirt of lemon.

The crowds that once inundated Joso's have thinned, partly because there are other good fish restaurants now, but also because Joso's prices tend to be high. The sting can be taken out of them if you go in a group and share calamari, a large pasta and a large grilled fish. The meal comes with a communal bowl of salad. There is no dessert to speak of, no wine list to boast about; any red wine that's available seems to be poured freely by the liter. Service is exuberant, friendly and helpful. Dinner for two will be about Can$130, but four, sharing as suggested, will bring that down to Can$90 per couple.
Open Mon.-Fri. 11:30 a.m.-3 p.m. & 5:30 p.m.-11 p.m., Sat. 5:30 p.m.-11 p.m. Cards: AE, MC, V.

Kahee Restaurant
349 Broadview Ave., Chinatown
• 463-6401, 463-6686
CHINESE

12/20

Kahee remains the most welcoming Chinese restaurant in Toronto. Its recently redecorated room sparkles, its service betrays none of the nonchalance of far too many other places, and its mostly Asian clientele doesn't seem to mind the intrusion of Occidental faces into their midst. The credit for a lot of this warmth belongs to the chef-owner Yee Shing Lo and his glamorous wife, co-owner/maître d', Oi Yuk Lo, who together run a happy, tight, family operation. The cooking is endearing and filling, but nothing to write home about. Nevertheless, the

RESTAURANTS

Kahee's many confirmed regulars return time and again. The low prices have something to do with it, and the consistency and generosity of certain, signature items doesn't exactly distract from the allure.

Shrimp won tons in MSG-free (if requested) broth are crunchy with chunks of the sweet seafood and the earthiness of tree ears. The stir-fried rice noodles, Malaysian-style, are chock full of enhancements like barbecued pork and sautéed shrimp, and are miraculously toothsome for a noodle that is famous for its softness. Seasonally available, blue crabs, sautéed in black-bean sauce make for a messy, delicious, hands-on feast that should not be missed except by the queasy.

For major appetites, Kahee offers a multicourse, pre-set meal that feeds up to four people and costs very little. It includes a daily soup, an appetizer plate of barbecued meats, al dente broccoli topped with mixed seafood, lobster in ginger and scallions, and an entire steamed pickerel (or buffalo fish, depending on the night), in a light sauce of oil, soya, ginger and cilantro.

Dining at the Kahee provides the opportunity for a visit to the Gerrard/Broadview Chinatown, which, while not as flashy as the bigger version on Dundas West, is colorful enough, and much more authentic for being less touristy. Dinner for two, with beer, shouldn't run higher than Can$35.

Open Mon.-Thurs. & Sun. 9 a.m.-midnight, Fri.-Sat. 8 a.m.-1 a.m. Cards: MC, V.

Last Temptation
12 Kensington Ave., Kensington Market
• 599-2551
MIDDLE EASTERN/ AMERICAN

9/20

Does one have to look like Sinead O'Connor in order to work at Last Temptation? It would seem so from just the briefest glance at all the buzz-cuts and black clothing affected by the staff. In any case, Last Temptation is a casual, cute, funky restaurant. The eclectic menu emphasizes Middle Eastern dishes, such as a good hummus dip served with pita bread, calamari with tzadziki, and a variation on the classic Greek salad, substituting watercress for the usual greens. Latin American touches include fresh salsa with tortilla chips, chicken grilled with more of that salsa and served on rice. Hearty sandwiches (crab, tuna, ham & cheese) and a roast chicken breast, sliced and napped with a creamy Dijon mustard sauce complete the choices.

For dessert, try the cheesecake; patrons are actually encouraged to linger over steaming cups of superb coffee (Toronto is one of the world's great, yet unsung, coffee towns). Dinner for two, with wine, is about Can$50.

Open daily 11 a.m.-2 a.m. (kitchen closes at 11 p.m.). Cards: AE, MC, V.

RESTAURANTS

Lee Garden Restaurant
358 Spadina Ave., Chinatown
• 593-9524
CHINESE

So many Chinese restaurants line the streets of Toronto's main Chinatown, they look like rivets on the side of a bus; without a map, the choice is overwhelming. Lee Garden will satisfy anyone who is put off by poshness and who thrives in places just this side of grungy. It's a true dive, with plastic tablecloths, paper notices on the walls and zippy service from waiters who seem not to understand a word you say, but then miraculously appear with everything you requested, and in the right order. Tell them to bring soft-shell crabs (when in season), crunchy on the outside, soft and steamy inside. For main courses, try the fat chunks of tender lobster in a pungent black-bean sauce; steamed fish, especially the seasonal northern whitefish called pickerel; and shrimp with sweet peppers. The English and Cantonese lists on the wall vary with the season and may include fresh oysters, mussels, eggplant or shrimp. Always have the steamed watercress and broccoli sprouts, and ask what other vegetables are available. Take the advice of the waiter, who knows which fish is achingly fresh and which vegetables have the perfect crunch. One Lee Garden specialty is the Mongolian hot pot, a huge meal for two or more cooked at the table, incorporating meat, seafood and vegetables. It is served only in the colder months, from October until it feels like spring outdoors. The place is a madhouse during the early dinner hours from Friday to Sunday; you'll do best after 8 p.m.

Open daily 4 p.m.-11:30 p.m. Cards: V.

Liberty Café
25 Liberty St., Downtown
• 538-1787
PACIFIC RIM

Tucked away from the flow of the action, Liberty Café on Liberty Street participates in the gentrification of this erstwhile light-manufacturing district on the backside of the Canadian National Exhibition fairgrounds. Now reclaimed by artists as loft residences, the area's buildings are beginning to refitted to meet urbane needs such as a place to meet with friends, listen to music and eat a good meal. Liberty caters to all of the above, and shines most brightly in the summer with a delightful, curbside patio from which to participate in the resuscitation of this idiosyncratic part of town.

The menu, which varies seasonally, stresses fresh-market items, with lean sauces and mostly flash-cooked meats. Soups are thick, with vegetable, borscht and black-bean all taking a turn in the rotation. Salads are dressed in perfumed oils such as hazelnut, and combine such upscale pairings such as green beans with smoked salmon and sea-scallops with coconut-chili dressing.

The main courses can be grilled liver with poached pear and red-wine sauce, sautéed veal paillard with a mango-lime salsa or

RESTAURANTS

grilled calamari with Szechuan sauce, scallion rice and Chinese cabbage salad. Also notable are the steak of the day, a rosemary-mint-garlic stuffed lamb baked with mushroom-brandy sauce, and a free-range chicken with Indonesian peanut sauce. Seafood is the prefered enhancement for pasta.

None of the cooking astounds, but neither does any of it disappoint. At last report, an effort was being made to improve the desserts, one of the restaurant's admitted weak points. The moderately priced wine list holds no surprises, just solid-value, popular French, Italian and Australian labels priced between Can$17 and Can$28. Dinner for two, with wine, will eat up about Can$75.

Open Mon.-Fri. 11:30 a.m.-3:30 p.m., Sat. 6 p.m.-10:30 p.m., Sun. noon-6 p.m. for extended brunch. Cards: AE, MC, V.

Going traveling? Look for Gault Millau's other "Best of" guides to Chicago, Florida, France, Hawaii, Hong Kong, Italy, London, Los Angeles, New England, New Orleans, New York, Paris, San Francisco, Washington, D.C. and more to come . . .

Lobster Trap

1962 Avenue Rd.,
Toronto
• 787-3211

404 Steeles Ave. West,
Thornhill
• 731-2263
SEAFOOD

12/20

Lobsters are industrial strength creatures with suits of armor. Assailing their outsides to eat their insides is a job best done at home, where newspapers may be spread on the table and the operation performed without concern for propriety. When Torontonians disregard that advice (why ever would anyone want to restrict their lobster eating to home?), they generally eat their lobsters at one of the Lobster Trap's two locations. That's because the restaurant does an efficient job of preparing fresh lobster at not much more cost than you could do at home, partly because lobster is the only item on the menu here.

The restaurant acknowledges the importance of privacy by seating most diners in small, boothlike sections. You can have your lobster either steamed or broiled, and we find the steamed version infinitely better. When the creature arrives at your table, it comes with enough hokey accompaniments that you'll be glad to be tucked away in a booth where no one can see you, with those sterno cans of warm melted butter and a plastic bib around your neck. The bib may be useful, but disregard the butter and opt for lemon juice or cider vinegar, which is the way that they eat them "down east" in Maryland. A good feed of lobster can be very rich. You should therefore have no qualms about disregarding the accompanying airline-quality iceberg-lettuce salad, the wimpy garlic bread, the plain baked potato or the

RESTAURANTS

appalling desserts. You don't come here for those anyway. A full dinner for two, that includes a two-pound lobster each, plus all the above-mentioned sides and a bottle of wine, will cost about Can$105.

Open daily 5 p.m.-10 p.m. Cards: AE, MC, V.

Lotus
96 Tecumseth St., Tecumseth
• 368-7620
PACIFIC RIM

If a meal is going to soar in a Toronto restaurant, this is where it will happen. Since opening this small, personal restaurant in 1988, chef-owner Susur Lee's name has become hallowed in Toronto's halls of gastronomy. Lee is Hong Kong born, and trained in formal French cookery. As the years go by, his platters have become less flamboyant and more focused on the primary—and successful—union of Chinese and Japanese ingredients prepared according to European techniques.

So, on this daily-changing menu there may be: deboned quail, cooked pink, stuffed with Chinese rice and flavored with a light black-bean sauce; or fish, like snapper, will be cooked just until the shine is off the flesh, then it will be laid beside velvet mashed new potatoes and surrounded by two poster-perfect pools: one, a purée of black olives, the other of red pepper. His soups and entrées often are anchored by flavorful vegetable crisps, crêpes and dumplings: a silken lobster bisque may have a dim-sum shrimp dumpling; an organic duck breast is cooked crispy with a miso-wildflower honey glaze and served with a hazelnut and taro crisp which melts as soon as it touches the tongue. The cookery is very health-concious. Dairy products are rarely used in dishes other than dessert and organic produce is nearly always in evidence.

Dessert might be a baked apple tart layered with crème brûlée and capped with a hazelnut meringue. That dessert may seem more cohesive than the chocolate mousses—one dark, the other white and banana, served with green tea crème anglaise—but usually, the wierd combinations work. There are misfires too: once an ill-advised mid-course granita of vodka and pear was mean and bitter. At another meal, vegetables, usually so lovingly done, were served as if they were an afterthought.

The wine list is not this restaurant's strength, though it is better than adequate with a mid-to-high-priced range of French, Italian and California wines. There may be a surprise in a well-chosen Oregon wine too. Service tends to be long and drawn out, so leave a full three hours for a meal. Lee sees his meals as an experience that compares with a night at the theater and expects his audience to give equal time. The restaurant is small, it seats only 30. The room is understated and gently

RESTAURANTS

decorated with one colored wall, Chinese scrolls and jars of preserves. Lee and his family live upstairs and he has been known to hush big-paying tables of patrons because the baby is sleeping. A quiet dinner for two will cost Can$140.
Open Mon.-Sat. 6 p.m-10:30 p.m. Cards: AE, MC, V.

Mad Apples Restaurant
2197 Bloor St. West, Toronto
• 761-1971
AMERICAN/SEAFOOD

10/20

Two friends, Donna Neil and Matthew Jamieson, set out to run a restaurant that each would feel comfortable with, and achieved one where just about everybody feels at home. As such, it's a phenomenon in Toronto: they invited the neighborhood to their small local eatery and the whole city came. The phenomenon is more sociological in nature than culinary; but the food is better than adequate and comes in generous portions. We like to make up a meal from the changing array of more than a dozen appetizers: deep-fried calamari, crisp on the outside, tender inside; mussels steamed with garlic and goosed with Pernod. One popular starter, crabcakes made "Maryland-style" employs canned crabmeat—a cardinal sin in Maryland—but tastes decent anyway. Among the main courses, we've found the best to be the pork medallions, which chef Jamieson sautées and serves with cooked apple slices and a Dijon cream. The fresh fish work well, too: swordfish is rubbed in black peppercorns, grilled and served with beurre blanc. As for the service, it's always kind and solicitous. As for the name? Mad Apples translates as the mythical Greek name for eggplant, though that vegetable actually is rarely on the menu. Neil changes the mostly French and Italian wine list every month. Most fall into the Can$20-Can$40 range, and quite a few can be had by the glass, too. Dinner for two, with wine, will reach about Can$80, less if you make a meal of appetizers.
Open daily 11 a.m.-4 p.m. & 5 p.m.- 11 p.m. Cards: AE, MC, V.

Madras Express Café
1438-A Gerrard St. East (& Ashdale St.), Cabbagetown
• 461-7470
INDIAN

Indian restaurants abound in Toronto, but this fluorescent-lit snack bar of a place is the one you'll remember. It is such a "find," that it's impossible to discover unless one knows exactly where it is. The Gerrard Street East address means little, as it is actually located three storefronts north on Ashdale.

Even after it's found, the first impression it evokes is "so what?" Not only does it appear dull, it has counter service, which is slow, and a menu whose breadth encompasses all of two items. There's idli and then there's dosa. Thing is, it is such idli and there is so much sheer pleasure to be had in the dosa, that if the already popular Madras Express Café offered anything else, it would be impossible to get inside its narrow doors.

49

RESTAURANTS

Both items spring from Southern Indian cuisine. They are composed of fermented rice flour and white-lentil flour. In the case of idli, the mixture is formed into balls and steamed, to be served submerged in sambhar, an intoxicating sauce of vegetables, oil, spices and cilantro. To make dosa, the mixture is thinned out with milk, and then baked on a flat grill, like a pancake. We've had this pancake many times (it's the favorite "any-hour" breakfast in most of India), but seldom is it created in so delicately gossamer a texture, nor with such a sparkling taste. The dosa be ordered plain, or folded over a choice of stuffings, most notably an onion-potato-mustard-seed mixture, which is called masala. The beautiful creation, big enough to be supper, is served with a bowl of the same sambhar, and a smear of coconut chutney. There is no alcohol here, but plenty of tropical juices and soft drinks. In the summer, a front patio with picnic tables allows for al fresco munching and great gazing on the action of Gerrard Street, the main drag of Toronto's sizeable Indiatown. Spicy smells, sitar music, men in turbans and women in saris; the scene floats by as in a magical dream of the subcontinent. Vegetarian, meal-size snacks for two, with beverages, cost something short of Can$20.

Open Tues.-Sun. noon-9:30 p.m. Cards: MC, V.

Mariko Japanese Restaurant
348 Danforth Ave. (in the Carrot Common), Riverdale
• 463-8231
JAPANESE

12/20

Tucked away inside the Danforth Avenue Carrot Common, a shopping mall dedicated to alternative-lifestylers and vegetarians, Mariko is eye-appealing in a rectangular and clean, very Japanese way. A couple of rice-paper screens, some minimalist artifacts and beautiful plants punctuate a cafeterialike plainness. During the day, the place is bathed in light from the many windows and skylights, but seems rather severe under artificial light after sunset. The cuisine is homey Japanese, with a wide selection of vegetarian items (to suit its location), and many flesh-bearing selections, for those of us who still eat the stuff. The vegetarian slant can be enjoyed by all because of its focus—unusual sushi makis, which translate as seaweed-wrapped rolls, normally filled with some form of sea creature. Mariko, on the other hand, favors fillings like tofu, ginger, radish, celery, dried melon and various pickles. They all taste fine, but for sushi purists, Mariko does stock a limited, but very fresh supply of fish and seafood.

Age dashi tofu, the light-hearted, fried bean curd in a miso sauce tastes excellent. Meal-in-one soba noodles in broth are properly garnished with aromatics, and delightfully crunchy

RESTAURANTS

with bits of fried-to-order tempura batter. Chicken and salmon teriyakis also figure on the menu, probably because they are always in demand by non-Asian diners. We don't bother with them. The grilled, robata-style fish, however, is beautifully prepared and again, very fresh. It changes daily, and we have enjoyed the king fish, the yellow-tail collar, and even the Spanish mackerel. These are all garnished with ground daikon, and warm, sticky rice. Dinner for two, with saké or beer, will be under Can$60.

Open Tues.-Sat. noon-2:30 p.m. & 5:30 p.m.-10 p.m., Sun. 5:30 p.m.-9:30 p.m. Cards: AE, MC, V.

Massimo Rosticceria

2459 Yonge St.,
Toronto North
• 487-2771
ITALIAN

This tiny, simple Tuscan "roastery" filled up fast when it opened in the fall of 1990. Everybody already knew Massimo's small pizza-and-pasta parlors (three in Toronto), and his fans were eager to try this more upscale place, with its rustic, heartwarming food, low prices and the city's best lick at chicken spit-roasted over an open flame, Tuscan-style. Signore Massimo makes it easy with a prix-fixe menu, so there are only three decisions to make, including whether or not to hang up your coat. Dinner includes four courses: salad, pasta, the main course and dessert. First courses range from a well-turned out fennel-and-orange salad to a satisfying minestrone to a superb risotto with radicchio. Alternatives to spit-roasted chicken for the main course might be roast pork in a milk bath, braised rabbit in a tart sweet-and-sour sauce or grilled fish. With your entrée, you also get polenta or roast potatoes and a platter of cooked vegetables. If you run out of the excellent homemade bread, just ask for more. A simple dessert, often fresh fruit and a hunk of Parmesan cheese, makes a perfect finish.

Don't plan an intimate dinner for two; with tables only for four or six, seating is semicommunal, though long table runners segregate sections of the table. Service is kind. At a fixed price of Can$25 a person, plus a bottle of house wine and coffee, a meal for two costs about Can$85. Though the atmosphere in this small eatery is rather austere, the exceptional food, along with a bottle of Chianti Classico, may well send you out singing "Volare."

Open Tues.-Sat. 6 p.m.-10 p.m., Sun. 5:30 p.m.-9 p.m. Cards: MC, V.

We're always interested to hear about your discoveries, and to receive your comments on ours. Please feel free to write to us, and do state clearly exactly what you liked or disliked. Be concise but convincing, and take the time to argue your point.

RESTAURANTS

Metropolis

838 Yonge St.,
Bloor-Yorkville
• 924-4100
CANADIAN

12/20

Who has ever heard of nouvelle Canadian cuisine? And to what end? Well, we are not so sure it'll become a craze like Cajun, or Pacific Rim, but the folks behind Metropolis are putting some terrific new spins on traditional Canadian dishes, as well as coming up with some impressive originals. Not only that, but the staff is genuinely inviting and friendly—you feel like a regular after only one visit. Metropolis prides itself on using only the freshest local ingredients and preparing everything from scratch; even the lamb sausage is made in the kitchen. Executive chef Terry Kennedy is only 28 years old, but knows his way around a saucepan. He comes from a family of farmers, which may explain his dedication to using the only the best produce, meats and such.

To begin with, the bread at Metropolis is positively dreamy—great, fragrant rations of both onion sage and cornbread—it's difficult not to eat too much of it. The rest of the dishes we tried didn't disappoint, either: crispy cornmeal fritters studded with Mennonite sausage, scallions and bell peppers, served with a sweet mustard dip; spicy Grand Banks cod cakes with bits of fresh rock shrimp with a tomato-cucumber mayonnaise, and potato-zucchini pancakes topped with either Woolwich goat cheese or birch-smoked salmon.

Some of the best middle-course dishes we tried were the creamed leeks with aged Canadian cheddar on that incredible grilled onion-sage bread—comfort food for sure, a three-mushroom toast napped with a peppery white-wine sauce, and sea-fresh mussels in a dry Niagara Peninsula Riesling broth, infused with fresh herbs and garlic.

Main courses may seem redundant after all that largesse, but don't skip them. There's some savory local lamb, grilled Atlantic salmon, served cold with a tomato-cucumber-chive mayonnaise with a new potato salad and bunny-soft baby greens, as well as free-range chicken dishes, aged strip loin or rib eye steaks, and a gargantuan burger of freshly ground beef, served with homemade condiments, a choice of toppings (the best: Canadian back bacon and Canadian cheddar), with excellent french fries.

Ready for dessert? The lemon pecan-loaf cake served with a puckery lemon curd tastes fine, as does the chilled maple cheesecake in a bracing strawberry-lemon sauce; the apple-custard pie is a homey sweet, the kind Mom would make, were Mom a master baker. A small but well-chosen selection of Canadian, Californian, French, Italian and German wines is offered at fair prices. Dinner for two, with wine, is about Can$80.

Open Mon.-Sat. 11:30 a.m.-3 p.m. & 5:30 p.m.-11 p.m. Cards: AE, MC, V.

RESTAURANTS

Mobay Caribbean Cuisine

200 Carlton St., Cabbagetown
• 925-7950
CARIBBEAN

12/20

Toronto boasts the largest Jamaican gathering in North America, and seems to have sprouted a roti shop or a jerk joint at every corner. Most of them achieve no more than fast-food mediocrity, but among the hoi polloi is a gem or two. Mobay is such a one, not only because its cooking is careful and clean, but also for its civilized dining room with the starched tablelinen, the picture windows and the art on the walls.

Jamaican cooking is a mixture of African notions with a solid measure of East Indian cuisine. This reflects the population, people who were transplanted to the Island from Africa and India and were ruled by the British at a time when that nation was seduced by everything subcontinental. The sample dishes consist of simplified curries of goat, chicken and shrimp, spiced and grilled "jerked" meats, deeply flavored stews of beef and oxtail, and the chapati-like, roti flatbreads, that are wrapped around any of the above.

When this standing-over-the-stove-for-hours-and-stirring type of cooking is practiced as conscientiously as Mobay does it, then it is stick-to-the-ribs, utterly heartwarming food. The exotic accompaniments incorporate coconut-rich rice and "peas" (actually red kidney beans), steamed bananas, fried plantains and raisin-studded coleslaw. The hearty soups are thick and thyme-infused. The one decidedly decent fish specialty is salted cod and ackee fruit, a surprising concoction combining the maritime flavor of re-constituted dried cod with the egglike texture of the ackee and the sweetness of fried onions. At Mobay they serve it every Sunday, as the main attraction of a brunch that also includes soup, dessert, and a guava cocktail. The inexpensive spicefest, which is best washed down with Jamaican Red Stripe beer, always sends us still swaying to the infectious rhythms of reggae, into the sweet air of Carlton Street in this cozy corner of Cabbagetown, one of Toronto's most progressive restaurant districts. Dinner for two, with beer, Can$40.
Open Mon.-Wed. 11:30 a.m.-11 p.m., Thurs. 11:30 a.m.-midnight, Fri.-Sun. 11:30 a.m.-1 a.m. All major cards.

Mövenpick

165 York St., Downtown
• 366-5234
SWISS/CONTINENTAL

10/20

What if Café Casino went to Switzerland? Well, more likely than not, Mövenpick would be the result. It's part of a Swiss chain, which has two North American branches, both in Toronto. If Heidi and her grandfather had visited Alice in Wonderland, Mövenpick might be what their story would look like. There are food stations piled high variously with fresh fruits and vegetables (Mövenpick prides itself on the freshness and goodness of the ingredients it uses), air-dried beef and other charcuterie, raclettes and fondues and desserts; you can dine buffet-style, or be served if that's not your thing.

This eatery is very popular (especially as a meeting place for

RESTAURANTS

breakfast, where the bowls of muesli are huge, and brimming with fresh berries), and while not as inexpensive as one might think, you do get a lot for your money. Mövenpick is rather slick and soulless, for all its attempted Alpine hokeyness, but if you enjoy a dollop of camp with your food, you won't be disappointed. Dinner for two, with beverages, is about Can$60.
Open Mon.-Sat. 7:30 a.m.-1 a.m., Sun. 7:30 a.m.-midnight. All major cards.

My Cahn

609 Queen St. West, Kensington Market
• 594-0261
VIETNAMESE

11/20

Located in Toronto's ethnic-rich Kensington Market district, My Cahn, an absolutely spotless—some might say austere—little restaurant comes off as an unpretentious jewel. Although there are some Chinese meals in the style of "choose one from Column A, two from Column B" restaurants, the best cuisine here remains, of course, Vietnamese. Sample the house specialties: chim cut roti, a dish of deliciously browned, flavorful roast quail (served in pairs); bo nuong vi, spicy, grilled beef; and bo nhung dam, a Vietnamese version of boeuf bourguignon. Other interesting dishes include the cua rang muoi, fried salted crab; bun chao tom nem nuong, succulent shrimp served on sugar cane, with vermicelli, and lau luon, a smoky eel hot pot. Soups are good, too, especially the traditional sup mang cua (asparagus crabmeat soup), and for the adventurous, there's a souplike stew concocted of frog's legs and lemon grass. Although wine is offered here, this food really goes best with beer, of which there's a decent selection, both domestic (Canadian), Vietnamese, European and American. Dinner for two, with beverages, will run about Can$30.
Open Mon.-Thurs. & Sun. 11 a.m.-11 p.m., Fri.-Sat. 11 a.m.-3 a.m. Cards: MC, V.

Nami Japanese Restaurant

55 Adelaide St. East, Downtown
• 362-7373
JAPANESE

Nearly every street corner in Toronto boasts a Japanese restaurant, but still only a handful have earned citywide approval. Nami is one of the favored few, partly for its dark, elegant good looks, partly for its very fresh sushi, but most of all for its stunning robata bar. Robata yaki (meaning "fire grill") is an enormous indoor barbecue, Japanese-style. Fifteen patrons at a time gather around the grill at a U-shaped bar, selecting raw foodstuffs (mostly very fresh fish and vegetables) that wait on a bed of ice. A cook deftly grills the items one at a time, as they are ordered. As at most sushi bars, there is no set meal and no set price. You just order away until you're satisfied, and the cost of the ingredients determines the price of your meal.

For example, point to a glistening chunk of fresh salmon. The cook will sprinkle it with sea salt, then toss it onto the flames to sear its outside and free its juices inside. You then dip it into finely grated white radish and soy sauce, and give it a squirt of

RESTAURANTS

lemon juice. Lobsters that look as if they're crawling around the bed of ice are not alive, but are almost as fresh. Order one of these, and a knife is quickly inserted between its head and thorax. The claws and tail go onto the flame, the head is sent to the kitchen to become the base for a fabulous soup made with sesame paste. The extensive selection of fresh fish and seafood presents the problem not of what to order, but when to stop.R Because the robata bar seats only fifteen, reservations are essential, especially on weekends. The restaurant also has tatami rooms and many western-style tables, with a menu of teriyakis and grilled fish and meats. The waiters will accomodate you if you wish to have robata or sushi at a table. But don't miss the bar experience: it's twice the fun. Eating without restraint, you can easily spend more than Can$160 on dinner for two, with saké and Kirin beers.

Open Mon.-Fri. noon-2:30 p.m. & 6 p.m.-10:30 p.m., Sat. 6 p.m.-10:30 p.m. All major cards.

Natalie's House
752 Queen St. West, Toronto
• 360-6564
CANADIAN

12/20

Look for simple fare here, in the domain of youthful Natalie Williams, Toronto's most postmodern chef. Sandwiches, soups and salads, big and beautiful structures, homey almost, put together with a kind of conscientious care that belies her spiked Mohawk hairdo, which can be pink one week, and lime-green the next. The same expertise and motherly affection go into Natalie's pastries, her foremost culinary metier. They're not the most refined cakes, but they're so obviously homemade that they always go down easy. She also prepares delicious breakfasts with freshly squeezed orange juice and yummy main courses like blueberry pancakes with sausages and real (Canadian) maple syrup. Tasty, inexpensive food, served by a vivacious owner/chef would normally be enough to attract the crowds, but this place offers more. Sally Ann furniture, used books and records (for sale), fine music, and the most relaxed, hippy-like atmosphere for miles around, are the bonuses.

Natalie's House is situated on a stretch of Queen Street West, which has become the official headquarters of Toronto's up-and-coming musicians and artists. There's an awful lot of strutting on the street, by poseurs with lace-up boots, tight jeans with suspenders, black leather and gravity-defying hairdos posturing to see who is the wildest of them all. When it's time for a rest, they all retire to Natalie's. It's where the 1990s return to the 1960s, but with a cleaner act. It's also the best corner from which to observe that they're only young, after all. No liquor license. Cappuccino and dessert for two, Can$10; breakfast or lunch for two with beverage and cappuccino, Can$20.

Open Tues.-Fri. 9 a.m.-9 p.m., Sat.-Sun. 9 a.m.-6 p.m. No cards.

RESTAURANTS

N44°
2537 Yonge St.,
Toronto North
• 487-4897
PACIFIC RIM

First off, let's deal with the idiosyncratic moniker. N44° refers to Toronto's latitude; the name is spoken as "North 44." The longitude remains a mystery. Whatever its map coordinates, N44° sizzles as the hottest of the hot among trendy Toronto eateries (or did, at least, at press time), with all the upsides and downsides that are attendant of such status.

The good news: the restaurant looks fabulous, consisting of three tiers, each of which afford a good view of the others. The dining rooms occupy the first two levels; a well-populated bar, host to some of the best-dressed folks in town, inhabits the upper tier. Everything's designed a little off center—even the chair backs are sheared off at an angle, perhaps an homage to David Lynch's *Eraserhead*, or possibly to Art Clokey's *Gumby*. There's lots of requisite sandblasted glass, a nutty mosaic-tile floor, pale, creamy-glazed walls, and huge, gorgeous windows set into massive copper casings. The wall sconces radiate with exotic ginger flowers à la Philippe Starck; even the host/hostess podium is a construct of bobby pins and scissors. More good news is the fact that the food here is mostly very good.

Now for the bad news: service leaves much to be desired. We weren't as bothered by the fact that we had to wait an hour for our 9 p.m. reservation (we weren't the only ones waiting, either). When we finally were seated, our waiter solicitously asked if we'd been waiting long. When we answered in the affirmative, he said "I'll make up for it." He then disappeared for about ten minutes. Go figure. There were long gaps between courses, and it was quite difficult to flag our waiter down when we needed coffee.

Chef-owner Mark McEwan (also behind the ultrapopular Pronto Ristorante) knows his way around a Wolf range. You can easily be tempted to make a meal of his appetizers—corn-fried oysters with sweet-pepper-and-jalapeño cream, saké-cured salmon rolls in a lime-ginger vinaigrette, served with a frizz of thin, fried leeks, tortilla spring roll with grilled chicken, shiitake mushrooms and mustard chili dip, and ripe tomatoes with an arugula oil vinaigrette and chickpea and goat-cheese fritters.

But don't eschew the main courses. The penne with pine nuts, squash and fresh tomatoes tastes delicious, as does the peppered veal served with a creamy risotto studded with chanterelles. There's also a wonderful barbecued rib-eye steak with curried onion rings and charred tomato salsa, and grilled scallops with beet frites in a yellow pepper sauce.

Desserts fulfill the promise of what came before them, and in a nice gesture, they were brought to the table gratis as an apology for our wait (as well as for sitting smokers next to us—in the nonsmoking section). Homemade ice creams and sorbets hit the spot, but the best sweet we had was the supernal mango-ginger upside-down cake with crème fraîche and lime sauce. The wine list at N44° is packed with international selections at reasonable prices. As of February 1991, you can also lunch here, at the convivial sandwich bar upstairs. As well as tasty sandwiches prepared in the same creative vein as the entrées, the menu includes many of the same pizzas and pastas that are served at night. A good value, too, as the top-priced dish costs Can$9.95. Dinner for two, with wine, is about Can$100.

Open Mon.-Fri. 11:30 a.m.-2:30 p.m. & Sat. 5 p.m.-11 p.m., Sat. 5 p.m.-11 p.m. Cards: AE, MC, V.

Orso
106 John St.,
Harbourfront
• 596-1989
ITALIAN

Long as we can remember, Orso's been a well-ordered space, comfortable and inviting. A many-windowed Victorian brick house, within walking distance of the theater area and the SkyDome, the dining rooms, set on two bright and airy floors, are packed with fresh detail and color. Pretty in peach-pink with marble accents, this good-looking restaurant is renowned for its splashy charming terra-cotta dishes filled with robust pasta preparations and earthy soups. Orso was one of the first to offer this city "designer" pizza—seriously thin, light and crisp with prosciutto and Parmesan, mussels and mushrooms, basil and black olives or just straight, with garlic, good olive oil and fragrant rosemary.

While the kitchen always has been hip to market freshness, until the arrival of chef Raffaello Ferrari, it occasionally suffered from inconsistency. Now it sings in a new key, as focused as Pavarotti on a good night, with exemplary grilled chicken, crisp and succulent, accented with a garlicky aïoli; grilled swordfish with ginger-infused cream and mango relish; robust veal shanks with navy beans; a flawless tenderloin of beef with creamy oyster mushrooms and a splash of red wine. Good vegetables abound here—green beans packed with pancetta, the oft-overlooked Swiss chard . . . the list goes on. A variety of pastas (long, flat, bowtie, spiral, skinny) may seem stiffly priced at upward of Can$14, but for your money they will arrive at table imaginatively matched with chunks of roasted chicken and peppers, or with shallots, wild mushrooms and cream, for example.

Splendid desserts include a satiny lemon flan with raspberries, a Marsala-heavy Mascarpone mousse and an intense semifreddo of chocolate hazelnut. Fresh fruit, cheese and Italian ices also make graceful conclusions to a meal here. Thoughtfully chosen Italian reds prevail on the wine list, as does a skillful, good-tempered wait staff. Dinner for two with wine runs Can$100.

Mon.-Sat. 11:30 a.m.-midnight, Sun. 5 p.m.-10:30 p.m. All major cards.

RESTAURANTS

Ouzeri

500A Danforth Ave., Danforth
• 778-0500
GREEK

Aristedes has repeatedly proven that it is possible to cook better with only one name than most owner/chefs can with two or three. This rambunctious, lusty and mercifully inexpensive eatery/drinkery is his 25th restaurant Canada-wide, and if not his best (his first, Vancouver's Orestes, claims that honor), then it comes awfully close. An indoor-outdoor ambience with lots of potted trees, multilevel seating, graffiti-art on the walls and see-through doors (that open onto the sidewalk in summer) create the ideal setting for the platefuls of shareable Greek fare.

This is cooking based on olive oil, garlic, phyllo, oregano, labor-intensive vegetable creations, grilled meats and fishes and quick-fried seafood. As is done in the Grecian prototypes, the mezze are best enjoyed to the accompaniment of shots of ouzo, the anise-flavored Greek firewater. A full cellar of wines (60 of which are also available by the glass) and a complete selection of high-voltage Canadian and imported beers are available to wash down the highly satisfying and astoundingly varied (for Greek) cuisine. The lengthy menu is divided into simple categories, such as "appetizers," "fowl" and "fish," with items mostly named in Greek. One must not be daunted. If the category fits, just order. Rabbit-and-pearl-onion pie in its thick, specially made phyllo dough is remarkable with its snow-white, tender rabbit and clove-cinnamon spicing. All the dips are meaningfully flavored and silky-smooth. The vegetarian dishes (in Greece, meat and fish are at a premium) taste wonderful as well. Note the orgiastic Turkish-derived dish of imam biyaldi—a conconction of eggplant, onions, pine nuts and raisins—worth ordering even for nonvegetarians. A preparation of prawns with mushrooms, garlic and lemon rind finds new horizons for that ubiquitous crustacean, and the various kebabs—chicken, lamb, beef—make you wonder why you ever settled for souvlaki. A bit too loud for some, Ouzeri is situated in the heart of "the Danforth," the high street of Greektown. It reveals a slice of the relentless sociability that has been the birthright of Greeks for millennia. Dinner for two, with ouzo or wine, falls around Can$60.

Open Mon.-Thurs. 5:30 p.m.-3 a.m., Fri.-Sat. 5:30 p.m.-5 a.m. All major cards.

THE TOQUE, CIRCA 1700

Have you ever wondered about the origin of that towering, billowy (and slightly ridiculous) white hat worn by chefs all over the world? Chefs have played an important role in society since the fifth century B.C., but the hats didn't begin to appear in kitchens until around the eighteenth century A.D. The toque is said to be of Greek origin: many famous Greek cooks, to escape persecution, sought refuge in monasteries and continued to pursue their fine art. The chefs donned the tall hats traditionally worn by Orthodox priests but, to distinguish themselves from their fellows, they wore white hats instead of black. The practice eventually was adopted by chefs from Paris to Peking.

RESTAURANTS

Le Paradis

166 Bedford Rd. (at Davenport), Toronto
• 921-0995
FRENCH

13

Bistros are so hot these days that every restaurant with a baguette or a bouillabaisse in its kitchen takes the name. Le Paradis is one of the genuine few, a casual and warm neighborhood spot that does a fine job at being a bistro. Its double bistro/brasserie billing allows a mix of wonderful dishes: seared veal kidney in a port glaze; rabbit stewed with rosemary, thyme and saffron; terrific lamb shoulder flavored with fresh ginger and bedded on couscous; slices of eggplant and soft wedges of red peppers, beautifully seasoned, charred and served over molten brie. There are charcuterie and cassoulet in the fall—bistro classics that cost peanuts at Le Paradis. Note the blackboard menu for the daily fresh fish. For dessert, the standout is a chocolate marquise in a pool of creamy custard sauce, the kind that disappears minutes after you taste it.

The place is popular with inhabitants of the designer offices and showrooms in the area. They fill Le Paradis to its limit on weekends, a result not only of the restaurant's popularity, but also of its set-up: the tables are tiny and the passageways too narrow. Small complaints for a swell spot.

Open daily 11:30 a.m.-11 p.m. Cards: AE, MC, V.

Pearl Court Restaurant

598 Gerrard St. East, Chinatown
• 463-8778
CHINESE

13

Every city has to have one: a precocious Chinese restaurant that is always crowded with extended Asian families blissfully munching on delightfully prepared delicacies; the place where you go for that excellent and authentic meal. The only problem with this kind of restaurant is that its service never rises above functional (often falling below courteous), it has loud lighting, a drafty entrance (where one has to wait mercilessly for a seat) and a hideous stack of plastic, disposable tablecloths on every table. Pearl Court, up three steps from the busiest stretch of Gerrard Street East, here in the commercial hub of this smaller but infinitely more enjoyable version of Toronto's bigger Chinatown, follows the above pattern to the letter.

We go here for the food only, and what we eat here is very good. When the execution of a faraway cuisine is this exciting, we expect no compromises, and at Pearl Court we get none. The stir-fry peanut oil sits puddly at the bottom of the plate as it should, instead of being tucked away by useless cornstarch. The garlic smells like garlic. The chilies burn the tongue. The cilantro is inescapable. The shrimps are juicy and briefly cooked, flooding the mouth with flavors, as do the baby clams, which are flown in daily from the West Coast and still think that they are in the Pacific Ocean. The steamed fish shimmers with toothsomeness as it falls off its back-bone, virgin-white and firm, into the ginger-perfumed oil. Chicken simmers in a Mongol hot pot, sauced smoothly smoothly in coconut cream and lemon grass. Beef is sliced thinly and tenderized (without MSG) in a

RESTAURANTS

sweet-and-sour sauce with chilies and onions. Pork and black mushrooms are served in the company of eel, for a combination that couldn't possibly please every palate, but that'll surely be a conversation piece for anyone who is not content with mere chow mein and yet another order of egg rolls. Dinner for two, with Chinese beer, Can$55.
Open Mon.-Thurs. 3 p.m.-3 a.m., Fri.-Sat, noon-4 a.m., Sun. 3 a.m. Card: V.

Peppinello
180 Pearl St.,
Downtown
• 599-6699
ITALIAN

11/20

The Royal Alexandra Theatre, SkyDome, the Roy Thomson Hall and office towers in downtown Toronto have drawn more restaurants per square foot than there probably are in any other area of Canada. Most of these are mediocre; a few are spectacular. Peppinello's falls comfortably in between: this upmarket pizza-pasta-gelati joint has better food than its neon-trimmed, cavernous, downtown decor would suggest. A clientele of young businesspeople and pretheater suburbanites gather to nosh on upscale city-Italian food. Pizza, which is of the crisp cracker-crust variety, comes with a blessedly simple choice of toppings, all competent. Best are the zippy Italian sausage and the five-cheese combination. A couple can order a "pizzette" (a quaint Italian nonword), which are smaller-sized but still plenty for two. Same for the pastas, which include spaghettini alla arrabiata, a moist tangle of slim pasta in an aggressively spiced tomato sauce, and petuci salmone marinato, a stack of broad noodles swathed in a soft vodka-caviar cream. Risotto changes nightly, and fresh batches appear every half hour. When these are good, they're very good, but the occasional misfire means you should sneak a peek at your neighbor's table to see how the risotto's looking before you order yours.

The main courses, mostly such standards as veal chop and grilled shrimp, are unspecial. Should your meal need rounding out, you'd be best with any of the antipasti—a long list that ranges from antipasto di vegetali (a lovely platter of assorted grilled, steamed, roasted and marinated vegetables) to frito di calamari aïoli (fried squid with garlic mayonnaise) to a range of cold insalatas. In the dessert category, the semifreddo (in this case, a cool, creamy custard) outshines the average tiramisu; the heavenly homemade ice creams outdo both. Downstairs, the same menu is offered at the wine bar, where a younger, livelier crowd meets to eat. Here, a wide-ranging list of mostly Italian wines in the middle-priced range are sold, many by the glass. Dinner for two with house wine will be about Can$65.
Open Mon.-Thurs. noon-2:30 p.m. & 5 p.m.-11 p.m., Fri. noon-2:30 p.m. & 5 p.m.-midnight, Sat. 5 p.m.-midnight, Sun. 5 p.m.-10 p.m. All major cards.

Peter Pan

373 Queen St. West,
Downtown
• 593-0917
INTERNATIONAL

12/20

Peter Pan's funky fun; is it a Greenwich Village hangout that's been transported to Toronto? The folks who work here are friendly and helpful; this is truly the kind of café that, if one lived near it, one would go to on a whim. An Oriental rug runner traverses the length of the room, and pressed-tin ceilings above highlight the long, narrow space.

"Eclectic" names the menu, with everything from a Caesar salad to scallops poached in coconut milk. In between, there's a good cold Thai noodle salad with fresh spinach, cilantro and peppers; delicious cold grilled chicken, tossed with pine nuts and fusilli in a honeyed vinaigrette; rich aguillettes of smoked goose with a mixed berry and port compote, and fragrant, almost caramelized, braised leeks with a saffron custard. Don't forget the main courses: tasty steamed shellfish with fennel, which includes leeks, lemon zest, carrots and a dab of saffron cream; hearty grilled game sausages with a tangy Dijon-mustard sauce, and half a grilled chicken with fresh orange and plum sauce. The burger served at lunch here comes to table fat and fabulous; desserts are a tastebud's temptation: among them are a tart raspberry pie, a sinful hot butterscotch sundae and a homey apple crumble.

Open Mon.-Wed. noon-2:30 p.m. & 6 p.m.-midnight; Thurs.-Sat. noon-2:30 p.m. & 6 p.m.-1 a.m., Sun. noon-11 p.m. Cards: AE, MC, V.

Peter's Chung King Restaurant

281 College St.,
Chinatown
• 928-2936
CHINESE

The only restaurants that endure are those that are operated hands-on by their owners. Whoever has the most to lose will work twice as hard to succeed. But what happens where there are two hands-on owners? When the two in question are as professional and picky as Yung "Peter" Chen and Tung Fun Szeto (remember those names; they come in handy), you get true excellence. Peter's Chung King Restaurant, on College Street near Spadina, outside the immediate bustle of Chinatown, cooks up food that can stand up against the better anywhere. Furthermore, its little battalion of chefs includes experts from several regions of China, and so it is possible to choose one's regional Chinese menu to suit one's mood. The opportunity is there for forays up and down the entire culinary map of the most ancient civilization on Earth. Hearty seafood soups, which could stand to shed a spoonful of the corn-starch binder, are meaningfully chunky with all manner of perfectly underpoached sea morsels. Meat-filled, fried dumplings are light and airy. Szechuan orange chicken is hot and juicy. Al dente, sautéed green beans come in a spare sauce. Mu shu, the popular fun food, bears all the right condiments and flavorful, just-made wrapping pancakes. Lobster comes crunchy and seductive in its black-bean/garlic/scallion sauce. An entire

RESTAURANTS

pickerel, ideally steamed and thrillingly fresh, is best in the ginger-green onion-soya oil. Dungeness crab, flown in kicking from British Columbia (to order, which must be placed a day in advance) tastes good any old way. The flesh of this crab is so delicate and moist that it seems ready to levitate and evaporate unless one quickly tucks it away. All this, plus a clean, if simple environment, and truly caring service. A must for anyone remotely interested in fine Chinese dining. There is a full license, but wine tends to get in the way. Beer or even tea make better partners to the cooking. A dinner of delicacies for two, with beer or wine, Can$55.

Open Mon.-Thurs. noon-10 p.m., Fri. noon-11 p.m., Sat. 1 p.m.-11 p.m., Sun. 1 p.m.-10 p.m. Cards: MC, V.

Le Petit Gaston

35 Baldwin St.,
Downtown
• 596-0278
FRENCH

11/20

Gaston Schwalb, the indisputable king of charmingly international Baldwin Street, makes a point of being immodest. This, even though he knows that every time he puts his foot in his mouth, he'll have to pay for it by working extra hard to maintain the consistent quality of his traditional, rural French cooking. He's not worried. He has been on the scene for two and a half decades, and in the process, has converted Toronto to the joys of eating garlic. A tall and stately chef, who intentionally wears an extra-long toque, Schwalb represents the sum total of his restaurant. He cooks everything single-handedly, while perusing the clients, who are dining in the indoor-outdoor, rustic courtyard. He makes frequent jaunts through his wards, to garner compliments and greet his fans, who remember him in many flamboyant roles, including a mayoral race in which he ran as the only candidate who owned a convertible Rolls-Royce. Need we say he lost?

But there is nothing to lose by eating this man's food, and everything to gain, including extra pounds. This is cooking in the fashion of the *grand-mère*: dishes soaked in butter, cream and wine for the main course, chocolate mousse for dessert. The fish soup is legend. Blended in the fashion of Marseilles, it comes properly garnished with a crouton and a dollop of garlic-redolent aïoli. The pâté is coarse and bold. It could perfectly fit into the lunch-box of a French worker, anytime. The rack of lamb has formed a crunchy crackling. It glistens underneath its red-wine demi-glace. The huge slab of salmon is moist and appetizing with its tarragon-cream sauce. The canard à l'orange is exactly as we remember it, when it we loved it before it lost its intrigue due to over-exposure. The meat is still red where it meets the bone, but the skin is crisp and meltingly sweet. The sauce, sour from vinegar, sweet from caramelized sugar and

RESTAURANTS

profoundly orangy from orange peel and a French-kiss of Cointreau, is the real thing. The baguette is crusty, the cornichons tiny, and the frites straight from the bistros of Paris.

Le Petit Gaston dispenses a tasty facsimile of a France that was. It is an eccentric kind of nostalgia that will always be à la mode. Schwalb provides a full range of French wines (nothing too distinguished nor expensive) to wash down all the calories. Dinner for two, with wine, Can$110.

Open Tues.-Fri. 11:30 a.m.-2 p.m. & 5 p.m.-9 p.m., Sat. 5 p.m.-9 p.m. Cards: AE, MC, V.

Pimblett's
263 Gerrard St. East, Cabbagetown
• 929-9525
ENGLISH

9/20

In the finest traditions of *Carry On* and *Monty Python*, Geoffrey Pimblett conducts himself in outrageous ways that translate as unexpurgated fun for his many devoted customers. Located in a cheerful, Victorian-era town house on Gerrard Street East, near Parliament, his self-named establishment boasts a formal dining room at ground level, and a typical pub in the semibasement. Both floors are decorated with found objects, with Britain and the Royal Family in mind. The gang's all here with many portraits of the Royals, including Victoria, prim amid much bric-a-brac, like unicorns, and antique biscuit tins. Thus the stage is set for dinners on china, no two pieces of which match. For the summer there is a curbside patio that is awash in Union Jacks. To top it off, Pimblett himself makes unpredictable but frequent appearances as some kind of empress, bedecked in black velvet and the family diamonds. The food, or "British haute cuisine," as Pimblett insists it is, remains rather disappointing. Suspicious mousses of kipper or salmon and cloyingly sweet soups are only the beginning. Main courses of don't-ask-what's-in-it forcemeat en croûte, congealed steak-and-kidney pie, and I-dare-you-to-eat-me black pudding with mud gravy will leave no doubt whatsoever as to this kitchen's lack of finesse.

The specialties can be suffered à la carte, or in ludicrously cheap dinner-deals. No one would trust them at all if they cost any less. There is also a daily roast, which though overcooked and blandly garnished, at least stands the best chance of being digestible. This is fortunate, because missing out on Pimblett's strictly because of the food would be a great pity. This is a slice of home, and, indeed, of Toronto, that must be experienced for its eccentricity. Besides, it's a pocketful of mirth that won't burden the pocketbook. A comprehensive selection of British beers (served warm on request), will help wash it all down. Dinner for two, with a pint or two, under Can$40.

Open Mon.-Fri. noon-4 p.m. & 6 p.m.-11 p.m, Sat.-Sun. 6 p.m.-11 p.m.; pub open daily 4 p.m.-1 a.m. Cards: AE, MC, V.

RESTAURANTS

Il Posto
148 Yorkville Ave.,
Bloor-Yorkville
• 968-0469
ITALIAN

[14]

In the early 1980s, Nella and Piero Maritano left their restaurant in London, England, to take over this space in York Square. Piero cooks and Nella runs the front of the house in her gracious and inimitable style. They made a few important changes to this not-so-small room—dusky rose walls, discreet lighting and table arranged in such a way as to provide a feeling of seclusion and privacy. Il Posto attracts a well-heeled crowd and rather faithful following of local politicians, high rollers, the expensive-lunch bunch, visiting celebs... you get the picture. All are in search of well-prepared classic northern Italian favorites.

Main courses please without taking too many risks: hefty veal chops are grilled with rosemary; scaloppine is gussies up with porcini mushrooms; chicken comes Sicilian style with eggplant; pastas don yummy ultrafresh sauces; and don't forget the masses of wonderfully fresh fish and shellfish—the huge gamberoni (prawns) are outstanding. In fact, someone will demonstrate the freshness of the shellfish by bringing them to your table.

We also checked out the dessert table on the way in and found perfect circles of perfect oranges in Cointreau, the freshest raspberries with cream, poached pears in chocolate. One dessert worth fighting for was a tasty slice of chocolate-banana meringue cake. The wine list is divided equally between good French and Italian picks, averaging between Can$30 and Can$50; for the high rollers, there are a few Château Mouton-Rothschild and Château Baron Phillipe bottles to be had.

Nella smiles, Piero cooks with distinction—most of the time—and all is right with the world. Except once in a while, when a nonregular feels slighted by a supercilious waiter. For two, count on Can$120 with wine.

Open Mon.-Sat. noon-2:30 p.m. & 6 p.m.-10:30 p.m. Cards: AE, MC, V.

Prego della Piazza
150 Bloor St. West,
Bloor-Yorkville
• 920-9900
ITALIAN

[13]

The piazza of the name refers to this attractive restaurant's appealing location in a small square behind an old church. Inside, the decor is bright bistro with an open showcase for Prego's deservedly touted appetizers and humorous quotes about food and drink scrawled over colorful walls. At night the tables don cloth and the atmosphere becomes more formal. Expect things to be busy: with this location near Yorkville customers include local and nonlocal moviemakers and media types, a busy breed. Owner Michael Carlevale was among the first Toronto restaurateurs to catch the Italian wave that began in the last decade. He's there smiling at you from the postered walls outside the piazza.

His menu is anchored by the appetizers, pizza and pasta, with a medium collection of main courses. Of these the best have been the earthy pasta dishes like Spaghettini con calamari

RESTAURANTS

carlevale, a recipe that's loaded with plum shellfish and wetted by a tomato sauce, with the kind of depth that shows it started with a good fish stock. Grills are also recommended: fish is carefully and lovingly done; chicken grilled with thyme is succulent. The antipasti can vary in quality, but Prego's signature has been the competently grilled and flavored vegetables that include onions, whole garlic and always a range of peppers with eggplant. Don't miss the dense and velvety fish chowder, if it is on the menu. Desserts aren't fancy. Dinner will cost Can$100 for two. There is an adjoining restaurant called Enoteca, where lighter courses and designer pizzas are served in a more casual but highly designed setting. The wine list emphasizes Italian and Californian wines in the mid-price range, though there are bottles to splurge with and many by the glass.

Open Mon.-Sat. 11:30 a.m.-11 p.m. All major cards.

Pronto Ristorante
692 Mt. Pleasant Rd., Rosedale
• 486-1111
ITALIAN

Chef Mark McEwan and his partners, Leslie Kubicek and Peter Costa, own two of North Toronto's hottest, trendiest restaurants. This one, a slick, very urban-looking space full of chrome and mirrors, burgundy and blue banquettes and blue-leather chairs, predated the other, N44° (spoken as "North 44"—see page 56) by several years. Both places have consistently attracted flocks of foodies, visiting movie stars and other assorted celebrities; with little prompting, Pronto's staff will tell about when Brian Dennehey, Stockard Channing and Liza Minnelli all turned up the same night. People come for the scene, but what they keep returning for is McEwan's cooking, which is inventive yet subtle, with excellent results.

The menu promises a few culinary extravaganzas, and though these dishes sometimes taste as good as they sound, the best success at Pronto is to be had with some of the simpler grilled meats and fish, and the pastas. Some of those simple grills are best known for the company they keep: McEwan sends the lamb out with a gorgeous risotto cooked with mission figs; he chars onions and serves them in a relish alongside tenderly done veal. An eclectic assortment of trendy veggies—baby carrots, miniature squash, infant potatoes—accompanies many of the main courses. Pastas change regularly and seasonally, with simple but intensely flavored sauces: one night, an angel-hair pasta with smoked Ontario duck, pepper squash, and fresh thyme; another night, fettuccine with charred leeks, water chestnuts, pickled ginger and sesame oil. You can easily make a meal from a collection of appetizers: there is a lovely platter of charred octopus and squid, surrounded by a grand array of grilled vegetables; a barbecued quail with seasoned beans; and barbecued shrimps, served with vegetables rolled in a crêpe with fennel butter.

RESTAURANTS

One tip: Torontonians are loathe to rubberneck. Bette Midler sat one night over one of Pronto's carnival fruit plates and it seems that no one noticed. What you can look out for are regular art showings on the walls. A lovely, heavily Italian wine list also offers Californian, French and even a few Australian bottles, with prices ranging from Can$20 to Can$90. Service is generally efficient and careful. Dinner for two, with wine, is Can$125.
Open daily 5 p.m.-10:30 p.m. All major cards.

Queen Mother Café
208 Queen St. West,
Queen St. West District
• 598-4719
INTERNATIONAL

11/20

The Queen Mother Café hangs loose, Daddy-O, and it serves good food, to boot. The wandering menu travels all over the map, from rather retro (yet delicious) whole-wheat bread, reminiscent of that nuts-and-berries era a couple of decades back, to more exotic Southeast Asian dishes. Look here for a good, well-flavored gazpacho; over there for grilled vegetables, roast lamb in a Dijon mustard sauce, fat shrimp in coconut-curry sauce. Salads come equally eclectic salads (Laotian, for example, with sprouts, cilantro and a light, lemony dressing). Let's not forget Italy: scampi in a garlicky tomato broth, and carpaccio. If you're in need of comfort food, though, there are such things as tuna melts and quiches. If you're in the area, this is a destination for a meal that, while not quite as fine as one you'd have at the somewhat similar Berkeley Café, is nonetheless very good. There's a limited but fairly priced wine list. Dinner for two, with wine, is about Can$70.
Open Mon.-Sat. 11 a.m.-12:30 a.m.

Queen of Sheba
1198 Bloor St. West,
The Annex
• 536-4162
ETHIOPIAN

[13]

The Queen of Sheba, which was the first of its kind to open in Toronto, reigns over all of the Ethiopian restaurants in the city. Fitted into an ex-tavern on this unexciting stretch of Bloor Street West, it very much feels like a drinking place still, but the reason it is packed every night is its inexpensive menu of authentic East African cuisine. Ethiopian food means simplified East Indian curries served on an idiosyncratic pancakelike creation called an injera, which is composed of a soured, yeastless, wheat-flour and rice-flour mixture and has a spongy, airy texture. The injera is laid down to line a platter, and the several curries of meats and vegetables (some hot, some even hotter) are piled decoratively on this surface. No cutlery is provided. We are asked to tear off chunks of the pancake and to use it like a scoop to pick up bites of the food en route to the mouth. It will never cease to amaze us: how intimate two people can get, when they share a common platter from which they are obliged to eat with their hands.

Sheba offers combination platters that include samplers of just about the entire menu. The noteworthy participants are yebeg

RESTAURANTS

kay alicha, a Berbers's (hot) lamb stew, and its (slightly) milder cousin, yebeg alicha. Kay watt and alicha watt are the two versions of beef curry. The mild kik alicha is a purée of yellow split peas, and yesimir watt are black lentils in a three-alarm sauce. The lemony, not in the least hot, gomen watt, a combination of kale, onions and potatoes, provides the only respite to the western palate, which quickly begins to crave a familiar taste.

The food doesn't leave you uninterested, but compared to the depths of Indian and Iranian cuisines, from which it seems to somehow spring, it will appear rather crude and mono-dimensional. Nevertheless, Sheba provides an excellent version of it, and eating by hand will always be something to remember. Ice-cold beer is the only quencher for this kind of blunt spicing; good cappuccino is the only available dessert. Dinner for two, with beer, won't be more than Can$35.
Open daily 11 a.m.-2 a.m. Cards: MC, V.

The Real Jerk
709 Queen St. East,
Cabbagetown
• 463-6906
CARIBBEAN

11/20

If it's an instant party you want, then this is the spot. Tuneful and sassy, the large space is under the spell of nonstop reggae and the undiminished spirit of expatriates eager to recapture a bit of the beloved Island. Back in Jamaica, this is the kind of place that one would retire to after a whole day of beach-frolicking, ready to be infused with renewed energy and a longing for the pleasures of the night. The bill of fare encompasses all the Caribbean standards, like curried goat, rice and peas, saltfish (cod) and ackee, fried snapper, shrimp creole, fried plantains, roti shells stuffed with curries, fried chicken, and the restaurant's eponymous, spice-grilled chicken and pork, the "real jerks." The curry goat and the jerk pork are consistent and satisfying. Unfortunately, all the rest has been erratic. Rice and peas, which can be creamy and comforting, has on occassion been dry and unappetizing. The fried fish often arrives looking unsavory, and the shrimp disgrace their delicious, tomato-pepper based sauce by having been cooked to death. Of the jerk chicken, we can say that the tender breast meat requires many toothpicks to unravel from the teeth, and even the generally more sturdy leg is seriously overcooked. Obviously, the kitchen has to cook too many meals, yet is popular enough not to have to watch its quality too carefully. But there is always the curry goat, which is tender and flavorful, and if lucky, the rice and peas will be having a good day, because a visit to this ultra-lively Caribbean transplant is a must for a gratifying dose of Toronto's thriving Jamaican subculture. The Queen Street East location, in the about-to-be-gentrified, working-class district is itself worth a look. Jamaican rum and beer are the drinks of choice here, and

RESTAURANTS

why not? They fit right in with the rest of the Island trimmings. Dinner for two with a few drinks will easily reach Can$50.
Open Mon.-Fri. 11:30 a.m.-1 a.m., Sat. 1 p.m.-1 a.m., Sun. 2 p.m.-10 p.m. All major cards.

Rivoli Café & Club
332 Queen St. West, Downtown
• 597-0794, 596-1908
THAI/ECLECTIC

12/20

Rivoli Café, or "the Riv," is the hangout of choice for the trendy Queen Street West folks and their admirers. The back room buzzes every night with either performance art, or the brand-newest underground music being played to a standing-room-only, admission-paying crowd. The narrow front room, which in the summer spills out onto a sidewalk patio, is just as popular with the avant-garde set. A hubbub of seven-syllable words prevails, punctuated by liberal drinking and a whole lot of munching. Rivoli's passable-quality Southeast Asian fare is always fun—and occasionally very good.

The delicate and greaseless Laotian spring rolls are stuffed to bursting with julienned vegetables and shrimp; the refreshing yam mamouang, a salad of julienned green mango and toasted coconut napped with a lemony Thai dressing, comes sprinkled with shrimp chips; the chicken saté is accompanied by the usual peanut sauce. For main courses, feel the eastern influence in dishes such as bah me hang, a swirl of noodles, chicken, barbecued pork, shrimp, bean sprouts, green onion and chopped peanuts in a lime-cilantro dressing, or an Indian-influenced dish of chicken marinated in fresh orange juice, ginger and spices. The overly fussy Southwestern chicken salad puts together smoked chicken, Parmesan cheese and blackened croutons, with a cumin—ancho chili dressing to round out the international theme. If all this isn't enough variety, you can also order a Caesar salad, a good burger and even a comforting grilled cheese sandwich, made with challah and that wonderful aged Canadian Cheddar. All of it is inexpensive, and the eavesdropping is priceless. Dinner for two, with drinks, is no more than Can$50.
Open Mon.-Thurs. 11:30 a.m.-11:30 p.m., Fri.-Sat. 11:30 a.m.-midnight. Cards: MC, V.

Roberto's
2622 Yonge St., Toronto
• 489-2153
ITALIAN

10/20

If you're in the neighborhood, and desire a hearty Italian meal for very few dollars, make a stop at Roberto's. Its cozy, convivial mood, along with delicious garlic bread and free-flowing Chianti, will ensure that you have a good time, even if the wait is long and the service unconcerned. (We once went on a weekend and waited a good hour, learning that it's a fine idea to call ahead here to assess the crowd.) Go early, pore over the southern-Italian menu and let the overpowering aroma of garlic entice you to stay. For starters, try the crispy fried calamari or the clam sauté in a mildly spicy, buttery sauce. Among the main courses, we've

most enjoyed the heady seafood pasta that overflows the edges of its plate. Other good bets include a suave tortellini in cream sauce, crespette (crêpes) stuffed with ricotta and spinach, and a rabbit cacciatore (an unusual twist on the chicken preparation, but it works), surrounded by mushrooms, peppers, onions and large chunks of potato. Veal dishes tend toward the mediocre, and desserts are best skipped. It's unlikely you'll find room anyway, after indulging in several pieces of the crispy homemade garlic bread, which we find positively addictive. As for service, the staff rushes around taking orders and delivering food in an offhand—sometimes brusque—manner, so go with your guard up. A dinner for two, with house wine, costs about Can$45.
Open Tues.-Sat. 5:30 p.m.-10:30 p.m., Sun. 5:30 p.m.-8:30 p.m. Cards: AE, MC, V.

Rodney's Oyster House
209 Adelaide St. East, Downtown
• 363 8105
SEAFOOD

There was a time when you couldn't go to Rodney's Oyster House; instead, he came to you. This maritime expat began his career in Toronto by catering parties with fresh oysters and lobsters he brought in from the Atlantic provinces. His impeccably fresh fare, so fresh that he might have caught and carried it in himself, quickly earned him a name. A fish expert he is; a designer he's not. There's nothing very homey about this basement hole-in-the-wall, even if he does call it a house. But never mind the ambience; you're here to savor seafood. A few bar stools are lined up in front of a long granite bar, and the oyster beds beckon behind. There are a couple of tables, too, but the few lucky customers who have nabbed one tend to cling like barnacles. They will be eating oysters quivering on a bed of shaved ice in a tangle of (inedible) black seaweed, and dipping them in the collection of intense homespun hot sauces, ranging from "white-boy soul sauce," made with red peppers to "Johnny Reb's Español hot sauce," with Jamaican peppers, Dijon and fresh ginger. Among the "mildest" of the dips is a Tabasco-based sauce, so watch out. To follow, there is lobster steamed in sea water, its armor lightly cracked for access. A few chowder and fish dishes finish the menu, but you don't go to Rodney's for those. To round out your dinner, baskets of fresh, wholesome bread come from the well-loved local Future Bakery. The only dish worthy of joining the lobster and mollusks is the extraordinary chocolate mousse. Service can best be decribed as catch-me-if-you-can. There are places such as Rodney's where people don't know to go unless they have been sent. Consider yourself sent.
Open Mon.-Sat. 11:30 a.m.-1 a.m. Cards: AE, ER, MC, V.

RESTAURANTS

The Roof Restaurant, Park Plaza

4 Avenue Rd.,
Bloor-Yorkville
• 924-5471 ext. 1109
FRENCH

13

Perched on the best vantage point of the city, the roof-top restaurant of this venerable hotel offers an interesting menu, tirelessly attentive service, rather plush surroundings, and very soft seating. The clientele tends to be older and well-heeled; the young and hip generally kept out by the retro dress code of no jeans (not even designer) and no sneakers (not even the Can$200 "pump"). Some culinary sins such as the watery texture of the marinated salmon, the overcooked dryness of the salmon trout and the expensive blandness of the salads (of both the green and fruit varieties) are tastily offset by the many near-perfect offerings of the modernist kitchen, which relies on ultrafresh ingredients and picture-perfect presentations. Lightly handled appetizers such as sautéed shiitake mushrooms with warm oysters and vanilla-scented lobster-filled raviolis prepare nicely for the tender lamb, the scarlet-fleshed, crispy-skinned duck breast with its blood orange sauce and the delicately grilled scallops on the less than satisfying beurre blanc. A calorific chocolate mousse/crème anglaise marquise, or a baked meringue/mocha butter dacquoise make for rich finales with which to admire the million lights of the city below.

The perfect location at the corner of Bloor West and Avenue Road allows access to (or from) the Royal Ontario Museum and the eclectic shops of Yorkville. An excellent, leather-trimmed bar, which shares the roof with the restaurant, and attendant big-hotel frills, such as a serious wine list (Chablis Fourchaume, 1986; Château Carreneau Fronfac, 1985), are added inducements to take that long elevator ride to the sky. Dinner for two, with wine, Can$130.

Open daily 5:30 p.m.-10:30 p.m. All major cards.

The Rosedale Diner

1164 Yonge St.,
Rosedale
• 923-3122
MEDITERRANEAN

12/20

Neither elegant nor chichi, in fact rather scruffy and down-to-Earth, the Rosedale Diner belies its precious, upper-middle-class area, while dishing out solid value and casual dining. Narrow and long, like a New York City "railroad" apartment, the premises include a bar area out front, a comfortable, snug dining room in the middle and a colorful, characterful patio in the backyard. The generous, low-priced fare includes samplers from the entire Mediterranean basin, from Israel to Spain, and adds a sprinkling of California-style touches for good measure.

Chicken makes many appearances, and is most enjoyable moistly char-grilled and flavored with rosemary. The smoked chicken, which is served at every opportunity and is at its best atop a zestily dressed green salad, is succulent enough to have been smoked in the restaurant's basement (which it was). Soups are always hearty, and salads so big that a couple can easily get away with one apiece and then a shared main course. Aside from the grilled chicken, fish specials, poached or grilled and mas-

sively garnished with rice pilaf and sautéed vegetables, constitute the best deals. Desserts are weighty affairs like chocolate-pecan pie and mile-high mousse cake. The wine list offers several interesting American wines alongside potable French and Australians, most of which are avaliable by the glass. A major beer list, from the international inventory completes this picture of a blissful time warp to an epoch when vibes were mellower and food was meant to fill the belly. Best of all, the 1990's await right outside the door in the guise of myriad, smart shops with lovely merchandise that very few can afford. Dinner for two, with wine, Can$80.
Open Mon.-Fri. 11:30 a.m.-1 a.m., Sat. 11 a.m.-1 a.m., Sun. 11 a.m.-11 p.m. Cards: AE, MC, V.

Sai Woo
130 Dundas St. West, Downtown
• 977-4988
CHINESE

11/20

Sai Woo fits the "absolute institution" category in Toronto. This gloriously old-fashioned Chinese restaurant holds no pretense toward modernity (or authenticity, for that matter). It harkens back to the grand age of westernized Chinese food in the best sense, akin to the wonderful chop suey and egg foo yung joints in Manhattan's Chinatown, rather than the proliferation of mediocre Chinese restaurants that abounded in the 1950s and 1960s, giving Cantonese cuisine a bad name.

Let's count the old favorites: fried rice is fine; the egg rolls, crisp and greaseless; Sai Woo ribs, tender spare ribs glazed with a honeyed garlic concoction tasted stickily marvelous. Don't expect any surprises at this thirty-five-year-old landmark, that's not the point. Sai Woo is a great place to take the kids—and the adults won't fare too badly, either. Dinner for two, with beverages, is about Can$40.
Open Mon.-Sat. 11:30 a.m.-2 a.m., Sun. 11:30 a.m.-1 a.m. Cards: AE, DC, MC, V.

Samovar Barmalay Restaurant
505 Mt. Pleasant Rd., Rosedale
• 480-0048
RUSSIAN/JEWISH

12/20

Gregory Bruskin, the Russian émigré who has run this charmer for the past seventeen years, describes his role as that of chef, but he's more like an effusive host at a private dinner party. He plays the room as easily as if it were a balalaika, filling empty hands here and there with glasses of vodka or wine, or, if these are already in good supply, he might shove in a tambourine. Some might view it all as a trifle too gushing, but it works for us, mostly because the food is very good. Borscht, served hot or cold, balances intense sweetness and sourness; it's loaded with fresh dill and topped with the requisite dollop of sour cream; pirozki (called pirogen by the Polish) are tender little mouthfuls of meat, wrapped in dough and doused with sour cream. Main courses are alive with garlic. The half chicken, for example, is pressed flat until its flesh succumbs and its bones weaken; then it's blasted with garlic and roasted until the flesh

RESTAURANTS

is charred and sweet. The rib steak is charred on the outside, rare on the inside, and coated with garlic; the lamb, which measures the length of the CN tower, gets grilled and brushed with oil and garlic. Best for dessert is a fresh crêpe with strawberries. Or, you could have more vodka, which comes in tiny, ice-cold glasses. Don't pick this place for that quiet, intimate dinner; though there may be subdued evenings, usually an enthusiastic singer and Gregory's antics will coax you into singing all the sentimental Russian and Jewish songs you want to learn. Dinner will cost about Can$85 for two.
Open daily 5:30 p.m.- 9:30 p.m. Cards: V.

Sanssouci
Sutton Place Hotel Kempinski,
955 Bay St.,
Toronto North
• 924-9221
CONTINENTAL

12/20

We're talking luxe here, on a grand scale. An ornate Prussian palace setting, which comes complete with massive, marble pillars, gleaming crystal and immaculately conceived place settings. Grand mirrors on lattice-worked walls reflect candlelight and the hyperelegance that good taste provides, with pastel-pink azaleas as far as the eye can see.

Add to this an impeccable company of servers who attend and anticipate whims, either real or imagined. And quite rightly so, when you're forking over these kind of rubles, a little well-placed bowing and scraping is definitely in order.

The big menu includes a Can$49.50 table d'hôtel, perhaps a savarin of hardwood-smoked salmon with shrimp surrounded by spinach leaves; double beef consommé with herb dumplings; spiced best-end of veal in bed with angel-hair pasta and pizzaiola sauce; or shrimps and scallops with Manitoba black rice in a sabayon of Champagne and tomato. Afters include a hot Grand Marnier soufflé and delectable friandises.

Left to your own devices, you might choose from a cold and hot appetizer grouping: one of the most successful, although a bit fatty, is the slivers of honey-glazed duck breast with shiitake mushrooms, redolent of sesame oil. Tomato and eggplant lasagne swimming in a beurre-blanc sea intrigues with its oddness, which is complemented by basil-tossed carrot and zucchini shaved into pappardelle-like ribbons. A sampling of salad leaves is ceremoniously prepared at your table with a suitably fine olive-oil dressing. A young lobster is market-priced (Can$39 when we dined here last), the sweet and succulent flesh resting on a plumping of spinach leaves made limp by a delightful sauce of Pernod-infused citrus butter. Dover sole—the real thing—could not be more classically treated, presented and skillfully boned at table. It shares the stage with a modest boiled potato and a pile of impossibly thin, crunchy green beans.

Later still, a three-tiered caravan of splendid proportions

RESTAURANTS

wheels by, laden with blackberries the size of damsons, strawberries and rasberries served with freshly whipped cream; deeply flavorful passion-fruit mousse gâteau, enrobed in dark chocolate, and a plethora of tortes and tarts. Sip a coffee or digestif while the pianist soothes. The tab for two with wine (of which there are some marvelous, pricy selections) will be at least Can$150.

Open Mon.-Thurs. 11:30 a.m.-2 p.m. & 6 p.m.-10 p.m., Fri. 11:30 a.m.-2 p.m. & 6 p.m.-11 p.m., Sat. 8 a.m.-10 a.m., 11:30 a.m.-3 p.m. & 6 p.m.-11 p.m., Sun. 8 a.m.-10 a.m., 10:30 a.m.-2:30 p.m. & 6 p.m.-10 p.m. All major cards.

Santa Fe
129 Peter St.,
Downtown
• 345-9345
SOUTHWESTERN

12/20

Santa Fe isn't just another Taos wannabe: chef Christopher McDonald studied at the booted feet of a master of modern Southwestern cuisine, Mark Miller. He learned his lessons well. Decor matches Disneyland with the Southwest. This high, wide and handsome two-tiered room is bright and whimsically decorated with oversized papier mâche lizards, bright colors and zany knicknacks—like a child's paintbox version of how a restaurant should look.

The menu gets a little more serious, though there are some dishes as fun as the decor. How about a version of Woolworth's Frito pie, a Caesar salad using the original, Tijuana recipe, and of course, guacamole with yellow and blue corn chips? They'll put some dust on your chaps. Another good starter is the richly spiced black-bean soup dabbed with sour cream and salsa fresca. For more complex dishes, try the spicy steak tartare with corn chips, or the hickory-smoked chicken quesadilla. And what's this? A chewy cornmeal pizza with bacon, fire onions and roast tomato that we dreaded at first, but actually enjoyed.

There are also some bang-up main courses: the tamale sampler platter offers a trio of tamales, Oaxacan chicken, pork carnitas, and plantain, served with tomatillo sauce. The poblano-chile relleno with a black bean chalupa, plantain tamale and potato empanada, served with a red chile sauce, is a well-modulated plate of textures and palate temperatures; the grilled tuna steak with grilled new potatoes, Japanese eggplant and watercress napped with a cumin-garlic vinaigrette may not be particularly Southwestern, however, it's still good. If there's posole, make sure you order this flavorful pork-and-hominy stew. The wine list is of decent size and price. Dinner for two, with wine, is about Can$70

Open Mon.-Sat. 11 a.m.-11 p.m. Cards: AE, MC, V.

RESTAURANTS

Savunth Restaurant

1 D 583 Parliament St.
(entrance on Amelia St.),
Cabbagetown
• 961-9748
INDIAN

10/20

Things don't get much cheaper than this. All of Can$4 buys a complete dinner of various Sri Lankan vegetable curries and condiments, which surround a mound of basmati rice and a crisply fried papadum. Known as thali in Southern India, the Savunth version is of the Tamil persuasion, as practiced in Sri Lanka. The curries, of potato, eggplant, okra, cabbage and lentils all seem to taste the same, but it is an authentic sameness, with freshly ground spices and slow, careful cooking. They also serve meat and seafood curries, which come in small, very inexpensive samplers. They are satisfying, if not exactly refined. Don't look for alcohol in this tiny place; enjoy the tree-shaded patio in summer, and the restaurant's wonderful location on quaint Amelia Street, just in from the corner of Parliament Street. The service is amateur but endearing, and the food so exotic and ultra-inexpensive; we tend to order the entire menu, thus ultimately overeating. A constitutional walk through the simpatico, florally accented cottages of Cabbagetown after indulging helps to settle the stomach. Dinner for two, with bottled tropical juice, can't possibly cost more than Can$20. *Open daily 11:30 a.m.-11:30 p.m. No cards.*

Scaramouche Restaurant/ Pasta Bar & Grill

1 Benvenuto Pl.,
The Annex
• 961-8011
PACIFIC RIM/SEAFOOD

13

Scaramouche, one of Toronto's grandest restaurants, deserves its long reputation for having the city's most imaginative chefs. That reputation has been augmented by the unique hilltop setting that overlooks downtown and, as such, has the best view of any local restaurant that doesn't revolve. That view may be oversold by the maître d' who may insist on seating you to face it, even though the seat may face a mammoth outdoor television antenna. There are times, too, when the kitchen's reputation also exceeds the quality of its food. That said, you can still expect a very high order of cookery from Keith Froggett.

Fish dishes are often the best of it, both as appetizers and main courses. Fresh calamari may be tenderly sautéed and served with shiitake mushrooms and sweet peppers; barely cooked swordfish may be crusted with ginger and cracked peppercorns and served as a first-course salad with lime vinaigrette. For the main course, there will be several fish, mostly from the Atlantic. Salmon, first smoked by Froggett, then grilled, comes with wild rice; halibut may be laid on a fennel sauce with potatoes, morels and Jerusalem artichokes. There is more chance for disappointment in the meat and poultry dishes. A menu listing of clay pot roasted chicken leads a winter-weary diner to eagerly expect a stewy, comforting and hearty dish, but this chicken is limp and austere; the waiter calls its accompanying fritters potato, and though they taste great, the flavor is corn. Better luck might be had with the rich veal osso bucco served with rosemary-scented spaetzle.

Dessert chef Joanne Yolles has elevated Scaramouche's fabled desserts to such heights that this year a pastry-making school has opened for the slavish adherents. Best of the desserts? Savor any of the rich berry constructions with puff pastry, most sensibly offered in the summer, or the coconut-cream pie, based on a recipe by San Francisco's Jim Dodge, which is available year round. When we've dined here, we've found service to be scrupulous throughout the meal. The wine list is wide and eclectic. There is an emphasis on French, Italian and American in the medium to upper price ranges, though there is wide geographical representation from other continents. Dinner for two will be about Can$160. Both the wine list and dessert menus are available in the adjoining pasta bar. That section offers a range of pastas and lighter dishes as well as a wonderfully quiet corner table that is sought by the city's table cognoscenti. *Open Mon.-Fri. 11:30 a.m.-2 p.m. & 6 p.m.-10:30 p.m., Sat. 6 p.m.-10:30 p.m. All major cards.*

Le Sélect Bistro
328 Queen St. West, Downtown
• 596-6406
FRENCH

12/20

Call here, and you'll get a taped phone message promising that this is the most authentic bistro this side of Paris. Come here for dinner, and the only shreds of bistro evidence you'll find are in the onion soup and the name. But that's not to say you can't get a good meal, in a chummy, hip setting. Since its beginnings as a smoke-filled, artsy hangout in the 1960s, Le Sélect has gone upscale and mainstream, and one room has expanded to three. One has a glass sunroof; all have colorful tablecloths, hanging baskets of bread, lots of cheer and no more smoke.

The kitchen has added every kind of fare from Thai to Italian, and though the trendiness can be cloying, much of the food is good enough to warrant a long, lingering lunch. Bouillabaisse is generous with a lovely rich broth and lots of fish and shellfish; salmon tartare receives joyful spicing with little chunks of fresh ginger; calamari are competently marinated in coriander, garlic and good olive oil. Stay away from the extremely fashionable fare, such as the black-bean pancake or wierd pasta mixtures. You can rely on the standards to be good—marinated rack of lamb brings small, tender chops on a crowded plateful of vegetables; tender bavette steak is accompanied by good, traditional fries. The wine list offers a wide selection of French, Italian and California labels in a range from Can$20 to Can$40. There are nearly two dozen imported and locally brewed beers. Le Sélect's popularity is also testimony to its location on the interesting Queen Street, Toronto's SoHo. Save time for a post-meal stroll. Dinner for two, with wine, can reach Can$80. A three-course prix-fixe dinner for two costs about the same. *Open Sun.-Thurs. 11:30 a.m.- 4:30 p.m. & 5 p.m.-11 p.m., Fri.-Sat. 11:30 a.m.-4:30 p.m. & 5 p.m.-midnight. All major cards.*

RESTAURANTS

Senator Diner

253 Victoria St.,
Downtown
• 364-7517
AMERICAN

12/20

Bob Sniderman forsook the opportunity to work for his father's thriving retail chain of Sam the Record Man stores, and instead took on an ailing, run-down diner right around the corner from one of them. Though renowned for its egg-salad sandwiches, The Senator Diner had fallen on hard times. But that was ten years ago, and since then Bob Sniderman has made the place sing again. You can still hop up onto a barstool or slide into a booth for the best egg-salad sandwich in town, plus juicy hamburgers, good crabcakes and creamy rice pudding by the bathtubful. Keeping in tune with the times, he has also added a number of pastas, somewhat out of place in a diner but very good nevertheless. An even stranger find in a joint that serves fries and sodas is the exceptional wine list, which has always been part of the diner. With an emphasis on California wines, the list has been named among Toronto's best. Our only caveat: you'll find that this restaurant has maintained the original ambience only in looks. The wine list and some of the menu items are right in step with the 1990s, and you may find that Can$85 for two, with wine, is more than you expected to pay in a beanery. *Open Mon.-Fri. 11:30 a.m.- 2:30 p.m. & 5:30 p.m.-10:30 p.m., Sat. 5:30 p.m.-10:30 p.m., Sun. 8 a.m.-3 p.m.*

Senator Steak House

253 Victoria St.,
Downtown
• 364-7517
STEAKHOUSE

13

As soon as his first baby, the ten-year-old Senator Diner (see above review), was humming with success, Sniderman opened this eatery next door. Now just past infancy and into its second year, the restaurant grandly revives the American steakhouse of the 1920s and 1930s. The room is done up in polished mahogany and mirrors, and booths with velvet curtains attract local celebrities and politicians, who draw the curtains and share delicious secrets. The food is served in generous portions, and some of it is fabulous: sirloin steak is as tender as a velvet cloche, and Caesar salad brings a generous bowlful made with whole leaves, the way it's said to be made at its namesake in Tijuana, Mexico. Cobb salad brings less of a thrill, on par with the politically correct but disappointingly tenacious "natural" beef.

Portions are so huge, you may not have room for dessert. Find some—Senator's deserts are superb. This restaurant also shares its sister restaurant's excellent list of mostly California wines. The Senator is the best restaurant in the area of the Pantages Theatre, which shows blockbuster Broadway musicals. If you plan to dine here before the theater, you must make reservations. A dinner for two, with wine, costs about Can$100.
Open Mon.-Fri. 11:30 a.m.- 2:30 p.m. & 5:30 p.m.-10:30 p.m., Sat. 5:30 p.m.-10:30 p.m. Cards: AE, MC, V.

RESTAURANTS

Shopsy's

33 Yonge St.,
Bloor-Yorkville
• 365-3333
JEWISH

12/20

You can't visit Toronto and not be aware of Sam Shopsowitz. Everywhere you go you'll see ads for Shopsy's, as well as Shopsy's hot-dog carts, Shopsy's this and Shopsy's that. Not to mention this deli that is Mr. Shopsowitz's kosher jewel, named—what else?—Shopsy's. It's a sine qua deli, something straight out of one of Toronto native Mordecai Richler's novels. The place feels comfortable and familiar; in fact, the only thing that may seem strange about Shopsy's is that the wait staff is friendly and polite.

Shopsy's makes its own hot dogs (and you must get one on the street from one of the carts), salami, and there's a full complement of deli classics—corned beef and pastrami sandwiches piled high, liver, cabbage rolls, potato pancakes, knishes, bagels and cream cheese and smoked salmon. Portions are hefty, and while Shopsy's won't make people forget New York's Carnegie Deli, it's definitely one of Toronto's best—and this is a city with no dearth of delis. Dinner for two, with beverages, is about Can$40.

Open Mon.-Fri. 7 a.m.-1 a.m., Sat. 8 a.m.-1 a.m., Sun. 8 a.m.-midnight. Cards: AE, MC, V.

Simcoe North

2 Rosehill Ave.,
Downtown
• 964-1293
INTERNATIONAL

12/20

The merchants in this area still stand with their mouths agape at the man who had the temerity to open a restaurant—a spiffy one at that—at the end of 1990, just as Toronto was slipping deep into the recession. The truth is, this place just *looks* expensive. So far, owner Richard Geddes' place is surviving quite well. It was built on the site of a former nightclub, Harry's New York Bar, and has kept that place's posh British men's-club facade. But prices are a polite average of Can$6 for appetizers and Can$16 for main courses. And what appetizers! Beef carpaccio is served up with marinated mushrooms and shaved Parmesan, on a bed of arugula. Szechuan linguine brings more happiness than these kinds of mixed marriages usually do; the warm roast peppers, goat cheese and olives, spiked with shallots, garlic and peppercorns, balance harmoniously. Another winner is the spiral pasta, in a light cream sauce scented with cinnamon.

We like to build an entire meal around the starters, but if you opt for an entrée, try the grilled salmon with hollandaise (or any of the good fish dishes) or the steak frites, a huge slab of meat under a scoop of herbed butter, served with a pile of lovely, crisp fries. For lunch, try main courses of lovely chicken livers pan-fried with crushed peppercorns and thyme, or the roast Italian sausages with peppers and goat cheese on Italian bread. The large restaurant also includes a snooker room and an adjoining lounge with dance floor and live music. Make sure you've scooped your last bite of tiramisu and savored your last drop of cappuccino by 10:30 p.m., when the snooker enthusiasts cue

RESTAURANTS

up to the beat of a drum.
Open Mon.-Fri. 11:30 a.m.-3 p.m. & 5:30 p.m.-11 p.m., Sun. 11 a.m.- 3 p.m. & 5:30 p.m.-11 p.m. All major cards.

Sisi Trattoria

116A Avenue Rd., Toronto
• 962-0011
ITALIAN

Owner-chef Leo Schipani left a career in civil engineering for one in culinary construction with astounding success: on weekends you can't get into Sisi without a crowbar's push. You can get in, however, with a reservation, and when you do, you'll say "Bravo!" Schipani has a simple formula: offer a short menu of southern-Italian classics, use fresh ingredients religiously, and keep the restaurant small and cozy, with minimal decor. The result is some of the city's best Italian grilled food in a casual but sophisticated setting.

Onions figure largely in Schipani's cooking, and the scent of them as you descend the few steps to the restaurant is a powerful draw. They shine on the grilled sardines, their flavor sweetening the balsamic vinegar. They join the same vinegar, plus sweet peppers, capers and garlic, to enliven grilled chicken. Simplest and best of all are the grilled fish, which change according to the market. Regularly available calamari are done whole with no greasy batter, an infinitely superior preparation, so tender that the knife slides through the meat with barely a nudge. Shrimp are plump and full of taste, and good grilling gives fresh salmon a crisp crust and an tender inteior. Be aware that the chef has a tendency to lavish the oil on a little too freely. Occasional oil slicks on otherwise delicious food may suggest that the restaurant needs an environmental assessment more than a review, but regulars know to request a light hand. Portions are silly in their generosity: risotto built for two could sleep three. There isn't much for dessert, but you won't need it. The sight of the lean, well-turned out clientele tucking into those heaping platefuls may be all the surplus entertainment you can handle. Sisi's wine list concentrates on lusty Italian wines, none of them expensive. Dinner for two, with a bottle of house wine, costs about Can$110.
Open Tues.-Sat. 6:30 p.m.-10:30 p.m. Cards: AE, V.

Southern Accent

595 Markham St., Toronto
• 536-3211
CAJUN/CREOLE

Southern Accent was one of the vehicles that brought the Cajun/Creole craze barreling into town in the mid-1980s, and it has not only survived the waning of the trend, but has also gotten better over the years. The food started off fair at best, and with encouraging applause from spice-starved Torontonians, has risen to the occasion admirably. Now there are such soul-satisfying dishes as blackened chicken livers, fat with taste from their crisp, spicy exteriors right through to their pâté-soft interiors; and corn fritters with the same texture contrast and abundant corn taste. The spicing of most dishes

RESTAURANTS

won't send anyone running, except for the extremely spice-phobic. Some dishes, plantation duck for example, tend to show more spirit than spice. But a few go for the real Cajun heat: shrimp piquante, the shrimps' flesh inflamed by a red-chili-and-lemon sauce, tastes good and burns long. Seafood gumbo roars in a rich mahogany sauce, with tender seafood and rice for respite. Skip the boring jambalaya and the bland corn muffins, which unfortunately don't measure up to the rest of the menu. For dessert, bourbon bread pudding makes a superb finish. The restaurant takes up two levels of a storybook Victorian house, and is done up with a fitting amount of chintz and whimsy. Service, however, remains strictly in this decade: young and hip, with the occasional green-haired server to boogy you through the menu. Like the food, the clientele is a spicy mix, from clamorous groups of young trendoids to subdued suburbanites in their 50s to smartly dressed professionals. The wine list offers mostly Spanish labels, and there's a multitude of beers as well. Dinner for two will be about Can$85. If you like this place, also check out its sister restaurant, the more casual Zydeco (see page 89).

Open daily 5:30 p.m.-10:30 p.m. AE, MC, V.

Tall Poppies

326 Dundas St. West,
Kensington Market
• 595-5588
PACIFIC RIM/
SOUTHWESTERN

Tall Poppies zooms straight out of a Robert Altman movie from the 1970s, and that's meant as a compliment. Owned by two sisters, and with a wonderful chef named Henry Schmidt at the helm in the kitchen, Tall Poppies could have been a little too precious and a little too serene, if it weren't for all the good humor and controlled, yet palpable energy here.

The centerpiece is a beautiful patio, open in the spring and summer, canopied with both fruit and nonbearing trees. There's nothing wrong with the interior, though, which is airy and light. Appetizers are a good part of the script: grilled corn cakes with avocado salsa and black beans (truly a hit), a marinated salmon roulade stuffed with a tasty smoked trout mousse and nori, accompanied with sweet-and-sour cucumber, and marinated grilled flank steak on Chinese greens with snow peas, bean sprouts and carrots.

For lunch, there's a yummy sandwich built of grilled eggplant and tomato, on earthy homemade sourdough bread spread with an aromatic pesto. At dinnertime comes an impossibly rich duck confit on mixed greens with poached pears and chèvre dressed with a balsamic vinegar and shallot vinaigrette (it's not nearly as fussy as it sounds), homemade ravioli stuffed with smooth chicken mousse, served with huge tiger shrimp, steamed Chinese sausage and a julienne of vegetables in a clear, clean broth, and a simply done, yet simply grilled marinated Cornish game hen with black rice and mango in a lime and ginger vinaigrette.

The denouement sometimes plays flat, but the crème brûlée satisfies the audience, as does the chocolate raspberry tart. The wine list is limited but nicely chosen, with wines by the glass available. Two tickets to dinner, with wine, costs about Can$70. *Open Mon. 11:30 a.m.-2:30 p.m., Tues.-Fri. 11:30 a.m.-2:30 p.m. & 5:30 p.m.-10:30 p.m., Sat. 5:30 p.m.-10:30 p.m. Cards: AE, MC, V.*

Tapas Bar
226 Carlton St., Cabbagetown
• 323-9651
SPANISH

Grazing, which is just catching on here, has been entertaining the hungry of southern Europe for centuries, and nowhere more religiously than Spain. Grouped generically under the label of tapas, these snacks run the gamut of Spain's down-to-earth cuisine, and are probably the most abused notion in all of restaurant cooking. Approximations and misinterpretations run rampant through the menus of our respected restaurants. The real thing is available in this originally tiny (and now expanded), cheerful cellar with its checked tablecloths, its Asturian owner, and its dedication to a meticulous re-creation of the fare back home. Priced cheaply, the tapas here are inauthentic only in size of portions, which are two to three times more hefty than their Spanish counterparts.

The two dozen or so blackboard suggestions, which change according to the vagaries of availability, include homemade chorizo sausage served in a variety of ways, and thinly sliced serrano ham. Octopus is tenderized in a paprika sauce; check out the fried salt cod, brought back to life through simmering in white wine, onions and red peppers. Chickpea-and-tripe stew, flavored through with chorizo spicing, is a favorite. A university of little fishes, such chanquettes, anchovies and sardines—centerpiece of Spanish cookery—are offered in all those inventive, thirst-creating, greasy, saucy preparations, to round out the list. The wines are strictly Spanish, with many good buys in the modestly priced list. Though scorned by some wine snobs, Spanish *vino* has enough grease-cutting power to do justice to the free-for-all, garlic-and-oil essence of tapas. Service is macho (in a benevolent way) and often unilingual (Spanish, that is). That and the tree-lined Victoriana of this Cabbagetown stretch of Carlton Street add to the illusion of a minijourney to an Iberian destination. A grazing extravaganza of several, shared tapas, with lots of wine, shouldn't cost more than Can$60.
Open Mon.-Fri. noon-1 a.m., Sat. 2 p.m.-1 a.m. All major cards.

RESTAURANTS

Thai Magic
1118 Yonge St.,
Toronto
• 968-7366
THAI

This place took over a space that had been occupied by more than a half-dozen restaurants in as many years, so when Thai Magic caught on within days of its opening, hardly anyone was happier than the landlords. Except, perhaps, the people that discovered the food here. An effusive welcome at the door recalls the real Thailand, as you're ushered into a comfortable, smallish room with hanging plants, textured walls and fabrics and accents in dark jewel tones, with lots of brass. The gracious service continues at the table, where you get down to the real business of this place: the food.

Barbecued shrimp are crunchy and spicy, with a tart-hot dipping sauce; hurricane kettle, a soup full of searing chili heat, lemon-grass flavor and abundant seafood chunks. Massaman lamb curry, and the "Very Special" curried beef are truly Thai, authentically (in other words, hotly) spiced. Scotch Bonnet, the Caribbean chili with a Sunday school name and the heat of hades, is employed mercilessly in many of the meat dishes. Chili-phobics be warned: in the curried beef, the searing green chili peppers look just like the innocent, sweet green variety, and both are in profusion. When the lights are dim and the night is sweet, mistakes are easy. You will remember one feckless bite of the wrong chili for years after you've forgotten the dinner. The fabulous seafood dishes pose less of a danger: whole steamed pickerel cooks just until its glassy flesh acquires an opaque sheen, then is lovingly teamed with lightly pickled vegetables. Coriander lobster comes in its shell, with a richly herbed sauce that will leave you sorting through crevices for flavorful nuggets long after the flesh is gone. Brass bowlfuls of rice keep the dishes company. One warning is that portions are small; two people will eat well by ordering four dishes and a few appetizers. The essential well-chilled beer is available in the form of several imports and several local brews (sorry, no Thai labels). Dinner for two, with beers, will bring your meal to Can$60.

Open Mon.-Sat. 5 p.m.-11 p.m., Sun. 4 p.m.-10 p.m. Cards: AE, MC, V.

Thai Shan Inn
2039 Eglinton Ave. West,
York
• 784-1491
THAI

No one will fault first-time visitors to this unabashedly modest Thai restaurant for being a bit dubious because of the place's interior. Even in Toronto's most authentically ethnic eating establishments, you'll probably find the odd plastic flower or even a wall calendar. Here, count on Formica-meets-plastic and not much else.

The good news is that the budget's reserved for the food, which excels. It will be difficult not to order from the appetizer list alone: satés of pork, chicken or beef come to table juicy with

RESTAURANTS

a kiss of heat, while the shrimp—stretched out on a wooden skewer—sock a garlic-salt hit so flavorful you'll want to eat the tail shell. The requisite dish of Thai peanut sauce, chock full of nuts, is served alongside, as is a serving of refreshing pepper strips and cucumber chunks. Shrimp egg rolls bulge, huge and greasy, with a diaphanous, thread-thin noodle mixture and one big shrimp, the tail of which protrudes at one end. Don't pass up the mango salad, in which fine, juicy slivers of green mangoes mingle with tiny bits of chicken, peppers, onions and a heap of flavor-complex coriander. This dish tastes deeply fruity, spicy sweet and utterly unique. The oddly named French Thai toast, fried bread topped with a pork-and-egg mixture, reminded us of Chinese shrimp toast. Whatever the nationality, it's tasty.

Rice and noodle dishes, you bet. The tasty standard, Phad Thai wows the tastebuds with its chilies, peanuts and green onions. There are nine rice offerings; we count among the best as being the zingy-hot rice with purple basil and the greasy-but-good crab fried rice with peas and hefty crab claws.

For a main course, sample the statement-making kaeng phed curry with your choice of meat, or the whole deep-fried fish, best ordered by two people because of the size. Thais aren't big on desserts, and your best bet here might be a sugary Thai iced tea, especially since there's no liquor license. Dinner for two ravenous appetites is around Can$60.

Open daily 5 p.m.-11 p.m. Cards: MC, V.

Tipplers Restaurant
1276 Yonge St., Rosedale
• 967-9463
FRENCH

While working as Susur Lee's trusted sous-chef in the well-known restaurant, Lotus, Chris Zielinski proved nightly that food, both in preparation and presentation, can indeed be art. Now his own boss as the chef of Tipplers and working on a narrower (less expensive) canvas, Zielinski continues creating artful deliciousness at this facetiously named drinker's bistro, that had never before been remarkable for anything but the unsteady gait of the clients heading home at the end of an evening. As the sun sets over the quaint and refined pretentiousness of this Rosedale stretch of Yonge Street, the double-decker dining rooms of Tipplers nowadays are filled with serious diners sitting at white-linen clad tables, tastebuds tingling with anticipation.

The rewards begin right away, with the puréed soups that, although uncharacteristic for their genre, are light and refreshing. Some kind of whimsical touch, like dollops of beet-pink crème fraîche or julienned green apple, as well as rounds of bruschetta on the side, complement the nourishing slurps. All the appetizers are blessed with subtle elegance and attention to detail: blood-red carpaccio with edible flowers, goat cheese and olive oil. Lobster-and-salmon terrine with a center of seaweed-

RESTAURANTS

wrapped lobster forcemeat, riding on a fresh tarragon mousseline; a deboned quail, stuffed with cheese and polenta on a blueberry sauce; soft-shell crab humanely fried and displayed on a mango-tomatillo coulis with fresh corn kernels. We ordered them all and had a grazing feast. The limited mainstays of the daily-changing menu include lamb, liver, salmon and swordfish, all of them expertly handled and appropriately sauced. The glory of these plates is in the vegetable and starch garnishes, which at last count included nine separate items, each one prepared to showcase its best advantage. Desserts, except for one or two a night, are brought in, and after such bounty, rather redundant. The wine list is endless and a fair sampling is available by the glass. Dinner for two, with wine, Can$105.
Open Mon.-Fri. noon-2:30 p.m. & 6 p.m.-10:30 p.m., Sat.-Sun. 6 p.m.-10:30 p.m. All major cards.

Tortilla Flats
429 Queen St. West,
Downtown
• 593-9870
MEXICAN/AMERICAN

9/20

Tortilla Flats calls itself a "Texas bar and grill." What it really looks like a Texican Hard Rock Café, catering to a young adult crowd that likes loud rock-and-roll, margaritas big enough to bathe in and large portions of mediocre food—a crowd whose members probably haven't read the John Steinbeck novel of the same name.

It's the perfect restaurant for college students: the food's fairly cheap; it's a good place to meet people; it's undeniably fun—as long as you're not too old for this kind of stuff. As for the food's finer points, there aren't any: students dig blithely into fajitas, burgers, awful chili, tostadas, quesadillas, tacos and enchiladas. There's even "Kitchen Sink Dip" (elsewhere known as seven-layer dip), a geological dig of refried beans, chili, Jack cheese, guacamole, sour cream, onions, olives, peppers and cilantro, which ends up looking less than inspiring after the third chip has been dragged through it. Dinner for two, with beverages, is about Can$40.
Open Mon.-Sat. 11:30 a.m.-1 a.m., Sun. noon-11 p.m. Cards: MC, V.

Trapper's Restaurant
3479 Yonge St.,
North York
• 482 6211
CANADIAN

The name and wilderness scenes might lead you to wonder if you'll be sharing your meal with a lumberjack in a macinaw and eating coffee on a stick for dessert. The food may well be hearty enough to fuel three hours of snowshoeing in the bush, but the comfortably elegant ambience and the menu, with its wide wine list, feel more urban than that. One of the reasons we love this place is simply its cozy warmth, its solidness—with cushy chairs and banquettes, heavy silverware and welcoming service. Trapper's is usually full, and sometimes there's a wait while early eaters linger over dessert. One of them might be Mme. Janet Boland, a justice who sits on Ontario's Supreme Court, and also

RESTAURANTS

the owner's mother. Her son, Chris, has described the menu as "North American/Continental," and here's what he means: barbecued, center-cut Ontario pork, stuffed with fresh fettuccine and aged Canadian cheddar and served with a brandy-fig sauce; northern-Ontario trout seared with cayenne, garlic and black peppers, finished off in the oven and served with grilled melon. Trapper's kitchen is big on Canadian Cheddar—and understandably so, for Ontario produces exceptional aged cheese. Cheddar-cheese soup has been a menu standard here for years. So has the onion soup, which receives a Canadian boost with onions that are first caramelized in maple syrup. Most of the dishes work very well because the chefs don't go overboard with patriotic whimsy. For dessert, there's a satiny and soothing white-chocolate mousse with hazelnuts, and a homespun deep-dish apple-apricot-pear cobbler. Owner Chris Boland has an active interest in wine and offers nearly 250 bottles between Can$20 and Can$40. Dinner for two, with wine, will be about Can$90.

Open Mon.-Fri. 11:30 a.m.-2:30 p.m. & 5:30 p.m.-10:30 p.m., Sat.-Sun. 5:30 p.m.-10:30 p.m. Cards: AE, MC, V.

Trata Psaro Taverna

1055 Yonge St., Toronto
• 924-1257
GREEK/SEAFOOD

12/20

Though Trata has never earned the worshipful endorsement from Toronto that its mentor restaurant, Mykonos, did in Montreal, it still attracts a good crowd of regulars, who come for the terrific grilled fish and a few outstanding appetizers. The culinary centerpiece is a wide variety of seafood—usually bass, sole, porgy, swordfish, lobster and shrimp—displayed on a bed of ice in front of the charcoal grill. Shortly after you're seated, your party chooses from among the fresh offerings, which are soon returned whole, perfectly cooked and expertly seasoned. The menu includes a couple of less exciting meat dishes, such as souvlaki and grilled lamb chop.

If this all sounds suspiciously as if it weren't quite the same taverna you loved in Athens, it's because it isn't. The cuisine might be called sanitized Greek, leaner and pricier than the real thing. Two specialities set Trata apart from the multitude of other Toronto restaurants that serve grilled fish and charge dearly for them. One, octopus, is marinated and then seared on the charcoal grill to succulence; the other, an appetizer for two—a pyramid of chiplike, paper-thin slices of eggplant and zucchini stacked over garlic-spiked homemade yogurt—is something to savor, linger over, and order again.

Trata's owner, Socrates Psarfoulias, encourages family-style dining in true Greek fashion, with roomy tables and shared

RESTAURANTS

platters. The friendly, rustic feeling echoes the restaurant's simple decor of checkered tablecloths and draped fish nets. Keep in mind that with family-style dining, everyone shares the food, while only the grownups get the bill. At Trata, that can be high. Making a meal from a collection of appetizers and a grilled fish will keep the tally down to about Can$90 for two, with house wine; if you order an entrée apiece, count on more than Can$110.
Open Mon.-Sat. noon-midnight, Sun. 5 p.m.-midnight. Cards: AE, MC, V.

Trattoria Giancarlo
41 Clinton St.,
Little Italy
• 533 9619
ITALIAN

12/20

This casual restaurant in the heart of Toronto's little Italy is a neighborhood sweetheart, loved for its coziness and good food throughout the year. During summer, its side-street patio fills with locals, who sip chilled rosé and watch the street life go by. Antonio and Eugenia Barata, a Portuguese couple and this trattoria's owners for almost three years, have added only a little of their own ethnic flavor to the menu, choosing to maintain the original restaurant's integrity and flavor. Pastas are fresh and varied; spaghetti might be simply done with Pecorino cheese or olive oil and garlic. Whatever the ingredients, dishes are of a good quality, and carefully prepared. Ask about the "surprise" pasta of the day; sometimes a restaurant's surprise can be your evening's demise, but Giancarlo's usually prove to be the best dishes offered on any given night. These range from spaghetti Nero, featuring cuttlefish and its black ink, shellfish and fresh coriander, to pappardelle with fresh herbs, chilies, and lightly sautéed vegetables. Grilled swordfish pops up as ubiquitously as tiramisu in Toronto's trattorias and ristorantes, and this is one place that offers a truly sublime preparation. The fat shrimp don't disappoint, either. Look for the wine list on a blackboard, which you have to get up to survey, since you can't see it no matter where you're seated. It's an intimate place, so you don't have far to walk. Ask about the ports; Antonio has several vintages stashed away in the basement and several more by the glass. If you're inclined toward dessert, there's a lovely crème caramel, or you can do what many regulars do, and stroll to one of the espresso cafés or the Sicilian Ice Cream Parlor down the street. Dinner for two, with house wine, will reach Can$85 to Can$95.
Open Mon.-Wed. & Sat. 5:30 p.m.-11 p.m., Thurs.-Fri. noon-3 p.m. & 5:30 p.m.-11 p.m. Cards: AE, MC, V.

RESTAURANTS

Truffles

Four Seasons Hotel,
21 Avenue Rd.,
Bloor-Yorkville
• 964-0411
INTERNATIONAL

[14]

The reputation of the Four Seasons Hotel in Yorkville precedes it and, we are happy to report, extends to the dining room. Truffles features a grand and sophisticated style without any risk-taking in decor. Dark-beamed ceilings, tasteful floral expressions, muted blue-velvet chairs, crisp white nappery and Old Master–style prints prevail. A few tables are partially recessed beneath a slight alcove, perfect for serious handholding or buisness chat. Service is genuinely friendly, thoroughly professional and helpful.

What about the menu? It's intriguing in style and content, listing one imaginative preparation after another. An appetizer of white-truffle spaghetti tasted deeply rich and intense. Two long bales of pasta, pale brown from frothy truffle juice, took center stage, encircled by truffle shavings. A trio of round raviolis with sculpted edges came packed with sweet lobster chunks. Fresh, fragrant cilantro shone through; the blend of tastes was hauntingly delicious. Seasonal greens created an edible garden of taste: buds of slender garlic chives, frisée, a riot of radicchio, watercress, even purple pansy petals in January. Then there was the perfect baked potato dressed with more truffles, that concealed a tiny quail.

Keeping up with the times, some main courses on the menu are followed by an asterisk, meaning that they are considered fair game for the low-calorie, low-fat, low-salt gang. Sublimely sweet veal tenderloin sitting amid plump, crunchy snap peas was accented by pink grapefruit slices and a Champagne caviar sauce. An oval of dark perfection, the beef filet came soothed by a royal demi-glace with bourbon—two crossed skewers of run-through vegetables and golden creamy saffron whipped potatoes cozily alongside. Dessert, tropical sorbets of pineapple, lime, orange, lemon and passion fruit, left our palates positively startled and absolutely refreshed. Dinner for two with a reputable but not exorbitant wine will run Can$150.

Open daily 6 p.m.-11 p.m. All major cards.

United Bakers Dairy Restaurant

Lawrence Plaza,
506 Lawrence Ave.
West,
Toronto North
• 789-0519
POLISH/JEWISH

12/20

In an unusual twist on the patron-restaurant relationship, this family-run operation had to pick up and move across town to where its customers lived. A beloved noshing spot in the mostly Jewish immigrant district since 1912, United Bakers suddenly found dim-sum palaces and noodle shops popping up on Spadina Avenue in the late 1980s. Now their old neighborhood is predominantly Chinese, and the restaurant has relocated to a grungy strip mall in North Toronto. Aesthetically, there's nothing to recommend the place, but looks aren't the whole schmear—gastronomically, now that's another story. First, there are the soups: the barley-bean, split pea with noodles and sweet-and-sour cabbage borscht are the best in the city—on a really sentimental day, we might even say the best in the world. Then there are the basics: potato latkes fit the bill; cheese blintzes are oversize crêpes stuffed with sweetened Toronto-style cottage cheese and served with applesauce and sour cream. Other worthwhile hot dishes include kasha stirred with sweetly fried onions, and cabbage rolls stuffed with mushrooms, onions and rice. Gefilte fish comes in biblical proportions, with ample horseradish to test your stomach's stamina. In fact, all of the portions are big: farmer's salad brings a mountain of cottage cheese and sour cream, piled with diced cucumber, tomatoes and onions. Lox, eggs and onions satisfies even the choosiest schlemeil, and is worth the Can$18-a-pound price of the smoked salmon. If you haven't noticed yet, there's no meat on the menu—but who needs it with this kind of food? Toronto's Jewish dairies produce some of the finest cream and cottage cheese on the continent, and if you want to find out for yourself, United Bakers is the place. Service may be challenging, but dinner for two will be less than Can$25. Another branch of United Bakers is at 390 Steeles Avenue West, in Thornhill (764-1149).

Open Mon.-Thurs. 7 a.m.-8:45 p.m., Fri. 7 a.m.-7:45 p.m., Sat.-Sun. 7 a.m.-9:45 p.m. Cards: MC, V.

Vanipha Fine Cuisine
193 Augusta Ave., Kensington Market
• 340-0491
LAOTIAN

12/20

North America's magnetic attraction for nationalities from around the world has brought a continuous stream of exotic new cuisines onto the conintnent. Among the newest to enter the scene is Laotian. Laos, which has influenced its neighbor, Thailand, in the kitchen, also has one thing to add to its neighbor's cuisine: more heat via more chilies. All Laotian food, as interpreted by Vanipha, this basementlike hole-in-the-wall on picturesque Kensington Market's Augusta Avenue, sizzles with extreme heat: definitely *not* for the timid. Those with cast-iron palates, who have the ability to discern tastes beyond the fumes, are regaled with subtleties of spicing and ultra-authentic expertise. Tom kha kai (coconut-chicken soup), sweet and creamy, is laced with lemon grass and curry leaf, and satisfies with chunks of moistly poached chicken breast. Spring rolls are thinly rolled and beautifully greaseless. Phad Thai, the stir-fried rice-noodles, are sweet and sour, a perfect sidekick to the marinated and grilled chicken ping kai, which literally spurts spicy juices when bitten into. Pla poaw is an entire fish, slow-grilled to maximize the taste of its tender flesh, which is napped with a powerful tamarind sauce. Lab kai is a knock-out stir-fry of chicken shreds with garlic, mint, coriander, lemon grass, onion and the inevitable chilies. Even sane people can enjoy this restaurant as long as caution (as in small bites) is exercised and an ample supply of the special, wonderfully bland, sticky rice with its sweet peanut

sauce is kept nearby to be nibbled whenever the alarms go off. At last report Vanipha's liquor license was still pending, but one of the many bottled, exotic juices will quench the fires. Dinner for two, with beverage, will come in under Can$35.
Open Tues.-Wed. noon-11 p.m., Thurs.-Sat. noon-midnight, Sun. 1 p.m.-10 p.m. Cards: V.

Vietnam Village
393F Dundas St. West, Downtown
• 598-3288
VIETNAMESE

12/20

It's cute. It's spotless. It's a haven of good Vietnamese food in a city positively studded with Vietnamese restaurants. Take, for example, a delectable appetizer of a shrimp and pork bun, very tasty, indeed. Or what they term "lasagne," which are long, flat noodles made from gelatinous rice with various fillings including spicy sausage, shredded pork, and shrimp. Fine, filling soups include a beef brisket soup, fairly clogged with brisket so tender, there's no need to chew in order to eat it; we also enjoyed a beef soup with zingy meatballs, shrimp soup, and a wonderfully rich sparerib soup. The noodle and rice dishes should claim your attention as well, especially the rice topped with grilled beef, lemon grass and hot (red alert) peppers, and the noodles with shrimp and sugar cane. House specialties include a saucy chicken sautéed with piquant ginger, barbecued quail (absolutely delicious), and sautéed and grilled snow crab. Plus, don't miss the fish of the day with tamarind sauce, that elusively flavored dressing, not quite sweet, not quite sour.

You can't imbibe here—there's no liquor license—but you'll do just fine with Vietnamese iced coffee (akin to Thai iced coffee, a nectar of caffeine and sweetened condensed milk), soda pop, or a virtuous, yet not half-bad, soy bean drink. Vietnam Village is a real treat, and the low tariff is just an added plus: dinner for two, with beverages, is about Can$30—and that's if you order a lot of food.
Open daily 10 a.m.-9 p.m. Cards: MC, V.

Yamase
317 King St. West, Downtown
• 598-1562
SUSHI/JAPANESE

12/20

A longtime favorite with local sushi mavens, Yamase has beckoned the fans of raw fish slices on Japanese horse-radish smeared, vinegared rice patties, to its narrow premises on King Street West ever since it opened. The steady flow of customers is more or less guaranteed by its location, which is minutes away from the Broadwaylike Royal Alexandra Theatre and the state-of-the-art Roy Thomson Symphony Hall, which dispense culture nightly. Despite the fairly authentic decor and geishalike service, the cooking of Yamase's traditional Japanese cuisine does not match the quality of its sushi, and is best left alone.

The sushi, however, and especially the numerous, unusual hand rolls come highly recommended (by us), particularly if you're lucky enough to land an empty seat at the small sushi bar, and watch the intrepid and skillful fingers of the sushi chefs. It

RESTAURANTS

is hard to go wrong with any of the hand rolls, since even the well-known items such as tekka-tuna or kappa-cucumber are prepared with flair and extra little treats. For the adventurous, there is the ono-maki with shrimps and al dente fiddle-heads, the Steve-maki's salmon eggs and cucumber, the Vito-roll, wherein yellow tail is spiked with a hot pickle, and the filling Toronto-maki with its quartet of tobiko caviar, avocado, crab and the surprisingly appropriate lettuce. Sake, as always, is the best solvent for sushi, and Yamase keeps those minicarafes of warm rice wine permanently filled. Sushi and saké for two easily mounts up to Can$90, depending on appetite and thirst.
Open Mon.-Fri. noon-2:30 p.m. & 5:30 p.m.-11 p.m., Sat.-Sun. 5:30 p.m.-11 p.m. All major cards.

Zydeco
583 Markham St.,
The Annex
• 536-1774
CAJUN/CREOLE

12/20

Zydeco, along with its parent establishment, Southern Accent (see page 78), a few doors away, are the only worthwhile purveyors of Louisiana-style cooking in Toronto. Considering that, at least Cajun cuisine has its roots in Canada, albeit a thousand miles away in Nova Scotia (Acadia), this would have to qualify as some sort of homecoming. The place is as lively and outgoing as the accordion-based music, from which it has borrowed its name.

The peppy cooking is determinedly southern, something that the owners and chefs cultivate with annual pilgrimages to New Orleans. And in truth, everything has been improving over the years, even the signature bo and jambalaya, which started out anemic and unpleasant, but have gotten full-bodied and eminently cravable. The kitchen's forte is "blackening," the highest profile process of the current re-discovery of Cajun cooking. The spicing is just right, and the pans must be just perfectly searing, because the meats and fishes arrive every bit as juicy inside and mysteriously dark outside as they should be. The lowly chicken livers taste best among the blackened items, though steak and fish have also satisfied. The best lunch at Zydeco is a crunchy, mouth-filling New Orleans sandwich, known as poor boy, which features cornmeal shrimp, spiked mayonnaise, lettuce and tomato in a minibaguette. A cup of deeply aromatic gumbo soup accompanies the sandwich very well, and wonderfully boozy, Louisiana bread pudding, with bourbon sauce closes it off in style. Zydeco recalls the South especially well in the summer, on its wide terrace in the middle of the action on happening Markham Street. The full license includes a wide selection of French and California wines, as well as beers for putting out those Bayou flames. Lunch or dinner for two, with wine, shouldn't exceed Can$70.
Open Tues.-Sat. noon-midnight, Sun. 11 a.m.-5 p.m. All major cards.

QUICK BITES

ASIAN FAST FOOD	92
CAFES	93
DELIS	97
HAMBURGERS & SANDWICHES	98
HIGH TEA	100
MEXICAN FAST FOOD	101
MIDDLE EASTERN	101
PIZZA & PASTA	102

ASIAN FAST FOOD

Kwangtung Dim Sum Restaurant

10 Kensington Ave.,
Kensington Market
• 977-5165

Toronto's Kensington Market district is a compact compendium of many of the world's cuisines—bustling, open markets, milling crowds, and lots of little cafés. Kwangtung Dim Sum Restaurant is small and spotless, offering a good selection of inexpensive dim-sum dishes. Especially good are the standbys such as har gow, shu mai and fried shrimp rolls, and so are the more exotic steamed soup in a pouch, beef tripe in a pungent ginger sauce, and the Chinese radish cake. About Can$15 for two.
Open daily 9 a.m.-8 p.m. No cards.

The Original Vietnam

842 Bloor St. West,
Bloor-Yorkville
• 531-8763

Fans of Vietnamese cuisine will like this place; its food is good and inexpensive (as evidenced by the preponderance of college students). We eschewed main courses in favor of appetizers, and were happy as curried clams with the pork-stuffed wonton-chicken soup, shrimp with rice and sizzling scallions with oysters. There is a huge selection of teas, and with a meal costing about Can$25 for two, you get a lot of bang for your Canadian buck.
Open Tues.-Sun. 4:30 p.m.-10:30 p.m. Cards: MC, V.

Sam the Chinese Food Man Tavern

371 Yonge St.,
Toronto
• 977-2100

This nutty restaurant, tucked away behind a narrow doorway and up a seemingly endless flight of stairs, offers a buffet has been attracting folks for its inexpensive, decent Chinese food for years. The fare is fresh and pretty tasty, considering that it's steam-table cuisine; try the honey-garlic wings, sweet-and-sour ribs and wonton soup. The price is certainly right—Can$6.95 for an all-you-can-eat dinner.
Open daily 5:30 p.m.-10 p.m. Cards: AE, MC, V.

Satay Satay

700 Bloor St. West,
Etobicoke
• 532-7489

One of Thailands best-loved cultural exports in the food department are its satés, those succulent skewers of beef, chicken, seafood and pork that arrive at the table sizzling on a hot plate, accompanied by the traditional creamy peanut sauce and a hot/cool cucumber salad. At Satay Satay, they go one better: you grill the satés yourself at a tableside hibachi. Though there are other dishes on the menu—including especially good soups—focus on the satés. A meal for two is about Can$24.
Open Mon.-Thurs. 5 p.m.-10:30 p.m., Fri.-Sat. 5 p.m.-11 p.m., Sun. 5 p.m.-10:30 p.m. Cards: AE, MC, V.

QUICK BITES Cafés

Yokohama Restaurant
326 Adelaide St. West,
Downtown
• 351-7538

This downtown noodle house shows an obsessive and welcome concern with the quality of its homemade broth and noodles. There are four kinds of broth—soybean, garlic/soy, miso and meat—and only one kind of noodle, which is made on the premises with imported flour. Enjoy a bathtub-sized bowl of satisfying broth loaded up with noodles and any variation on vegetables and meat. The best is Yokohama soup slopping over with piles of dense, slurpy noodles that vie for space with sliced egg, corn niblets, vegetables and slippery sheaves of seaweed. It will take nearly a half hour to finish the soup, for which you pay just Can$8.45. This is as genuine a noodle house as they come in these parts. The staff speaks a little English, punctuated by lots of happy noodle slurping.
Open Tues.-Sun. 5:30 p.m.-11 p.m. Cards: AE, MC, V. Full license.

CAFES

Abundance Restaurant
81 Church St.,
Downtown
• 368-2867

Don't you love this name? Abundance is the perfect restaurant for pre- or posttheater dining—a very pretty room, gently lit and brimming with greenery, and a kitchen that offers some very tasty, very homey food. Best bets are the chicken pot pie with french fries, the wonderfully creamy macaroni and cheese and the Cajun meatloaf with real mashed potatoes. Service is friendly, and prices reasonable: a meal for two runs about Can$24.
Open Mon.-Thurs. 11:30 a.m.-10:30 p.m., Fri.-Sat. 11:30 a.m.-11:30 p.m., Sun. 11:30 a.m.-8 p.m. Cards: AE, MC, V.

Amsterdam Brasserie & Brewpub
133 John St.,
Downtown
• 595-8201

The bar menu at Amsterdam, though it changes regularly, remains a fabulous one, and considerably less expensive than the dinner menu. This deservedly popular pub brews its own beer on the premises, and the atmosphere is lively and fun, but to us, the food is the real draw. The menu changes every few months or so, and we always enjoy the perfectly crisp and light fish-and-chips, tender skewers of chicken saté with spicy Thai peanut sauce, home-smoked barbecued ribs and fried calamari in a tangy lime-and-cumin aïoli, with sweet-potato fries. A bar snack—actually a real meal—runs about Can$22 for two.
Open Mon.-Sat. 11:30 a.m.-2:30 p.m. & 5:30 p.m.-10 p.m. Sun. 11 a.m.-midnight. Cards: AE, MC, V. Full license.

QUICK BITES Cafés

Cake Master Ltd.
1281/2 Cumberland St.,
Bloor-Yorkville
• 921-6353, 925-2879

Yes, you'll want to focus on the cakes, cookies and other delectable sweetmeats (the shop is locally famous—for its their dense, moist poppyseed danish and sinfully delicious mocha-meringue cakes), but you can also enjoy some very tasty sandwiches. Sit at one of the outdoor tables, which are stepped down from the street, so you can eavesdrop and ogle folks passing by. It's a nice spot in which to sit and rest your tootsies for a while—the shopping in Yorkville is a full-time pursuit, and sipping a cappuccino and nibbling on a home-made sandwich cookie at Cake Master is a splendid way to refuel. Sweets and cappuccinos cost about Can$12 for two.
Open Mon.-Sat. 8 a.m.-5:30 p.m. No cards.

Chez Cappuccino
3 Charles St. East,
Bloor-Yorkville
• 925-6142

The primary attractions of this café are its 24-hour schedule and its charming patio, which is a popular ogling spot for its views of the best-looking men and women in Toronto (courtesy of several work-out palaces in the vicinity). Chez Cappuccino is located on the cutting edge of the action on Charles Street, around the corner from the main drag of Yonge Street, near many hotels, entertainments and shops, making it an ideal pit-stop for an eponymous cappuccino and a quick bite. The sandwiches are filling and inoffensive, but there's nothing here that couldn't be slapped together in two seconds in a hotel room. The salads, especially during the bounty of summer and early fall, constitute a good value, but again nothing special. The pastries are all brought in and commercial. The cappuccino is drinkable and the best of the same anywhere in this area (which isn't saying much). The people-watching makes up the difference. Not a drop of alcohol, though. The premises does not have a license. Coffee snacks for two won't run you more than Can$15.
Open daily 24 hours. No cards.

Croissant House
10 Dundas Square,
Downtown
• 598-1124

You'll find basic fast food at this café-cum-bakery, but the goods are more than decent; if you have to catch a bite on the fly this does just fine. There is a variety of croissants, croissant sandwiches, danishes and coffees and teas—they even serve Rice Krispie squares here, crunchy-chewy mementos of child-hood after-school snacks. Though the bulk of the business here is of the take-out variety; several tables allow for dining in. Lunch for two is about Can$12.
Open Mon.-Fri. 7:30 a.m.-8 p.m., Sat. 7:30 a.m.-6 p.m., Sun. 7:30 a.m.-noon. No cards.

QUICK BITES Cafés

Kensington 73 Café
73 Kensington Ave.,
Kensington Market
• 971-5632

Aside from being a rich trove of ethnic markets and eateries, the Kensington Market district is also home to quite a few hip, upmarket shops and cafés—not unlike New York's Greenwich Village. Kensington 73 is cute and funky, chiefly offering breakfast, lunch and snack victuals—heavy on the salads, sandwiches, pastas and desserts. The food won't send you into raptures, but it's good, and the service is friendly and fun, making this a good pit stop for a break from trying on used Levi's and 1950s party dresses in the neighborhood's many vintage clothing stores. About Can$20 for two.
Open daily 9:30 a.m.-6 p.m. No cards.

H. Rooneem's
484 Queen St. West,
Downtown
• 366-1205

Wonderful bakeries and cafés dot Toronto, and H. Rooneem's is a local favorite. It's been around since 1949, supplying the locals with ornate, European-style birthday and wedding cakes, as well as earthy, chewy dark-rye and Estonian sauerbrots. But look more closely, and you'll notice a lunch counter at the back of the shop, offering cold-cut sandwiches, hot dogs, burgers, schnitzel and french fries to fill up on before you hit the buttercream icing. Don't miss the few outdoor tables (weather permitting), which complete the northern-European feel of this café. Lunch for two is about Can$16.
Open Mon.-Fri. 6:30 a.m.-5 p.m., Sat. 6:30 a.m.-6 p.m. No cards.

Hungarian Goulash Party Tavern
498 Queen St. West,
Downtown
• 863-6124

A quick bite at this long, narrow restaurant goes a long, long way—this is real stick-to-the-ribs, -hips and -thighs stuff. Things can get pretty raucous in the evening, hence the "party" in its moniker, but that just aids in getting your digestive juices flowing for the onslaught of garlic spare ribs, roast beef, goulash, schnitzel and oniony chicken. Things are quieter at lunch time, but the portions are just as huge, so be prepared to nap after eating. Lunch for two is about Can$20.
Open Mon.-Sat. 11 a.m.-11:30 p.m., Sun. 11 a.m.-10:30 p.m. Cards: AE, MC, V.

Marky's Fine Dining
355 Wilson Ave.,
Toronto
• 636-0163

Marky's (formerly Greenfields) produces Glatt kosher fare that's right up there with the best of them. Don't come looking for blintzes and borscht, things are little more Continental at Marky's (is the name a play on "mockie," Yiddish for a greenhorn fresh off the boat?). You'll find good pastas, fresh fish, steak, Cornish game hens, duck and various salads on the menu, and be sure to try the homemade ice cream for dessert. A meal for two, with sodas, will run about Can$32.
Open Thurs.-Sun. 11:30 a.m.-10 p.m. Cards: AE, MC, V.

QUICK BITES   Cafés

OBoy
287 Richmond St. West, Downtown
• 971-5812

OBoy, oh boy, it's a vintage diner with a lunch counter! OBoy has been co-opted by enterprising New Wavers. The look of this little nook is strictly Edward Hopper-esque; the feel is decidedly bohemian coffee house. There's a brisk take-out business here, but it really is fun to eat in. The menu offers various breakfast specials of the egg-bacon-toast combo variety, as well as sandwiches, salads, soups and desserts—and a full complement of coffee beverages (cafe au lait, cappuccino, espresso and so on). Lively, hip and inexpensive at about Can$15 for two, OBoy is really a treat.
Open Mon.-Fri. 8 a.m.-5 p.m.; Sat. 10 a.m.-4 p.m. No cards.

> *We're always interested to hear about your discoveries, and to receive your comments on ours. Please feel free to write to us, and do state clearly exactly what you liked or disliked.*

Simply Delicious
279 Queen St. West, Downtown
• 971-5863

Very cool, very friendly and with some of the best sweets you'll find in Toronto, Simply Delicious is just that. In fact, it's nearly worth a trip from anywhere in Toronto for its supernal, mile-high praline-and-cream pie, surely a dessert that is served in heaven. The people who work here are so friendly, it's infectious—and you'll get pretty giddy from the Italian-strength cappuccinos as well. There are fabulous fruit pies and lots of other sugary goodies, all served up until the wee hours of the morning. A snack for two is about Can$12.
Open Mon.-Thurs. 8:30 a.m.-3 a.m., Fri. 8:30 a.m.-4 a.m., Sat. 10:30 a.m.-4 a.m., Sun. 1 p.m.-1 a.m. No cards.

Tea Masters International Café
10 St. Mary St., Toronto
• 924-1799

Part of a chain, Tea Masters sells a variety of whole coffee beans by the pound, as well as teas from around the world. It also offers a more extensive menu, including a good variety of soups, sandwiches, salads, quiches, bagels, muffins and the like. Friendly service compliments the shop itself, which is spotlessly slick, yet charming. It's a nice place for a respite from all the shopping you'll find yourself doing in this neighborhood. Sandwiches and tea for two costs about Can$15 for two.
Open Mon.-Sat. 7 a.m.-10 p.m., Sun. 10 a.m.-8 p.m. Cards: AE.

DELIS

Centre Street Deli
1102 Centre St.,
Thornhill,
York
• 731-8037

It's a bit of a trek from downtown Toronto to Thornhill, but the Centre Street Deli's top-notch smoked-meat sandwiches are worth the trip. That's because the meat isn't from these parts at all, but from the famous Snowden Deli in Montreal. Old fashioned smoked-meat sandwiches have slightly spicy meat piled as high as the CN Tower. Next best are the corned beef and roast beef. All are served on chewy rye bread with hot mustard, if you want, for about Can$5 a pop. This is a full-service restaurant where you can find a range of Jewish deli foods and salads, but you're not going to drive to Thornhill just for a salad. Beer and wine is also served.
Open daily 11 a.m.-8:45 p.m. Cards: MC, V.

Druxy's
1 Bloor St. East,
Bloor-Yorkville
• 925-5885

Basically a fast-food deli, Druxy's has several locations (including one in the Byzantine Eaton Centre), all in well-trod areas, where folks are looking for a quick place to refuel. Deli sandwiches (corned beef and roast beef, ham, salami, tuna), salads (Greek, Caesar, tossed, coleslaw) and soups hit the spot, especially since the prices are low. The feeling here is a bit reminiscent of McDonald's, but it does the job. Count on Can$16 for lunch for two.
Open daily 6:30 a.m.-7 p.m. No cards.

The Pickle Barrel Restaurant and Deli
595 Bay St.,
Downtown
• 977-6677

This big deli draws folks with big appetites; nobody who complains about not getting enough food. The food is more quantitatively worthwhile than qualitatively, but it's a hit with kids and those who like value for their Canadian dollar. As anyone who has spent any time in Toronto knows, natives are mad for chicken wings, and you'll get a mess of them at the Pickle Barrel; ditto for the combo plates, fish-and-chips, Caesar salad and a gloppy, yet filling, tub of French onion soup. Lunch for two runs about Can$20.
Open Mon.-Thurs. 10 a.m.-midnight, Fri.-Sat. 10 a.m.-1 a.m., Sun. 11 a.m.-9 p.m. Cards: AE, MC, V.

Switzer's
322 Spadina Ave.,
Chinatown
• 596-6900

Toronto's chockablock with delis, and if you're in the art gallery/city hall area, and are hungering for a tasty hot dog, this is the place. A real, old-fashioned deli, Switzer's has been around for quite a while, feeding hordes of hungry folk its corned beef

QUICK BITES Hamburgers & Sandwiches

and burgers, and a host of hot dog preparations: knockwurst and beans, wieners and sauerkraut, and their "Coney Island" naturals. Friendly and efficient service matches the lively atmosphere. In case you wonder what a nice deli is doing among all these Chinese markets and noodle shops, this district was once predominantly Jewish. Lunch for two, about Can$16.
Open Mon. 8 a.m.-10 p.m., Tues.-Sat. 8 a.m.-midnight, Sun. 9 a.m.-8:30 p.m. Cards: AE, MC, V.

Tutti Frutti
64 Kensington Ave.,
Kensington Market
• 593-9281

Tutti Frutti excites, merchandise-wise, as much as the Little Richard song bearing the same name. You'll find everything from searingly hot Indonesian pastes and dried shrimp to smoked trout and Russian sturgeon. There are various fish and game pâtés from around the world, a multinational panoply of gorgeous cheeses, baked goods, smoked duck and goose from Eastern Europe and more than a dozen varieties of halvah. You can get sandwiches constructed from various charcuterie, as well as prepared salads, but the real fun here is in cruising the cases and getting a little of this and a little of that. After your repast, why not stroll around the neighborhood, which is one of Toronto's most colorful districts, and search for an ice cream cone? Lunch for two is about Can$20.
Open Mon.-Sat. 9 a.m.-7 p.m., Sun. 10 a.m.-5 p.m. No cards.

HAMBURGERS & SANDWICHES

California Sandwiches
244 Claremont St.,
Toronto
• 366-3317

This tiny, wonderful place is run by twelve members of the same family. It's called California Sandwiches because the family felt that the name had a nice ring to it, not because they actually serve anything from that sunny state. What they do serve is just fine—once you find the place. As one fan reported, "This isn't one of the easiest places to find, but then, neither are pearls." Enter through the side door and you'll see a counter, a few small tables placed around a big room, a few video machines and lots of other folks. Most of them stand outside to eat or take their sandwiches into the nearby Monarch Tavern and order a beer. This is why they bother: The hot veal and sausage sandwiches are huge and superb. Sauce drips from the major-league kaiser buns, made by the bakery just down the road. The veal patty overhangs its sandwich bun and the peppers inside are searing

and unforgettable. These sandwiches are the crowd's favorites, if you can judge by the random wall scrawls of the sports figures and politicians who've eaten here. The highest compliment bestowed upon California Sandwiches came in the form of a letter from the city's detective department, and you'll see the letter framed, hanging proudly on the wall. As for the other fare, the steak sandwich isn't special in size or taste, but the sausage one remains memorable. Veal sandwiches and sodas for two costs Can$11.
Open Mon.-Sat. 10:30 a.m.-7 p.m. No cards.

French Fry Freddie's
1240 Bay St.,
Bloor-Yorkville
• 963-4330

You can pretty well guess what French Fry Freddie's is all about. While the red-hots, burgers and sausage sandwiches are all tasty, the fries (fat, crisp and homemade) are revelatory. Served Franco-Belgian style with a good selection of toppings and dipping sauces (gravy, barbecue sauce, chili and mayonnaise), we easily consumed two large orders. While the young lady working behind the counter on our visit was a tad befuddled (she didn't know the stand's phone number—or address—when we asked), she sure did know how to fry up a mean batch of spuds, and that's what really matters here, right? A snack for two is about Can$6.
Open Mon.-Wed. 11 a.m.-7 p.m., Thurs.-Sat. 11 a.m.-2 a.m. No cards.

Gypsy Hungarian Restaurant
Village by the Grange,
105 McCaul St.,
Downtown
• 598 1650

There are lots of schnitzel sandwiches in Toronto, but few have the heft and integrity of those from this stand in the food court in Village by the Grange. A hefty portion of seasoned veal is laid between two huge slices of rye, then piled with lettuce, tomato, pickles, peppers and an optional slice of Edam cheese. Count on about Can$5 a head. It is take-out only, but there are tables nearby to hold up both you and the sandwich when your strength fails.
Open Mon.-Sat. 10 a.m.-7 p.m. No cards.

Harvey's
27 Carlton St.,
Downtown
• 971-9207

Harvey's reigns as the McDonald's of Canada—except that Mickey-D could take a few lessons from its northern neighbor. For a fast-food burger, the version here is quite impressive—the meat tastes like beef, the condiments and garnishes are fresh and snappy, and the real-life french fries are crisp, nongreasy and delicious. A meal for two is about Can$20.
Open Mon.-Sat. 7 a.m.-midnight, Sun. 8 a.m.-11 p.m. No cards.

QUICK BITES   High Tea

Lick's
285 Yonge St., Downtown
• 362-8020

Lick's may tout its barbecued chicken and ribs, which are very good, to be sure, but the homemade burgers remain your best bet. Tricked up like a cute little cottage, Lick's is full of comfy, well-worn furniture to lounge upon with twangy music playing in the background. Lick's has them lined up for its good, honest grub. At about Can$18 for a big meal for two, it's easy to see why.
Open Sun.-Thurs. 11 a.m.-11 p.m., Fri.-Sat. 11 a.m.-midnight. Cards: AE, MC, V.

Toby's Goodeats
Eaton Centre
(Yonge & Queen Sts.), Downtown
• 591-6994

Navigating Toronto's Eaton Centre for the first time can be somewhat akin to traversing one of Hong Kong's jumbo malls, which requires the stamina and Zen patience of a Sherpa guide. You can quite easily whirl and twirl through this enormous, bustling commercial center for hours. Need a burger after all the shopping? Go to Toby's. There are actually several Toby's scattered throughout downtown Toronto, but this location is a perfect fit in Eaton Centre. The burgers taste yummy (especially the Brobdinagian, ten-ounce state-of-the-art charbroiled model), and there's decent chili, Caesar salad and macaroni and cheese. Lunch for two is about Can$12.
Open Mon.-Sun. 11:30 a.m.-1 a.m. Cards: AE, MC, V.

HIGH TEA

Windsor Arms Hotel Fireside Lounge
22 St. Thomas St., Downtown
• 979-2341

All of the major downtown hotels serve an afternoon tea based on the true British model of the cream tea. The Windsor Arms, a small inn on a side street in the midst of Toronto's prime shopping district, was one of the first to begin the time-honored ritual, and its full tea remains among the most satisfying. The repast is served every afternoon in a cozy chintz lounge dominated by a large fireplace, surrounded by overstuffed chairs and Victorian antique tea tables. Loose tea is served in a large china pot, with hot water on the side so that you can replenish the pot. A waitress in a frilly white apron presents an array of slender sandwiches, sans crust—usually smoked salmon, cucumber and watercress. The scones (minus raisins), with whipped cream (no Devon clotted) and strawberry jam, anchor the meal, and though they're never as good as you will find them at the Connaught in London, they will do. Assorted biscuits and a small range of French pastry tops off the tea. For two, it costs about Can$36 (which we might add, is about Can$8 more than

you'd pay at the Connaught). Afternoon tea is best taken slowly. It is served until 6 p.m., just about the right time to tip you into the cocktail hour.
Open daily 3:30 p.m.-6 p.m. All major cards.

MEXICAN FAST FOOD

La Mexicana
229 Carlton St.,
Downtown
• 929-6284

Toronto isn't exactly awash in enchiladas and burritos, but a few good ones can be found. One place to go is La Mexicana, a small spot that vibrates with fiesta fun; the food's yummy, too. Tortillas are homemade, as is the mole sauce; the tamales and tacos taste as light, fresh and delicious as do the accompanying homemade guacamole and salsas. A meal for two will run about Can$30.
Open daily 11:30 a.m.-11 p.m. Cards: MC, V.

MIDDLE EASTERN

Falafel Falafel
1280 Bay St.,
Bloor-Yorkville
• 962-0639

You won't empty your wallet on the very good eats at this sweet, bright little café. The yummy falafel crunches on the outside, fragrant with chickpeas, parsley and spices on the inside. The salads are good, too. Don't miss the tabouli or the heavenly hummus. Two can dine as pashas do, for about Can$30.
Open Mon.-Sat. 10 a.m.-10 p.m. No cards.

Kensington Kitchen
124 Harbord St.,
Kensington Market
• 961-3404

This charming spot, with its large, pretty patio dining area serves some of the best Middle Eastern food in town; the falafel are especially wonderful. This is a great place for vegetarians, since many of the dishes are meatless. Even carnivores will love the hummus, tahini, salads and other zesty—and inexpensive—dishes.
Open Mon.-Sat. 11:30 a.m.-11 p.m., Sun. 11 a.m.-10 p.m. Cards: MC, V.

PIZZA & PASTA

Cappuccino Greek & Italian Food
200 Bay St.,
Bay Street Mall,
Downtown
• 865-0372

Whether you've been a-malling, or you need a quick bite before a game at the SkyDome, Cappuccino Greek & Italian Food is bound to have something you'll like. Everything's homemade here, down to the dressings and sauces. Good bets are the spaghetti and the veal parmigiana, as well as the items on the Greek side of the menu, including souvlaki, sausage and lamb. A meal for two is about Can$20.
Open Mon.-Fri. 10 a.m.-7 p.m., Sat. 10 p.m.-4 p.m. No cards.

Massimo's
504 Queen St. West,
Toronto
• 867-1803

302 College St.,
Downtown
• 967-0527

2459 Yonge St.,
Toronto North
• 487-4449

A branch of a small (three locations) chain, pizza-noshers remember Massimo's for its pizza, which is quite good (they make the dough for the crust with spring water). A cute café with the requisite checkered tablecloths, this spot will also charm the kids. There's the usual gang of suspects among the toppings, as well as more esoteric additions, such as clams, goat cheese, smoked salmon, tuna, Gorgonzola cheese and capers. Pastas, as well, cry out for attention. And what about those huge, overstuffed calzones! A meal for two will run about Can$32.
Open Mon.-Fri. 11 a.m.-11 p.m., Sat.-Sun. 4 p.m.-11 p.m. Cards: MC, V.

Pat & Mario's Restaurant
35 Church St.,
Downtown
• 366-7800

This spot is made for pretheater dining, especially if you have hungry children on your hands. Pat & Mario's tends to fill up during the shank of the evening, due to its lively bar, but you'll have no trouble getting in if you arrive early, around 6 p.m. The pastas taste good, including the linguine primavera and the fettucine with veal, and there's a burger (though bunless) for the young ones. A meal for two is about Can$25.
Open Mon.-Fri. 11 a.m.-1 a.m., Sun. noon-11 p.m. Cards: AE, MC, V.

HOTELS

INTRODUCTION	104
HARBOURFRONT	106
DOWNTOWN	109
BLOOR-YORKVILLE & VICINITY	118
TORONTO NORTH	122
EAST YORK & VICINITY	124
AIRPORT	126

INTRODUCTION

NORTHERN HOSPITALITY

Of all the world's great cities, Toronto is probably one of the easiest to enjoy. The heart of the city, where most visitors want to go, is so small and compact that within a day or two you'll be finding your way around with ease. Better yet, most sightseeing attractions are within walking distance of each other. Even when they're not, the city's fast and efficient bus and subway system gets you there in fifteen minutes or less. So that leaves just one question: Where to stay? Well, for a mid-sized city, there's an amazing range of hotels from which to choose.

If you like big, there are giant minicity complexes that belong to corporate chains and specialize in convention business. If you prefer small, there are pleasant four-story family-owned hotels. Some are luxurious and exclusive retreats for the wealthy; others are plain, practical hostelries that won't stress your budget.

Not only is there something for everyone—well, almost everyone—but Toronto's hotels are scattered through most areas of the city, regardless of price or quality. Whether you lean toward the Harbourfront's tourist-oriented recreational opportunities, the hustle-bustle of downtown or Yorkville's exclusive shopping, finding a hotel in your price range is a certainty.

In recent years, a spurt in hotel building has changed the face of Toronto's hotel industry. In 1990 alone, two thousand new rooms were added to the city's stock, forcing older hotels to undertake massive remodeling to stay competitive. Amenities once considered "extras" are now standard in the better hotels, such as swimming pools, fitness centers, two-line telephones with the call-waiting feature, cable television, complimentary shampoo and lotions, minibars, nonsmoking floors and business centers equipped with fax machines, copy machines and secretarial services.

Spurred on by preservation groups, some famous old granddads jumped on the bandwagon as well and were restored to their original splendor. The palatial Royal York stripped away the tacky trappings of six decades to rediscover its former elegance, and the classic King Edward, built in 1903, was saved from oblivion, then recreated in its former image from photographs.

But despite the improvements, some surprises are in store for international travelers familiar with the bold architecture and exciting decor in vogue at newer resort hotels. Innovative architecture is virtually unknown. The rule is big cement monoliths, virtual squared-off fortresses with small windows and plain facades, designed, one suspects, to keep out the cold. Nor is the interior decorating refreshing or novel. Most hotels, it seems, have opted for staid, English-influenced styles: traditional furniture, mousy color schemes, and flowery printed drapes and bedspreads.

HOTELS Introduction

A word about prices: The so-called "rack rates," the standard prices that we've quoted here, are just guidelines. As one reservations clerk whispered to us, "They don't like to talk about it, but most hotels here change their prices depending on availability of rooms, sometimes every week." When demand is strong—during holiday weeks, major conventions or the annual film festival held in September—hotels charge what the traffic will bear. But during slumps, rates are discounted by as much as 33 percent. We suggest choosing a couple of hotels based on location and services, then comparing prices.

What about bed-and-breakfast inns? American B&Bs are completely different from the Torontonian variety. In Ontario, a B&B is not a dolled-up Victorian charmer run as a business, but the home of a person who rents out guest rooms to earn extra money. For broad-minded travelers it's a marvelous way to meet real people, but luxury may not be part of the bargain. And you may have to share a bath. If you're still interested, contact the Midtown Toronto Association of Bed and Breakfast Guesthouses (153 Huron St., Toronto M5T 2B6; 416-598-4562).

Finally, we've concentrated on reviewing hotels in the heart of Toronto. But for travelers visiting outlying areas or staying at the airport, we included several suburban choices. The list is by no means exhaustive.

SYMBOLS & ABBREVIATIONS

Note that some hoteliers put as high a price on charm or modern facilities as others do on pure luxury. In other words, don't assume that "charming" means "cheap." Conversely, don't assume that hotels falling under the "Luxury" heading are truly luxurious: the place may position and price itself as a luxury hotel, but that doesn't mean it delivers the goods. Our opinion of the comfort level and appeal of each hotel is expressed in the following ranking system:

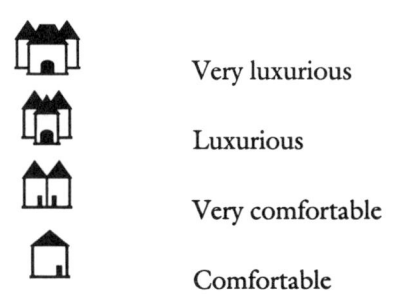

- 🏰🏰🏰 Very luxurious
- 🏰🏰 Luxurious
- 🏠🏠 Very comfortable
- 🏠 Comfortable

Credit Cards are abbreviated as follows:
  AE: American Express and/or Optima
  DC: Diners Club and/or Carte Blanche
  MC: MasterCard
  V: VISA

HARBOURFRONT

Hotel Admiral
249 Queen's Quay West,
Harbourfront
M5J 2N5
• 364-5444
Fax 364-2975

If you're one of those people who'd rather be sailing, you'll feel right at home at the Admiral Hotel on Pier 4 overlooking Lake Ontario. The theme at this small, elegant 175-room hotel is strictly nautical. The main lobby gleams with dark, polished wood and glass panels, like the posh lounges in the newest generation of luxury cruise ships. The rooms feel like a ship's cabins, with mahogany dressers and chests, brass fixtures and lamps and built-in cupboards. The latch-style handles on the doors are the same that you'd find at sea.

In the hallways and lobbies hang etchings, watercolors and paintings—each one different—of yachts, battleships, sailboats, fishing junks, harbors and famous battles. And to complete the illusion, desk clerks and bellhops outfitted in gold-trimmed, navy-blue uniforms handle your registration and luggage. Like it is aboard any good ship, of course, there is food aplenty: The Commodore Dining Room serves Continental cuisine, the Galley Café offers informal family fare and the Bosun's Bar provides a cozy refuge at cocktail hour.

The hotel management stresses an intimate atmosphere and personal service, and though we didn't see anyone swabbing the decks, the immaculate carpets and gleaming bathrooms suggested that someone was performing those chores. The outdoor pool and deck are especially nice, built on an upper floor over the water. From a patio chair it looks just like the ocean. The Admiral gets some business travelers, but we thought its prime location on the water appealed more to vacation travelers. This is the heart of the Harbourfront, a developing recreational area with craft shops, boutiques, restaurants, and cruise ferries. A park nearby is a good picnic spot, with its tables and sea air.
Singles: Can$150-Can$180; doubles: Can$165-Can$200; suites: Can$350. Weekend packages available. All major cards.

Novotel Toronto Centre
45 The Esplanade,
Harbourfront
M5E 1W2
• 367-8900
Fax 360-8285

Those French-speaking guests you'll hear checking into the quiet, elegant Novotel are not from Quebec, but France. They're here, apparently, because the Novotel chain, a French company, advertises the "European" charms of its properties at home, to French travelers planning to visit Canada. And just what is a so-called European hotel? It's a small, scrupulously clean hotel, with a blend of upscale charm and low-profile budget features that pleases the sophisticated tastes yet economical pocketbooks of many Europeans travelers.

HOTELS Harbourfront

At the 266-room Novotel, the lobby is tiled with gleaming white marble, but the reception desk is an understated *très moderne* natural oak, finished with a low sheen. The high ceilings and second-story balcony are very Italian villa, but the seating arrangement is a casual collection of comfy navy-blue-and-white overstuffed armchairs and sofas. A wide, white marble staircase goes up to the mezzanine above—where the modern meeting rooms are located. Nowhere are there superfluous tables or chairs or paintings; just straight smooth lines and cool, pale colors. The bedrooms are more of the same: simple, casual and pleasant, with separate sitting areas and good light. Because this is a new building, the bathrooms are larger than you'd usually find. Each offers a little supply of shampoo, soap, lotion and a sewing kit, plus a hairdryer and telephone.

The Novotel is not on a major street, but by itself on redeveloped land south of the Gardiner Expressway. Shops, restaurants, Union Station and Front Street are a bit of a walk north past empty lots and under the expressway through a tunnel. There isn't much traffic down by the water, and it's quiet at night, but you may miss the bustle of downtown. Nonetheless, a good value.

Singles: Can$134-Can$160; doubles: Can$149-Can$154; suites: Can$185-Can$215. Weekend packages available. All major cards.

SkyDome Hotel
45 Peter St. South,
Harbourfront
M5V 3B4
• 360-7100
Fax 341-5090

Calling all sports fans: The 346-room SkyDome Hotel, a semicircular hunk that clings to the outside of the SkyDome sports stadium, is an event, a happening, a tourist attraction and, yes, ever since it opened in March 1990, even a hotel. Tacked on to the stadium as "an afterthought," the SkyDome advertises itself as "an adventure." And it can be, sometimes. Pray for strength; if your room is at the far end of the semicircle, you can count on a hike to get there.

But all this is trivial, compared to the thrill of entering the SkyDome's futuristic lobby, a heady swirl of polished black granite and burnished metal panels. Overhead, a bank of television screens with sports action in living color flickers above the reception desk. What rivets your eyes and grabs your attention are the row of big plate-glass windows ahead and the scene beyond. Out there, the brilliant emerald green of artificial turf encircled by rows and rows of seats—a baseball diamond or football field, depending on how it's configured—glows like phosphorus in the night. The view is so compelling and so many tourists come to gawk, that when a game starts, curtains are drawn over the windows to keep the lobby free of crowds. This frustrates the guests, who discover they have to buy a ticket to see the game just like all the other looky-loos.

There are, however, 70 "stadium-view" rooms or suites, with wall-sized windows looking onto the field—your own personal press box, as it were. If you book in advance you may be able to get one for a game night. However, the windows are not—we repeat, *not*—one-way glass, a fact which one affectionate couple discovered too late. The incident, which entertained a capacity crowd of 54,000, made the headlines and became the hotel's first historic anecdote.

If only city-view rooms are left, ask about the "Adventure Package," which includes a ticket to a game and a couple of beers. The irregular guest rooms, each one a slightly different shape, are decorated in austere pale gray with plexiglass and stainless-steel accents. Shades of a science-fiction movie set. As we said, it's an adventure.

Singles: Can$130-Can$199; doubles: Can$130-Can$199; suites: Can$350-Can$550. Weekend packages available. All major cards.

Westin Harbour Castle
1 Harbour Square,
Harbourfront M5J 1A6
• 869-1600
Fax 869-0573

When you give the cab driver directions, just say "Harbour Castle," and don't mention the Westin. With the "musical hotels" game being played in this city, the locals forget that the Westin and Hilton swapped properties quite a while ago. What the Westin got was a giant of a place, with a sprawling entrance under the building (out of the rain and snow), a huge grand lobby with marble floors and parrots in tall cages, two separate towers, 955 rooms that look alike and meeting rooms in abundance.

The Harbour Castle is a city-in-one, a clone to all the other, similar giants in world-class metropolitan areas. The location is a little isolated, right on the lake, but the grassy park out front and lakeside view more than compensate. And every service you could want is right there: beauty salon, barber shop, car-rental agency, currency exchange, florist, furrier, dress shop and drug store. Besides, it's only a ten-minute walk to the center of downtown.

The North Tower was completely renovated in 1989 in tasteful peaches, blues and moss green, with handsome furniture. Renovations on the South Tower, which has a better view of the lake, began in 1991. In the meantime, however, the South Tower is a bit run-down, so the room rates are regularly discounted.

The Executive Club, for business travelers on separate floors, offers a private concierge for check-in and check-out, business services and complimentary amenities.

Singles: Can$95-Can$150; doubles: Can$95-Can$170; suites: Can$250-Can$500. Weekend packages available. All major cards.

DOWNTOWN

Best Western–Primrose Hotel

111 Carlton St.,
Downtown M5B 2G3
• 977-8000
Fax 977-6323

The Primrose Hotel, a modern, moderately priced hotel a couple of blocks east of Maple Leaf Gardens, is a good choice if you want to be located on the east side of downtown. The 338-room Primrose has its regular clients—they seem to have grown fond of the spaceship look in the lobby: it's a sort of ersatz black-glass trim, molded synthetic paneling, reflecting metal ceiling strips and Star Trek–style lighting.

On the upper floors the decor is more subdued, with well-lit corridors carpeted in tan and mauve and tidy guest rooms decorated in muted pastels. The bathrooms are very small but adequate; the standard complimentary sundries are doled out daily. For business travelers, there's a daily newspaper and complimentary Continental breakfast, free limousine service downtown between 7:30 a.m. and 10 a.m. The bargain meal is the buffet "businessman's lunch," for just Can$5, served Monday through Friday.

Singles: Can$99-Can$129; doubles: Can$109-Can$159; suites: Can$250. Weekend packages available. All major cards.

Bond Place Hotel

65 Dundas St. East,
Downtown M5B 2G8
• 362-6061
Fax 360-6406

Though almost every Toronto hotel boasts about how convenient and close it's located to that vast shopping extravaganza known as Eaton Centre, very few are actually a hop, skip and a jump away. The Bond Place Hotel, across the street and down the block, truly is.

The 286-room hotel, a tall thin structure similar to hundreds of others downtown, is not the place to be if peace and quiet is what you crave. But for visitors in search of big-city excitement, the seedy hustle and bustle that likens the intersection of Yonge and Dundas streets to Times Square, the plain, practical Bond Place Hotel is in the right place for the right price.

Here, on the east side of downtown, the sidewalks are alive with humanity: Window gazers strolling, shop clerks on lunch break, street vendors peddling trinkets, delivery boys on bicycles, professionals carrying briefcases and crowds of tourists taking it all in. A short walk away, the hotel's front door, flanked by glass windows and opening directly onto the sidewalk, could be mistaken for a store front. Within, however, is a spacious lobby, plain but clean. In the rear is the Garden Café, a pleasant place, at any hour, to grab a family-style meal.

Built in 1975, the hotel was renovated in 1988 with new furniture, carpets, drapes and bedspreads, all in pastel prints.

HOTELS Downtown

Some, however, are ready for some rejuvenation. In compliance with a city ordinance, some rooms are reserved for nonsmokers. Be sure to specify your choice when making reservations.
Singles: Can$59-Can$89; doubles: Can$69-Can$109. All major cards.

Carlton Inn
30 Carlton St.
Downtown M5B 2E9
• 977-6655
Fax 977-0502

The Carlton Inn has price and location going for it and not much more. A 23-floor cement monolith with 536 cubicle-like rooms, this hotel makes no bones about gearing its services for budget travelers and tour groups.

The cavernous lobby, tiled from top to bottom in gray and white marble, looks like a first cousin to a Roman bath. The guest rooms are small, the bathrooms are scrubbed down.

The hotel is located cheek-by-jowl with Toronto's rowdy sports palace, the Maple Leaf Gardens, on the east side of downtown, quite handy, really, if you've got tickets for an ice hockey game or are nursing a blood-lust for a boxing match. If not, you may find this hotel too spartan and cold to be worth the extra dollars saved.

The neighborhood is uncomplicated by trees, shops or cafés. There's a car rental office, beauty salon, travel agency and notions shop; a parking garage is directly below.
Single: Can$59; double: Can$69; triple: Can$79. Weekend packages available. All major cards.

Chestnut Park Hotel
108 Chestnut St.,
Downtown M5G 1R3
• 977-5000
Fax 977-9513

Brand spanking new as of April 1989, the chic Chestnut Park Hotel's architecture is a refreshing departure from the straight lines and monotonous flat facades typical of most of the city's older hotels. Faced with warm terra-cotta-colored brick, the exterior boasts plenty of large windows set in an eye-teasing pattern of angles and curves. With 520 rooms, this is a big hotel, but the careful shaping of space in the small but airy lobby, frequent use of natural blond woodwork and paneling—raw in some places—and casual comfy furniture lends a warm, intimate air to the interior. A splendid touch are the fine pieces of Asian art—lacquered chests, gold Buddhas, porcelain vases, antique screens and framed silk embroideries—that decorate the lobby and corridors. Both objets d'art and the hotel belong to Fred Braida, a well-known collector of textiles and Asian art, and the owner and builder of the well-known "Museum of Textiles" next door. The bedrooms are charming, adorned with country French furniture crafted of natural and whitewashed pine, and decorated with bright blue and peach prints. If the rooms weren't too small, the hotel might earn top ratings.

The Gallery Lounge serves Continental food, and the China Grill, on the mezzanine overlooking the lobby, serves a luncheon buffet that draws crowds of local businesspeople. The airport shuttle bus stops across the street at the Holiday Inn. *Singles: Can$130; doubles: Can$130; suites: Can$175-Can$400. All major cards.*

Delta Chelsea Inn
33 Gerrard St. West,
Downtown M5G 1Z4
• 595-1975
Fax 585-4393

At the time of this review the Delta Chelsea Hotel was in the middle of a vast building and remodeling project which, when finished, will make the 1,600-room hotel not only the largest hotel in Toronto but also the largest in all of Canada, surpassing even the Royal York. The Delta's location at a city nerve center—the busy but shoddy district around the intersection of Yonge and Gerrard streets—ought to attract all sorts of guests: business people, conventions, tour groups and individual tourists. According to the plans, the final product will be a slick, glitzy minicity with services, shops and eateries galore, and countless meeting rooms. The new big-kid on the block hopefully will bring much needed élan to a lackluster neighborhood. *Singles: Can$80-Can$90; doubles: Can$100-Can$120; suites: Can$200-Can$300. Weekend packages available. Cards: DC, MC, V.*

Essex Park Hotel
300 Jarvis St.,
Downtown M5B 2C5
• 977-4823
Fax 977-4830

The Essex Park Hotel, a sleek, sophisticated small hotel in a quiet location across from Allan Gardens—the area used to be called "millionaires' row"—is a fine example of what an innovative designer can do with limited space. The hotel was formerly a ho-hum 1930s apartment house with low ceilings. Now it is a chic 102-room hostelry with small but gracious rooms and a philosophy of personal service to guests. The upper floors were redesigned to make single rooms and suites, but the old moldings and ceiling details were kept. Some rooms have been papered with patterned prints, others were repainted. Traditional furniture is upholstered in tans, peaches and greens. In the minisuites—very "mini" indeed, but competitively priced—French doors separate the bedrooms from the sitting rooms.

The Essex Park is building a large health club in its new building next door. Due for completion in late 1990, the complete sports complex will have a pool, squash courts, billiard room, spa and sauna. For joggers—or thinkers—Allan Gardens, right across Jarvis Street, is a multi-acre grassy park shaded by mature trees, with pathways, landscaped flower beds, fountains and park benches.

Singles: Can$110-Can$125; doubles: Can$115-Can$140; suites: Can$155-Can$220. Weekend packages available. All major cards.

HOTELS Downtown

Hilton Toronto
145 Richmond St. West,
Downtown M5H 2L2
• 869-3456
Fax 869-1478

If you collect the autographs of famous sports figures, you might want to bed down at this Hilton and await your golden opportunity. The 601-room hotel, is a favorite with sports teams: The Quebec Nordiques, the L.A. Kings, the Montreal Canadiens, the Oakland A's and others. This Hilton is much like other Hiltons around the world: Big, gray on the outside, beige on the inside, very clean, comfortable and efficient.

Down on the lower level, convention attendees in power suits can be seen on break between sessions, toting thick notebooks and noshing from plates of luncheon fixings. The Hilton is definitely a business travelers' hotel, which explains why the rooms have coffee pots, why the pool is open year-around, why there's a fully equipped workout room, why the gift store features items such as toothpaste and razors.
Singles: Can$119-Can$229; doubles: Can$119-Can$259; suites: Can$415-Can$900. All major cards.

Holiday Inn Downtown
89 Chestnut St.,
Downtown M5G 1R1
• 977-0707
Fax 977-1136

The Holiday Inn is a tad overpriced for what it offers, which is small, no-nonsense guest rooms decorated in basic brown and beige, and furnished with motel-modern chairs and chests. But honestly, the 715-room hotel, a tall, squarish building in a central downtown location, is so friendly and familiar that if you're booked here on a tour or have found a discount deal on room rates, there's no reason to fret. The lobby is large and pleasant, you can swim year-round in two big pools, both indoor and outdoor, and the fitness center's exercise room is a regular stable of stationary bicycles, stair-climbers and weights. From here, west downtown, you're close to public transportation and a short walk from the financial district. The Holiday Inn is also one of the airport shuttle's stops, another small bonus.

If all this doesn't soothe your frazzled nerves, the Muzak that's piped over loudspeakers might—unless it drives you crazy. Happily, the desk clerks and bellboys, mostly smiling younger people, are some of the most courteous and helpful in any of the city's hotels. As in most Toronto hotels, children 12 and under sharing a room with their parents stay free.
Singles: Can$130: doubles: Can$145. Weekend packages available. All major cards.

L'Hôtel
225 Front St. West,
Downtown M5V 2X3
• 597-1400
Fax 597-8128

One of three Canadian Pacific hotels in town (the other two being the Royal York and the SkyDome), this grand, 587-room establishment on Front Street is a classic big-city hotel, with a multilevel lobby, restaurants on different levels and escalators to the meeting rooms below. Business travelers like the location near a clutch of tall office buildings, and with Union Station in the next block, getting to appointments is a snap. Another plus—for convention attendees—is the Toronto Metropolitan

HOTELS Downtown

Convention Centre next door. For all the grandiose, gleaming marble, however, L'Hôtel feels uncluttered and serene. Goups of sofas and wing chairs cluster comfortably around small area rugs, enhanced by discreetly placed Asian lacquered chests and porcelain vases. L'Hôtel may also win the prize for owning the city's largest chandelier. Hanging dead-center over the escalator, this leviathan of a light fixture is a fifteen-foot by twenty-foot panel from which hang thousands of long, slender, glittering glass crystals. The Asian theme in the lobby—no doubt reflecting the "Pacific" in "Candian Pacific"—is echoed in the elevators, which are paneled with black lacquer screens.

The hotel's 588 rooms are thankfully less showy. Recently renovated, with dark mahogany tables and decorative brass hinges and handles, they are dressed in hues of moss green highlighted with peach and pink. Enormous bathrooms add the final luxurious touch.

Singles: Can$180-Can$220; doubles: Can$195-Can$240; suites: Can$295-Can$1,900. Weekend packages available. All major cards.

Hotel Ibis
240 Jarvis St.,
Downtown M5B 2B8
• 593-9400
Fax 593-8426

There's something appealing about a budget hotel that doesn't try to disguise itself with useless frills. The 294-room Hotel Ibis, a country cousin to its more elegant sister, the Novotel on the waterfront, doesn't claim to provide much more than a clean, comfy room, and we like it a lot better for its honesty. For instance, the lobby doesn't pretend to be any more than a place to sign your name and get a room key. There's no need to wait in long lines to ask about room rates; they're posted on the wall behind the registration desk along with daily exchange rates for Canadian and American dollars. The small guest rooms provide the basics and no more—a bed, dresser, chair and television—but they are neat and clean. The bathrooms are smaller than average. The wall-to-wall carpet is green—after seeing most of Toronto's hotels, we're convinced that a local factory must have held a giant close-out sale on green carpet not too long ago.

One obvious downside to the Ibis is its drab location east of downtown, a six-block walk from the subway. But we liked the feel of this older area; because its old houses, two-story apartments and rambling office buildings have a relaxed, suburban feel. Eaton Centre is a brisk fifteen-minute walk west on Dundas Street through a seedy area that ought to be next in line for rehabilitation. When the city fathers finally get on the dime, we hope that the quaint two-story brick and clapboard houses dotted around Church Street will be designated historic buildings and restored.

Singles: Can$94; doubles: Can$109. Weekend packages available. All major cards.

HOTELS Downtown

Hotel Victoria

56 Yonge St.,
Downtown M5E 1G5
• 363-1666
Fax 363-7327

The Hotel Victoria, a golden oldie dating from 1906, could be a little gem if it were restored and remodeled in the formal style so popular around the turn of the century. The lobby still has those wonderful high ceilings and the original moldings still remain in their elegant detail. With only 48 rooms, the hotel has retained a small, intimate atmosphere that, with a boost, could easily make the leap from folksy to fabulous. But the most recent renovation, in 1988, only made it to the halfway mark. The hotel was left clean and tidy, but also off-balance and strangely impersonal: new paint freshens the lobby, a few flags fluttering over an inappropriately modern entrance, functional furniture and nondescript colors flatten the look of the bedrooms.

On the other hand, the location on the subway line, near the financial and theater districts, is convenient; the hotel has a small café; and the lobby bar is quiet and pleasant. There's no hotel parking, but four public lots are in the vicinity. And there is a nonsmoking floor. The hotel is privately owned, but managed by the Howard Johnson chain.

Singles: Can$99-Can$120; doubles: Can$114-Can$135. Weekend packages available. All major cards.

The King Edward

37 King St. East,
Downtown M5C 1E9
• 863-9700
Fax 367-5515

The elegant and historic "King Eddie," a nine-story Edwardian palace overshadowed by taller buildings, is not Toronto's biggest, nor most glittery, nor even most luxurious hotel, but it's the place where anyone who is anyone eventually wants to stay. Past guests have included Rudyard Kipling, J.P. Morgan and an archbishop of Canterbury. More recently, occupants have included queens, prime ministers and business magnates, most of whom opt for the Royal Suite (at Can$1,850 per day), a luxurious contemporary apartment decorated with Asian art. Lesser notables—film stars, journalists and the like—who end up in one of the comfortable but undistinguished standard rooms are happy to be there.

Built by George Gooderham in 1903, the King Eddie was once the city's most fashionable, impressing the local citizenry with the lobby's soaring 80-foot ceiling, a stately grand marble staircase leading to a balustrade above, seventeenth-century tapestries and numerous objets d'art from around the world. After World War II, however, the hotel fell on hard times. By the 1970s, the King Eddie was headed for demolition, but architectural historians discovered the ornate, molded ceiling panels intact in the dining room and began a campaign to save them. The hotel was declared a historic building and restoration began based on original photographs. The hotel reopened in

1981 as part of the Trusthouse Forte hotel group. At press time, a proposed renovation of the 338 guest rooms and suites was awaiting approval to be redone in "English country garden."

Presently, elaborate ceiling moldings, wainscoting and quality fixtures look like originals but are brand new; the rooms are charmingly furnished with traditional wing chairs, tables and four-poster beds. To please modern tastes, a chichi health spa gives massages and offers soothing sauna and whirlpool soaks. There are also exercise facilities. You might try afternoon high tea at the King Eddie, a tradition in this oh-so-English city. On most afternoons the Consort Piano Bar lounge is full of people sipping oolong or Monkey Pick tea and nibbling on scones and cucumber sandwiches. Alas, the scones are small and tough—to be avoided. Tea is served between 3 p.m. and 5:30 p.m. daily. *Singles: Can$199-Can$289; doubles: Can$219-Can$289; suites: Can$360 and up. Weekend packages available. All major cards.*

Royal York Hotel
100 Front St. West,
Downtown M5J 1E3
• 368-2511
Fax 368-2884

For sheer size, ornate decor and a history as big as all Canada, no other hotel rivals the Royal York Hotel. Since 1929, when it was built to the tune of Can$20 million, visitors from around the world have gathered to gape at the vast and colorful lobby and mingle at political receptions or charity balls in the sumptuous ballrooms and concert halls. The 1,200-room hotel, a Canadian Pacific Hotel property directly across from Union Station, was built to attract foreign visitors, who would buy, it was hoped, railway tickets going west from Toronto. A Can$95 million restoration program begun in 1988 brought the old hotel's eclectic splendor—a blend of French and Italian Renaisssance and oodles of late-late Victorian frippery—blazing forth anew. The result is a riot of color, pattern and design that revels in diversity. Green marble panels hidden in the 1930s because they seemed too "shiny" have been uncovered and repolished. Designs on the huge beams over the lobby have been repainted. Sturdy lobby furniture is re-upholstered in green velveteen and fringed with six-inch tassels, the fresh-painted gold capitals on the Greek columns glitter, and giddy, floral-print rugs (that hardly match anything) cover the marble floors.

The guest rooms are also being redecorated with antique reproductions and flowery fabrics. The smallest rooms are gone, combined with others to make spacious suites, a move that reduced the room count by 200 and toppled the hotel's onetime "biggest in Canada" rating.

With Toronto's reputation as "Hollywood East," it's not surprising that the hotel has often been a movie location. The

most recent film was hardly worthy of this great hotel: "The Queen of Mean," the (vapid) story of convicted hotelier Leona Helmsley. A tip: for an unobstructed view of Lake Ontario, request a room above the fifth floor.
Singles: Can$140-Can$189; doubles: Can$160-Can$200; suites: Can$275-Can$650. Weekend packages available. All major cards.

The Sheraton Centre
123 Queen St. West,
Downtown M5H 2M9
• 361-1000
Fax 947-4801

If your vacation destination just *has* to be a whirlwind of activity to earn that perfect ten, you'll like The Sheraton Centre. The buzz and bustle of constant comings and goings against a continuous hum of background noise is the daily fare at this megahotel a block from the Hilton. Pick any hour and you'll find people going up and down the lobby elevators, convention attendees coming in and out of meeting rooms and tour groups arriving and departing. With 1,400 rooms, there's space at this inn for all kinds of people and all sizes of groups. Some of the guest rooms are in the ten-floor Richmond Tower, others, including a section with private concierge and special amenities, are in the 43-floor Queen Tower. The standard rooms are pleasant but ordinary. Some are definitely overdue for refurbishment. A major renovation planned for 1991 will enlarge the lobby, move the elevators, reposition the concierge and check-in desk and redecorate the guest rooms.

This neighborhood, between Queen and Richmond streets, next to City Hall and Nathan Phillips Square, is central to almost everything. Just north is a grassy park, a delightful place to stroll and a respite from urban claustrophobia. The "Waterfall Gardens," a courtyard garden inside the hotel grounds, is refreshing to look at, even if you never go in. As if there wasn't enough elegant shopping to go around, you can go directly from the hotel to an underground shopping area with 60 stores and two movie theaters.
Singles: Can$155-Can$279; doubles: Can$205-Can$349. Weekend packages available. All major cards.

Strathcona Hotel
60 York St.,
Downtown M5J 1S8
• 363-3321
Fax 363-4679

Someday, the 200-room Strathcona Hotel may be an exclusive and pricey place to stay, thanks to its great location on York Street across from the mighty Royal York. For now, however, location is almost all it has going for it. Occasional remodels have tried but failed to stem the tide of nicks and scratches from constant use, the lobby makes a poor pretense at hospitality and the corridors are a tired combination of dingy paint and commercial carpet. Admittedly, there are telephones and tele-

HOTELS Downtown

visions and the beds are decent, but the rooms are so small and dim that a few minutes with your favorite book before lights-out may be too depressing to attempt. So why stay at the Strathcona? It's an unbeatable value for the area. And, if you don't like the coffee shop's menu or the clientele hanging out at the bar, no problem. Head across the street to the bright lights at the Royal York. The trains, subway and buses stop nearby, the airport shuttle stops at the Royal York, the financial and theater districts are close and the waterfront is a fifteen-minute stroll away. And after all, you aren't going to Toronto for the view inside your hotel room, are you?

Singles: Can$59; doubles: Can$69; triples & quads: Can$95. Weekend packages available. All major cards.

> *Remember to call ahead to reserve your room, and please, if you cannot honor your reservation, be courteous and let the hotel know.*

Sutton Place Hotel Kempinski
955 Bay St.,
Downtown M5S 2A2
• 924-9221
Fax 924-1778

The elegant Sutton Place Hotel, an oasis of European style in a bustling business neighborhood on Yonge Street, has a special affinity with the arts and film. In fact, so many actors and directors can be spotted here, chatting over afternoon tea or doing deals in the restaurant, you'll feel as if you're in Hollywood. In truth, you won't be far wrong, because Toronto's labor costs are still affordable, so many films are made in the city nowadays that the folks in "the business" call it "Hollywood East."

Each September, during the annual Toronto film festival, the Sutton Place books its 280 rooms and suites weeks ahead. The rest of the time, ordinary travelers get a chance to enjoy the scads of marble in the lobby, crystal chandeliers, huge tapestries, curvaceous Louis XVI furniture and elaborate Persian rugs. The hotel isn't much to look at outside, just another big sterile building, though the white and gold signs and brass lamps out front hint of opulence within. There's a covered driveway for limo pickups (not all the city's hotels are so endowed), several large, elaborate lounges and an indoor swimming pool. The numerous ballrooms and meeting rooms boast different themes, the most memorable being the Amsterdam, a seventeenth-century re-creation of a Dutch parlor. The pleasant bedrooms more than suffice, and there are some lovely large suites on the Regency Floor.

Singles: Can$170-Can$280; doubles: Can$170-Can$280; suites: Can$260-Can$1,500. Weekend packages available. All major cards.

BLOOR-YORKVILLE & VICINITY

The Brownstone Hotel
15 Charles St. East,
Yorkville M4Y 1S1
• 924-7381
Fax 924-7929

The Brownstone Hotel represents a genre—the so-called boutique hotel—that seems to be thriving in Toronto. These are small properties in great locations that keep their prices moderate by limiting amenities. The location in this case is in the bustling, upscale shopping district at the intersection of Bloor and Yonge streets, on the fringe of Yorkville. The 108-room Brownstone itself is a tan-brick, ten-story building a block off Bloor. Unpretentious outside, its small but attractive lobby is furnished with traditional antiques and Persian rugs. The rest of the hotel follows suit, with an emphasis on *small*. The Brownstone's rooms will satisfy those who don't require more than the minimum space, and they're fairly clean, each with a minibar and TV. The minuscule bathrooms can induce claustrophobia. A loyal but unusual mix of clientele stays at the Brownstone: Canadian businesspeople from the provinces, ballet dancers, theater performers and musicians. A member of the Clarion hotel group, the hotel, built in the 1940s, was partially renovated in 1985 and will be overhauled again in 1991.
Singles: Can$90-Can$110; doubles: Can$100-Can$120; suites: Can$105-130. Packages available. All major cards.

Four Seasons Hotel
21 Avenue Rd.,
Yorkville M5R 2G1
• 964-0411
Fax 964-2301

If you've stayed in Four Seasons hotels around the world, you know that gracious living and courteous service are a given at this top-rated Canadian-owned hotel chain. In Toronto you can sample the crème de la crème of the company at its flagship property, a block north of Bloor Street in the heart of Yorkville. With a staff-to-guest ratio of 1 to 1.25, if you aren't pleased and pampered it's entirely accidental. The 382-room hotel—including 160 suites—routinely appears in the top-50 lists of various travel and consumer publications, cited for luxurious accommodations and consistent and attentive service. Surprisingly, the lobby combines multicolored marble, antique tables with elaborate flower arrangements, a life-size figure on a pedestal, big mirrors and flowery carpets. The hotel's exterior is a work-a-day affair, a square hunk typical of northern climes. The banquet and sitting rooms upstairs, rich with Persian rugs, crystal chandeliers and classic furniture, are favorite places for wedding receptions and balls. The spacious bedrooms, decorated in simple colors and flowery prints, are furnished with traditionally

HOTELS Bloor-Yorkville & Vicinity

English tables and sofas. Firm beds and their plumped-up down pillows guarantee a good night's sleep. The bathrooms—of average size—are fussed up with piles of soft towels and a little tray of perfumed soap and lotions, shampoo and assorted goodies. Chocolates at turndown and a complimentary shoeshine makes guests feel like lords and ladies.

For top-floor views and top-drawer luxury, you might try one of three penthouse suites, where such regal guests as the Queen Mother, Robert Redford and Clint Eastwood have stayed. Can$1,800 a night buys genuine antiques, a four-poster bed, a wet bar and a bird's-eye view of the city and Lake Ontario. On a clear day you can see the United States. A large business center allows you to send faxes, make photocopies, phone locally and use the secretarial services, all free. And there is an indoor-outdoor pool and workout room.

Singles: Can$225-Can$325; doubles: Can$280-Can$325; suites: Can$410-Can$1,800. All major cards.

Hotel Inter-Continental
220 Bloor St. West,
Yorkville M5S 1T8
• 960-5200
Fax 960-8269

When you start from scratch, you have a once-in-a-lifetime chance to break the mold. The beautiful and intelligently designed Hotel Inter-Continental, which opened in March 1990, did just that, shunning the current trend toward rococo glitter, acres of marble tile and and gold-framed mirrors. Instead, the interior design firm brought in from Atlanta, Georgia, chose a rich, warm, cherry-colored wood, and accented rooms with brass fixtures and dark-green fabrics. The result is truly handsome—sleekly opulent, but simple. The eight-floor terracotta-colored hotel surrounds a garden courtyard, whose delicate trees and flower beds are visible from some of the rooms.

The Inter-Continental makes no bones about catering to business travelers and not to families. An extensive fitness center on the top floor, with a sauna, massage rooms, a changing room with oak lockers and a workout room packed with machines, a swimming pool and a 36-foot lap pool, is obviously geared toward fitness-minded business travelers. The bedrooms are of average size, but tastefully decorated in comfortable traditional furniture and bright pastel prints. If you want to hole up in your room and work, a two-line phone and data-port phone jacks for a fax or telex machine make it easy.

The location, on Bloor Street across from the Royal Conservatory of Music and the Royal Ontario Museum, is prime: close to Yorkville's chichi shops, good restaurants and the park.

Singles: Can$205-Can$265; doubles: Can$225-Can$285; suites: Can$325-Can$1,000. Weekend packages available. All major cards.

HOTELS Bloor-Yorkville & Vicinity

Hotel Selby
592 Sherbourne St.,
Toronto M4X 1L4
• 921-3142
Fax 923-3177

Like so many great old houses that stayed rooted in the old neighborhood when their owners moved on to greener pastures, the Hotel Selby is a Queen Anne Victorian mansion in a stately area now gone seedy, on the edge of Cabbagetown. The area seems to be in the throes of early gentrification, and a number of charming older homes have been gussied up. But the neighborhood still attracts a transient population of singles and gays and the businesses catering to their lifestyle—coffee shops, small markets and little nightspots. It's a lively place, if you're looking for something offbeat.

The price of a night here is certainly right. The Selby's 67 rooms are a good value for a northeast-central location a half block from the Sherbourne Subway Station. And the atmosphere is warm and homey. Better yet, for Can$85 per night, cheap for the experience, you can stay in the "Hemingway Suite," where the young Ernest lived during his stint as a reporter for the *Toronto Daily Star*, in the 1920s. Plus, there's the arguable value of staying in a historic landmark. Some of the Selby's original interior is intact, notably the fifteen-foot ceilings and the stained glass above the main staircase. Don't miss the the chandelier in the lobby, which once hung in the Chrysler Mansion in Gross Point, Michigan.

Complimentary Continental breakfast is served in the parlor in the morning. Eleven of the rooms share a bath; all have a TV and telephone. For longer stays, a weekly rate is available.
Singles: Can$45-Can$55; doubles: Can$55-Can$75; suites: Can$85. Weekly rates available. Cards: MC, V.

Journey's End
280 Bloor St. West,
Yorkville M5S 1V8
• 968-0010
Fax 968-7765

The Journey's End hotels have a concept that they call "limited service." Proof that the pudding is a success can be seen in the brand new 214-room Journey's End on Bloor Street, a gracious, modern hotel that keeps prices moderate by dispensing with extras they think value-minded travelers can do without. Conspicuously absent are such goodies as blow-dryers, bathrobes (you can bring your own), a swimming pool and workout room, a gift shop (stores are everywhere), a beauty salon (plenty in the neighborhood), a cocktail lounge and business center. Instead, the hotel concentrates on providing comfortable well-lit rooms decorated with light blond furniture and a green and gray color scheme, a safe, central location on Bloor Street, a self-park garage for guests, free local telephone calls, and data-port phone jacks for portable computer users.

The philosophy appears to be successful, if one is to judge by the number of people checking in and out. So far, the place seems a favorite of European travelers. At press time, the hotel was planning to add a restaurant on the ground floor, conceding

HOTELS Bloor-Yorkville & Vicinity

that this service was in demand.
Singles: Can$94; doubles: Can$109. Weekend packages available. All major cards.

Park Plaza Hotel
4 Avenue Rd.,
Yorkville M5R 2E8
• 924-5471
Fax 924-4933

The Park Plaza is blessed to have the three things that make prime real estate so valuable. They are, of course, location, location and location. The 264-room hotel sits on prime Yorkville property, at the corner of Bloor Street and Avenue Road across from the Royal Ontario Museum. The Royal Conservatory of Music is a block away, and the surrounding neighborhood is a hotbed of antique shops, designer stores, leather boutiques, bed-linen emporiums, and jewelry stores. But until the Park Plaza finishes the renovations now under way, make sure your room is one of those already remodeled, specifically those in the Plaza Tower. Its elegant suites have splendid architectural detailing around doors and windows, crystal chandeliers and antique armchairs and chests. The north tower, the Prince Arthur Tower, isn't finished, and gives you an idea of the transformation undergone in the rest of the hotel: when we visited, the corridors were dim, the plaster walls cracked, the wallpaper peeling and the carpets worn through. Future plans also call for an arcade of posh shops, a solarium with lots of greenery and trees and a patio area. When the place is completely finished, the Park Plaza should provide stiff competition for its neighbor, the Four Seasons Yorkville.
Singles: Can$175-Can$225; doubles: Can$195-Can$245; suites: Can$295 and up. Weekend packages available. All major cards.

Ramada Renaissance Hotel
90 Bloor St. East,
Yorkville M4W 1A7
• 961-8000
Fax 961-9581

To find the hotel is not easy; actually locating the entrance entails quite a search. Once found, however, it's obvious that the Ramada has a wonderfully convenient location near the intersection of Bloor and Yonge streets. A giant Hudson's Bay Company department store is next door; if you can't find what you want at the "Bay," other yuppie-style stores line Bloor in both directions. And, if you don't watch your step, you may fall into the subway entrance, it's so close.

The 234-room Ramada was renovated in 1990, with plush but predictable thick carpets, pastel prints and expensive furniture. The television and minibar are, also predictably, hidden in a big commode. Several floors are reserved for the Renaissance Club, whose members, mostly executive travelers, expect the little extras that make frequent business trips less tiresome: amenities include a private concierge for check-in and checkout, separate lounge, Continental breakfast and newspaper, afternoon tea and cocktail-hour hors d'oeuvres, all on the house. The lobby is contemporary and very functional—you won't stop to sit, as there are no chairs or sofas, at least not yet. *Singles: Can$155-Can$190; doubles: Can$175-Can$210; suites: Can$230-Can$1,000. Weekend packages available. All major cards.*

Venture Inn
89 Avenue Rd.,
Yorkville M5R 2G3
• 964-1220
Fax 964-8692

For casual charm at a reasonable price in a great Yorkville location, the Venture Inn steals the gold. From the street, the intimate 71-room hotel looks as if it were just another storefront on the sidewalk. That is, until you walk through the two white French doors into a small, cheerful lobby decorated in rustic knotty pine and country prints. To one side is a small living room, with a sofa and matching chairs grouped around a fireplace—which unfortunately can't be used, because of local fire regulations—but it does add to the cozy feel of the room. The walls are covered in natural oak wainscoting and navy blue wallpaper with a tiny white print and the floor is polished brick. On the other wall is a coffee and tea service, where a hot cup is available all day, and where complimentary Continental breakfast is served in the morning.

The same western ranch theme is carried out in the bedrooms, with heavy, knotty pine furniture that is a tad too massive, and blue-and-white ranch-style quilts. The hotel has no restaurant or gift shop but here, in Yorkville, these services are available close by. Nor is there a pool or fitness center. Nor is there a parking lot, but a city lot next door costs Can$9 for 24 hours. The hotel, beneath all its charm, is an economy choice.
Single: Can$89; double: Can$99. Weekend packages available. All major cards.

TORONTO NORTH

Bradgate Arms
54 Foxbar Rd.,
Toronto North
M4V 2G6
• 968-1331
Fax 968-3743

In a fashionable neighborhood just north of central Toronto, the Bradgate Arms has earned a reputation among the locals as an exclusive hideaway, but it's hard to figure out just why. The former apartment, built in the early 1900s, was converted to a six-story hotel in 1983 and the former living units were rearranged into 110 guest rooms and suites. Some suites are charming, retaining the warm, homey character of the previous residences, with welcome extras such as fireplaces (strictly for decor; they don't work) and screened-in porches. Much of the rest of the space, however, was chopped up into tiny rooms and stuffed with second-rate antiques. Change is in the wind, however, for a major renovation is planned, and the color scheme will be lightened and brightened with warm pastels and splashy prints. The corridors are already finished, and the glowing ivory walls and gleaming pink woodwork are a promising start.

The hotel's best feature is the glass-roofed courtyard in the center of the building, which does triple-duty as a reception desk, lobby and patio. During daylight hours the sunlight filters down on chairs and tables in a garden of delicate trees and potted plants. On the far side of some brick, vaultlike arches are the cocktail lounge and piano bar. The Bradgate Arms is a distance from downtown, so you may want to rent a car. Also, public transportation is within walking distance.

Singles: Can$140-Can$160; doubles: Can$150-Can$170; suites: Can$230-Can$600. Weekend packages available. All major cards.

Roehampton Hotel

808 Mt. Pleasant Rd.,
Toronto North
M4P 2L2
• 487-5101
Fax 487-5390

Once in a while—when you're visiting relatives, for example—even back-to-basics hotel accommodations look better than the family guest room. So if your activities are based in the business district north of downtown, you may be glad you chose the drab but very adequate 110-room Roehampton Hotel. It's about the only hostelry in the immediate neighborhood, which may be why the management doesn't fuss over little niceties. The lobby, a large room paneled in new, natural wood, has that impersonal feel of a large post office. The guest rooms are shabby, but the furniture is comfortable and the sheets clean.

There are some redeeming features that compensate for the lack of luxury. An outdoor pool and sundeck are pleasant, and because this is in the suburbs, you can park your car in the lot out front. But our favorite item here is Champs Bar, the next best thing to a corner pub, where, it seems, not only travelers but local chaps gather to lift a pint and swap sports stories. Who could refuse to patronize a bar that has strips of plastic Budweiser flags dangling from the ceiling, a wall-mounted television beaming hockey and football contests into the room, and a resident chef who carves a rare roast of beef on a trolley? According to local hearsay, the Four Seasons Hotel Chain once owned the Roehampton, in the dim, dark past. One can see why they moved on to better pastures.

Singles: Can$85-Can$95; doubles: Can$85-Can$95; suites: Can$105. Weekend packages available. All major cards.

EAST YORK & VICINITY

Four Seasons Inn on the Park
1100 Eglinton Ave. East,
East York M3C 1H8
• 444-2561
Fax 446-3308

The advantage of staying in the huge area of greenbelt and suburbs northeast of downtown Toronto is that there's no shortage of fresh air and elbow room, an important consideration if you're traveling with children. The Inn at the Park, a Four Seasons resort hotel that began in 1963 as a Hyatt, glommed on to a piece of that open land when it was still affordable. The hotel that emerged was a regular space hog, shaped like a big flat star; there have been remodels and additions that have brought the room count to 338 since then, but the star remains unchanged. At the points are meeting rooms and restaurants; in between are the guest rooms; connecting the parts is a regular rabbit warren of doorways and passages running hither and yon.

But the real attraction here is the out-of-doors. In the center courtyard, children and adults can play in a grassy two-acre park with shade trees, flower beds, a spiffy children's play yard and a meandering pond spanned by a quaint, wooden bridge. When the dogwood blooms in spring, the bridge doubles as a wedding chapel. There are also two swimming pools, squash and tennis courts, a game room and a health club with a spa and sauna. Across the highway is a 600-acre public park, for horseback riding in summer and cross-country skiing in winter.

The decor in the corridors and lobbies is a throwback to the 1960s, with its tacky but inventive styles. A shopping complex full of wonderful shops is definitely state-of-the-art, and the plush guest rooms bathe you in a luxurious, pampering warmth. It makes the whole Alice in Wonderland adventure a real one.
Singles: Can$118-Can$275; doubles: Can$138-Can$295; suites: Can$440-Can$555. Weekend packages available. All major cards.

Prince Hotel Toronto
900 York Mills Rd.,
North York M3B 3H2
• 444-2511
Fax 444-9597

If "Don't Fence Me In" is your theme song, or you and your spouse have the kids in tow, you'll like the serenely spacious and exclusive Prince Hotel, on fifteen acres of grassy lawns and woodlands in the Parklands. At any time of year the trees and gardens are lovely, but around Christmas the grounds become a fairyland, lit by 17,000 tiny white bulbs strung in the tree branches. With so much space, the Prince Hotel is able to provide the kind of resort activities that makes traveling with the family fun: a putting green, walking trails through the woods, a big indoor-outdoor pool with a spacious sundeck, a complete fitness center, a billiards room, table tennis and an kid's recreation area. The Parklands is also convenient for day outings to local family-style attractions, such as the Ontario Science Centre, the zoo, Black Creek Pioneer Village—a re-creation of an early settlement—and Canada's Wonderland, a Disney-ish theme park. You'll need a car for all this; happily, parking is free in the 700-car lot.

The interior of the 407-room Prince, with its 22-floor tower and two wings, reflects its Japanese ownership. In the vast lobby, pale colors and subtle textures create a quiet, meditative mood. Peach-toned walls, a moss green carpet, brass railings, black bamboo furniture with white cushions and potted palms are arranged in small seating areas. There are no walls between the lobby, café and lounge, rather the space is defined by varying levels and railings. Since the Prince has no close neighbors, you'll probably want to eat some meals in the hotel. Among the choices: The Coffee Garden Lounge dishes up informal food, Le Continental serves gourmet cuisine, Katsura prepares sushi and teppanyaki-style taste-treats, and the Brandy Tree piano bar is the place to relax before or afterwards.

Singles: Can$130-Can$140; doubles: Can$145-Can$155; suites: Can$285-Can$1,250. Weekend packages available. All major cards.

The Sheraton Toronto East
2035 Kennedy Rd., Scarborough M1T 3G2
• 299-1500
Fax 299-8959

This hotel's best feature is a huge, vaulted airy atrium at the back of the hotel, a giant greenhouse, really, with an all-glass outer wall. A little rain forest of tropical trees and ferns, it's a testimonial to humankind's efforts to defy cold, wet, snowy weather. On the ground floor is the pool, shaped like a clover with big lobes and fed by a constant waterfall, and at the far end are the squash courts. Perhaps it's this feature, plus the surrounding grass and trees, that somehow make this plush Sheraton with only 388 rooms look more spacious than it really is. In the Parklands area, close to the intersection of Highway 401 and the Don Valley Parkway (404), the Sheraton taps a combination market of families and small conventions. The Executive Tower is geared for business travelers, with complimentary Continental breakfast and a separate concierge for check-in and check-out. And of course, there are meeting rooms for small conventions. Since the largest seats one thousand, the hotel has become a favorite locale for day programs put on by local businesses.

The Garden Café, on a mezzanine floor, hangs lik a big, open-air tree-house above the pool. The constant sound of running water gives diners the feeling they're in an outdoor café.
Singles: Can$89-Can$135; doubles: Can$85-Can$160. Weekend packages available. All major cards.

AIRPORT

The Bristol Place Hotel
950 Dixon Rd.,
Rexdale M9W 5N4
• 675-9444
Fax 675-4426

You know what airport hotels can be like: cold, sterile, strictly functional, designed on the premise that people traveling for business are too busy to expect comfort. Well, the Bristol Place Hotel rightly considers that to be a lot of malarkey, which approach is why the 287-room hotel is so popular with frequent flyers. It has been, in fact, for fifteen years, but you'd never know it wasn't brand-new from its handsome, spacious lobby, with marble-tiled floors and a free-standing staircase climbing up to the mezzanine level above. Grouped here and there are cozy seating areas, with big comfy chairs arranged around coffee tables, each separated by leafy potted plants carefully positioned to create private conversation zones. The rooms are warm and attractive, with upholstered armchairs, flowered, quilted bed covers and matching dust ruffles. The bathrooms are scrubbed clean and annointed with little bottles of shampoo and conditioner. Almost half of the rooms are reserved for nonsmokers.

In recent years, the area around Pearson International Airport has become a thriving commercial district in its own right, creating a need for good business hotels. The Bristol Place has tapped into this market by anticipating the needs of traveling executives. To that end, there's Koko's cocktail lounge, a cozy spot for after-hours relaxation; Zachary's, a formal dining room serving cuisine good enough to entertain clients; and Le Café, for quick breakfasts or lunches. For lap-swimmers, there's a large, heated indoor/outdoor pool. The hotel, a five-minute ride from the airport terminal, operates a free shuttle bus every few minutes from 5:30 a.m. until 2 a.m.

Singles: Can$170-Can$180; doubles: Can$185-Can$195; suites: Can$190-Can$590. Weekend packages available. Cards: AE, MC, V.

The Toronto Airport Marriott Hotel
901 Dixon Rd.,
Rexdale M9W 1J5
• 674-9400
674-8292

This 425-room hotel, a five-minute ride from Lester B. Pearson International Airport, seems cloned from all the other large, bright, contemporary and comfortable but not terribly original hotels that have sprung up like mushrooms wherever business parks are located. Since most of the Marriott's guests are business travelers calling on commercial companies close to the airport, the hotel provides the required amenities in order to compete with the other hotels near the airport.

For instance, there is a health club, with sauna, indoor pool and squash courts. And free parking—if you have a rental car—is

HOTELS Airport

right out front. The hotel constantly operates a shuttle to the airport terminal. And in compliance with the law, the hotel reserves several floors for nonsmokers.

Singles: Can$154; doubles: Can$164. Weekend packages available. All major cards.

NIGHTLIFE

BARS	130
CABARETS	136
COMEDY & MAGIC	137
DANCE CLUBS	139
JAZZ	141
LOUNGES	143
MUSIC CLUBS	144

During the day, metropolitan Toronto pulses to the beat of its own heart. The downtown core, the expansive parklands, the varied neighborhoods and ethnic communities add an extra zip to the life pumping constantly through the city's sprawling arteries. But when the sun goes down and those arteries light up like a carnival midway, the steady pulse becomes a rhythmic dance beat and Torontonians take to the streets in search of an evening of entertainment. The choices are as varied as our capacity for fun and our financial status. Toronto is a lively city after dark, and its residents like to play with the same open, honest energy as that with which they work.

BARS

Amsterdam Brasserie & Brewpub
133 John St.,
Downtown
• 595-8201

As Toronto's first combination brewery/pub, opened in 1986, this is the hot spot for single mingling, seeing and being seen. The crowd, and we don't use that term lightly, particularly on a Friday or Saturday night, is strictly upscale yuppie. At first glance, it looks like there'd be lots of room for them with the soaring warehouse ceilings and exposed brickwork walls punctuated with paneless windows for discreet crowd cruising. But just try wading through the clothes-horse set, three deep at the bar, filling the aisles and spilling out onto the patio, in season or out. Sampling the one-hundred-plus brands of beer (four of them brewed on site) are Queen West artists, university students in jeans and loafers, stockbrokers outfitted *GQ*-fashion and runway models, all packed in shoulder to shoulder, phone-booth style. A small dining room section serves standard pub fare. Beware of lineups that can start as early at 5:30 on a Friday afternoon.
Open daily 11:30 a.m.-1 a.m., Sun. 11 a.m.-1 a.m. No cover. All major cards.

Cap's
572 Jarvis St.,
Cabbagetown
• 924-8555

Easy and relaxed, this small neighborhood bar can't keep up with the expanding neighborhood. Crowded on any night, it caters to a variety of nightcrawlers, offering darts, shuffleboard, video trivia, live R&B on the weekends, pinball and, the main attraction, the Big Game that seems to be continuously in progress on the big screen. The baby-boom generation from Rosedale, just across the ravine, and a crowd of those who like to coach the team and call the plays from their barstools make up the roster of regulars who indulge happily in Tuesday Wing Ding (suicidal chicken-wing-eating competitions) and Jughead

NIGHTLIFE Bars

Wednesday's 99-cent miniburgers. Sweatshirts, sneakers and a healthy appetite for sports and fun are the requirements here. Forewarned is forearmed: lineups are a frequent hazard on game nights and weekends.
Open daily 11 a.m.-1 a.m., Sun. noon-1 a.m. No cover. Cards: AE, MC, V.

Consort Bar
King Edward Hotel,
37 King St. East,
Downtown
• 863-9700

An upper-crust, posher-than-posh bar with expensive drinks and a staid, oh-so-elegant atmosphere. This place seems even stuffier than the Oak Room in New York—except when the piano player moves into the smokier blues numbers in an extensive repertoire. Then the stiffly starched flight attendants and the traveling business tycoons start to relax and show real potential for truly spontaneous fun.
Open Mon.-Fri. 11:45 a.m.-1 a.m., Sat. 5 p.m.-1 a.m. No cover. All major cards.

Grossman's Tavern
379 Spadina Ave.,
Chinatown
• 977-7000

No designer could come up with a decor more suited to the blues than this. In this greasy beer joint par excellence, the arborite table tops, plastic chairs, truck-stop memorabilia and the never-ending pool game in the front room are the perfect setting for some of the best lives blues and alternative hard rock in town. Always more than just a little quirky, Grossman's may never be respectable but is sure has a reputation and a loyal following. University students love it, bikers hang out in it, punks exhibit the latest depression around its pinball machine, the world-weary wile away the afternoons in it and the draft flows incessantly. To experience Grossman's is to experience life, the habitués are wont to say.
Open daily 11 a.m.-1 a.m. No cover. No cards.

Madison Avenue Pub
14 Madison Ave.,
Toronto
• 927-1722

The four floors and two terraces of this Victorian-mansion-turned-party-house are a whirlwind tour of the universe of youth. Once catering only to the university crowd, the clientele has expanded to include the junior urban landed gentry and a dense pack of singles, easily identified by incessant boy-meets-girl banter such as "So, what do you do?" and "So, where do you work out?" The scene is loud and raucous in any of the bars; we use the time spent in the long lineup to decide on the room in which we'd like to sit. Because of Ontario liquor-board regulations, capacity of the rooms is restricted so switching between bars is prohibited. Once inside, the exuberance of youth is infectious and pervasive. These people really know how to have fun, whether it's in the relatively quiet dining room in the basement, the rowdy piano bar on the main floor or the jocks' playpen (better known as the dart-and-game room) on

NIGHTLIFE Bars

the second floor, which is littered with male egos and mute television sets tuned to today's sporting event.
Open daily 11:30 a.m.-1 a.m. No cover. All major cards.

The Queen's Head Pub
263 Gerrard St. East, Downtown
• 929-9525

If that slightly dotty aunt we don't talk about in polite company had an attic, it would look like The Queen's Head. Victorian clutter and mismatched bric-a-brac vie for space with mounted heads and bashed-in French horns, broken toys and dolls, heavy oil paintings with varnish so old and thick it might be tar, and ancient silk lampshades that look most natural askew. Once-elegant portraits of British regency cower behind fly-blown glass in faded gilt frames; the wallpaper behind would make even those who don't bother with such things wince. As British pubs go, this is the quintessential eccentric watering hole. Fans of Coronation Street, expat Brits and university students quaff pints of Watney's Ale and revel in the tackiness and curiosity-shop atmosphere of this fun place.
Open daily 4 p.m.-1 a.m. No cover. Cards: AE, MC, V.

Remy's
115 Yorkville Ave., Bloor-Yorkville
• 968-9429

The Yorkville hotspot with style and elegance, Remy's isn't just a bar with a brass door, it is all that the renovated Yorkville neighborhood stands for. Once the haven for the hippie generation and flower children, Yorkville's renovated image is nowhere better captured than here. The rich and famous, and those who are on their way to being so, come here to chat and mingle, not be seen. Here they can relax and enjoy the good life they've earned without the inconvenience of rubbernecking tourists or star-spotters. The elegant decor is understated and warm. Business is checked with our coats at the door and relaxation is the first order after a cocktail. The vast rooftop patio is a popular favorite in the summer with locals and visiting celebrities.
Open Mon.-Tues. noon-midnight, Wed.-Sat. noon-1 a.m., Sun. noon-11 p.m. No cover. All major cards.

Rivoli Café & Club
332 Queen St. West, Downtown
• 596-1908

If Queen Street West had to be defined, The Rivoli would best sum it up. The designer bistro at the front encourages those long, long, late-night discussions on the state of the world. Big on conversation, the narrow room is also a showplace for local artists whose photos and colorful art hang in an everchanging exhibition on the walls above the tables. Most of the art is for sale. At the tables, other art is being worn as the room is also a showplace for the latest fashion trends, fads and eccentricities. Jeans and sweatshirts don't cut it here. In the performance space at the rear of the café, things get back to basics. The stage and dance floor find a variety of uses throughout the week from stand-up comedy acts to new-wave theater, poetry readings to

cool jazz, variety benefit shows to experimental films and performance art. Some nights, it's just a dance hall with the best of the new music. The crowd cuts across the barriers and enfolds black leather jackets as easily as it does blue pinstripe suits. The attitude and the ambience are definitive Queen West. This is the area and the movement summed up in one venue. Be assured, any fluctuation in either is tested and felt first at the Rivoli, the real beating heart of Queen Street West.
Open nightly 9 p.m.-1 a.m. Showtimes & covers vary. No cards.

Le Sélect Bistro
328 Queen St. West,
Downtown
• 596-6406

In this bustling restaurant bar, privacy is at a premium—but it is available. So are the best new beer and wine imports. Currently, the bar stocks 300 different wines in its huge cellars. The Parisian-bistro atmosphere is augmented by an exuberant staff that shows minimal attitude and lots of interest in our conversations, joining in at the drop of a bar rag with a charm, style and wit that makes the whole experience agreeably inoffensive.
Open daily 11:30 a.m.-1 a.m. No cover. All major cards.

GAY BARS

Metropolitan Toronto's gay and lesbian population is reputed to be, per capita, the second largest in North America after San Francisco. As in the City by the Bay, Toronto's gay community is active in the arts and in the merchandising, fashion and service industries. The venues catering to the community, which is centered around Church and Wellesley streets, offer a wide range of entertainment and diversions that never seek to exclude the rest of the population. Of course, the clientele at downtown's leather bars is almost exclusively gay, but straight visitors are made to feel welcome in any of Toronto's cabarets, showrooms or gay dance clubs.

The Barn
83 Granby St.,
Downtown
• 977-4684

The chosen leather bar of Toronto's gay ghetto, the Barn offers a steamy, crowded dance floor on which, early in the evening, you'll find these muscled dudes doffing shirts so they can sweat more freely. Catering to a denim and leather crowd, this is basically a harmless version of the rougher leather bars. Lots of university students, urban cowboys and outrageous leather costumes show up on the weekends.
Open Mon.-Thurs. 8 p.m.-1:30 a.m., Fri.-Sat. 8 p.m.-3:30 a.m. No cover. No cards.

Chaps
9 Isabella St.,
Downtown
• 960-1200

A two-story building with a reputation as the premier gay bar in Toronto. As tastes differ, some quibble about the unofficial title, but there is no denying the crowds that fill the smoky rooms every night of the week. The downstairs bar is all oak and brass with a small dance floor and banquette seating, as well as a few stools at the bar. This is where you'll meet someone through conversation rather than mutual ogling. Upstairs, the pounding disco beat has the preppy set sweating in their fashionable togs or posing in the glare of the flashing light show. Downstairs, Chaps restaurant (serving Continental fare) is popular with locals as a place to see and be seen; its patio in summer affords a great view of never-ending parade on nearby Yonge Street.

Open daily noon-1 a.m. No cover. Cards: AE, MC, V.

Club Colby's
5 St. Joseph St.,
Downtown
• 961-0777

A veritable smörgåsbord of decadence beckons from the dark, smoky depths of Club Colby's. Just inside the door, the first thing you see, once your eyes have adjusted to the dim light, is a G-string-clad dancer twining himself around the brass pole atop one end of the bar. He doesn't pay much attention to anyone but himself, despite the fact he poses directly over people's heads. It's all part of the show. The dancer at the other end of the bar, meanwhile, is behaving in a way that may or may not be illegal. And looking is what Colby's is all about: there are dancers on the bar, strippers on the dance floor, players around the pool table, X-rated videos on the soundless monitors around the room, table dancers on call, drag entertainment on the stage and pretty boys with chiseled cheekbones five deep at the bars. Sexuality hangs in the air like a cloud of smoke so intense you can almost see it. But this decadence has an air of innocence about it that makes all this heavy breathing seem silly. A relaxed ambience and a laissez-faire attitude prevails.

Open daily 11 a.m.-1 a.m. No cover. Cards: AE, V.

Komrads
1 Isabella St.,
Downtown
• 924-7853

Be assured, the volume is pumped up on Komrads's vast stainless-steel dance floor. So are the boys. The energy level is as frenetic as the strobes and the high-tech light show when the massive sound system is pushed into overdrive, which is not a rare occurrence. Focusing primarily on its role as an after-hours dance bar, Komrads caters to a youthful clientele that loves the mix of musical exotica and ancient disco hits. Faded denims mix comfortably with bursts of sartorial splendor and extravagance, which only those seated along the tiered sidelines, taking a break from the craziness of the dance floor, are sure to notice. That's the fun of sitting one out: watching. When the decibel level passes beyond deafening and verges on offensive, you can retreat to the quietly elegant front bar and enjoy the relative peace of rock videos and the comfort of air conditioning.

Open nightly 8 p.m.-3 a.m. Cover Can$2 after 1 a.m. Cards: AE, MC, V.

NIGHTLIFE Bars

Trax Toronto
529 Yonge St.,
Downtown
• 962-8729

This palatial gay bar possibly suffers from an identity crisis. The mazelike halls and steep staircases that wind endlessly through the building connecting the six rooms and two decks give no clue as to what lies beyond. The front bar on the street level features barn board and wagon wheels under a sculpted plaster cathedral ceiling. The one-way window onto Yonge Street is popular with the lunch and afternoon crowds. Beyond that is the big-screen television bar with two levels, and at the back, the showroom offers live dance bands on weekends, drag extravaganzas, the always-packed Tuesday night game shows (in case you didn't see enough on TV before you left home) and regularly scheduled variety shows featuring live acts such as The Mamas and Papas, The Platters, Leslie Gore, The Shirelles and Mary Wilson.

Up one flight, the softly lit, pastel-hued piano bar provides one of the best Broadway-musical repertoires around, and the games bar keeps the guys happy with darts, video games, pinball and shuffleboard. Across the outdoor deck, a pool room hums with clicks of pool sticks and the best in country-western music. An outdoor deck upstairs is the perfect spot to wind down at the end of the night. This bar attracts an older, more established crowd with specific tastes in entertainment; cruising and dancing are not high priorities.
Open Mon.-Sat. 11 a.m.-1 a.m., Sun. noon-1 a.m. No cover. Cards: AE, V.

The Rose Café
547 Parliament St.,
Downtown
• 928-1495

The bar of choice for Toronto's gay women, this expansive, casual place has two pool tables and a games room downstairs, and a dance space and bar upstairs. A crowd that includes a smattering of men gathers to unwind to sounds mixed by a live deejay, and on Sundays to dance to live entertainment that ranges from country-western to rock-and-roll. A mostly vegetarian restaurant upstairs serves up soups, salads and pastas at very reasonable prices, for tuckered-out revellers in need of a light bite.
Open Mon.-Sat. 7 p.m.-1:30 a.m., Sun. 11 a.m.-1:30 p.m.

Woody's
467 Church St.,
Downtown
• 972-0887

The new kid on the block, Woody's was only eighteen months old at press time, and already it has a dedicated following. Those elusive ingredients—location, timing and ambience—all came together to make a successful venture in an era where so many nightspots fall by the wayside after the novelty has worn off. Woody's exudes charm and friendly warmth, from both the staff and patrons. The exposed brick, polished-wood floors, silk-shaded lamps and faded Oriental rugs create a genteel, clublike ambience. The music, an eclectic mix of popular favorites both old and new, is kept low so as not to intrude on conversations.

This is a true neighborhood bar if ever there was one. It caters to a wide range of ages and interests in the community which surrounds it but, like the staff-hiring policy, stresses personality and warmth.
Open daily noon-1 a.m. No cover. Cards: AE, MC, V.

CABARETS

An Evening at La Cage
279 Yonge St.,
Downtown
• 364-5200

For a night of campy fun and illusion in a Las Vegas–style supperclub with a deceptively small cabaret stage and runway, join the boys and girls of the chorus as they welcome all those show-stopping favorites: Diana Ross, Joan Rivers, Dionne Warwick, Tina Turner or Marilyn Monroe. The operative word here, of course, is illusion. The girls of the chorus are boys, truly some of the finest female impersonators on the North American club circuit. The humor is raunchy, the costumes rival those of Bob Mackie, the sets have enough glitter and glitz to blind a Vegas blackjack dealer and the impersonations are breathtakingly convincing. These guys take their jobs seriously. Often the choreography is cramped and rough around the edges and the boys of the chorus obviously feel more comfortable dancing in high heels, but no one really cares because fun is the byword here. This show is not for children; the enthusiastic audience consists mostly of tourists and group-party bookings who readily join in the high-camp fun to make the evening a unique and memorable one.
Open Tues.-Thurs. 6 p.m.-10:30 p.m., Fri. 5:30 p.m.-10:30 p.m., Sat. 5:30 p.m.-1 a.m.; Sun. noon-10 p.m. Shows Tues.-Fri. 8:30 p.m.; Sat. 8 p.m. & 11 p.m.; Sun. 2 p.m., 5:30 p.m. & 7:30 p.m. Admission varies (Can$15-Can$38). Cards: AE, MC.

His Majesty's Feast
1926 Lakeshore Blvd. West,
Toronto
• 769-1165

Join King Henry for a royal feast in this lavishly costumed recreation of Medieval times. As you dine in the great hall, the Jester provides continuous, unrelenting entertainment and buffoonery, the lords and ladies of the court provide a visual charm and delight with authentic period dances and songs. Pages and serving "wenches" offer a taste of regal feasting in the way it was done in Merrie Olde England. If you love theater, this is for you. The youthful, energetic company is made up of top-notch local headliners who perform with the utmost energy and enthusiasm for a full three and a half hours. Be prepared to eat with your fingers and be drawn into the ribald merriment.

NIGHTLIFE Comedy & Magic

Open Tues.-Sat. 7:30 p.m. Shows Tues.-Sat 8 p.m. Cover Tues.-Thurs. Can$26.95, Fri. Can$30.95, Sat. Can$32.95 Cards: AE, MC, V.

Limelight Dinner Theatre
2026 Yonge St.,
Toronto North
• 482-5200

This 200-seat dinner theater recreates the musicals of Broadway, using local talent with a guest celebrity in the lead role. Specializing in such standards as *Singin' in the Rain*, *42nd Street*, *Me and My Girl* or *Hello Dolly*, the productions lack polish but the family and group bookings don't seem to mind; they enjoy the show as much as the youthful, enthusiastic cast. Dinner and theater packages available.

Open Mon.-Fri. 6 p.m.-11 p.m., Sat. 5 p.m.-1:30 a.m. Shows Mon.-Fri. 8 p.m., Sat. 7 p.m. & 10:30 p.m. Dinner & show Mon.-Thurs. Can$50, Fri. Can$55, Sat. Can$60 (late show, no dinner Sat. Can$30). Cards: AE, MC, V.

Stage West Hotel and Theatre Restaurant
5400 Dixie Rd.,
Mississauga
• 238-0042

A dinner-theater facility designed in the traditional style with a 60-foot gourmet buffet table, tiered seating for 600 and an elegant, theatrical atmosphere and ambience. The production lineup includes current hit comedies or classic musicals, such as *Double Act*, *Accomplice*, *Steel Magnolias* and *Season's Greetings*. Small casts of local professionals feature film or television personalities in the lead roles. Well rehearsed and professionally presented, these productions have developed a staunch local audience of theatergoers as well the tourist and group-booking trade. The limited table service is at all times fast, friendly and, most important, unobtrusive, which adds to the feeling of theater.

Open Tues.-Sun. 6 p.m.-11 p.m. Shows Tues.-Sun. 8:30 p.m. Cover varies. Cards: AE, MC, V.

COMEDY & MAGIC

Harper's Restaurant and Dinner Theatre
26 Lombard St.,
Downtown
• 863-6223

The show, *A Little Night Magic*, has been running for seven years and providing a fabulous and fun-filled evening's entertainment for tourists and Torontonians alike. We never tire of being amazed at sleight-of-hand or grand illusions when presented in this elegant setting which, with only 200 seats, allows for tableside magic during our meal. The stage show does not rival Las Vegas but is professional, fast-paced, fun and stylish. The humor is broad and the audience loves every minute of it, even if most of us have heard the jokes and seen the trick done

NIGHTLIFE Comedy & Magic

before. This is a great evening out that the whole family can enjoy.
Open Tues.-Fri. 6 p.m.-11 p.m., Sat. 5:30 p.m.-1 a.m. Shows Tues.-Fri. 8:30 p.m., Sat. 8 p.m. & 10:30 p.m. Cover (dinner & show) Tues.-Thurs. Can$26.95, Fri. Can$30.95, Sat. Can$32.95 Cards: AE, MC, V.

The Second City
110 Lombard St., Downtown
• 863-1111

A unique evening spent with The Second City cast will satisfy your palate and tickle your funny bone. The satirical revue performances, loosely strung on a theme which may or may not get lost during the evening's pointed, and definitely barbed, humor, are a hit with a wide cross-section of dinner theater devotees. The show has a strong local audience, particularly when offering a new show, about four times a year, and is a delight for the tourist trade. The theater is housed in a renovated fire hall so the ambience is relaxed and casual. This is not a show for stuffed shirts or children. The actors can be counted on for outrageous ad libs and a full evening of top-notch professional comedy.
Open Mon.-Thurs. 6 p.m.-11 p.m., Fri.-Sat. 5:30 p.m.-1:30 a.m. Shows Mon.-Thurs. 8:30 p.m., Fri.-Sat. 8:30 p.m. & 11 p.m. Cover Mon.-Thurs. Can$27.95 (dinner & show), Can$12.50 (show only); Fri.-Sat. Can$32.95 (dinner & show), Can$17 (show only). All major cards.

Theatresports
• 756-2444

Improvisational comedy for the masses presents stand-up comics in training for public viewing and humiliation, maybe even a few laughs if you're lucky. On the whole, this rampage of verbiage from the mouths of the untrained is strictly for those who don't get out much. If you visit the corner store even once a week, you'll find this a tremendous bore. But for those who like comedy with not just raw but completely frayed edges, this is the place for you. The rest of us will be on the other side of town at Yuk Yuks or Second City, where the comedy is just polished enough to make it that much funnier.
Shows Wed. 8 p.m. at York Quay Centre, 235 Queen's Quay West, Harbourfront. Admission Can$7. Workshops upstairs in The Loft every Mon., by audition only. Phone for details.

Yuk Yuks
2335 Yonge St., Toronto North
• 967-6425

Following in the tradition of comedy clubs in the United States, Yuk Yuks is an open mine field for stand-up comics who want to try out new material or see if they've got what it takes to tell jokes for a living. It has the potential for being a great evening's entertainment but on some nights, we feel deeply embarrassed for the beleaguered would-be comics fending off hecklers and rude college students. On these nights it becomes a Roman circus, with the crowd cheering each downed victim and calling

NIGHTLIFE Dance Clubs

for more. This style of comedy may appear sadistic and unappealing to some; others line up in the rain or snow for it. It's a matter of personal taste here. There is a regular schedule of professional comics to soften the harsher reality of show-biz hopefuls. The original Yuk Yuks still stands at 1280 Bay St., Bloor-Yorkville; Yuk Yuks West is at 5165 Dixie Rd., Mississauaga. Call 967-6425 for shows.

Yonge St. branch: open Tues.-Thurs. 7 p.m.-midnight, Fri.-Sat. 6:30 p.m.-1:30 a.m., Sun. 7 p.m.-11 p.m. Shows Tues.-Thurs. 9 p.m., Fri.-Sat. 8:30 & 11 p.m. Cover Tues.-Thurs. Can$23.25 (dinner & show); Fri. Can$27.95 (dinner & show), Can$12 (show only); Sat. Can$29.75 (dinner & show), Can$14 (show only). Cards: AE, MC, V.

DANCE CLUBS

Dancing is a favorite way to unwind in Toronto. A wide variety of venues offers a broad selection of musical styles, club atmosphere and varying degrees of elegance or degeneration. Whatever our mood, we can always find a spot to express it on the dance floor.

The Big Bop
651 Queen St. West,
Downtown
• 366-6699

Don't Fix It If It Isn't Broken, is the adage by which The Big Bop is run. This enormous danceteria hasn't changed its look, policies or music since it opened more than four years ago. Why should it? It makes money, and the legendary nightly lineups attest to its popularity with the young and young at heart. The three floors of ear-splitting entertainment inside the purple facade cater to definite factions of the rock club crowd. The first floor features 1960s and 1970s nostalgia with moldy oldies from Led Zeppellin to Aretha Franklin. Up one flight, we encounter the 1980s mania for manic twitch and gyrate to the synthesized sounds of bands such as Depeche Mode. The third floor is a television lounge of sorts where, by the familiar flickering blue light, bona fide couch potatoes can feel right at home. The Big Bop is definitely an acquired taste, but those who love it live by it.

Open Wed.-Sat. 8 p.m.-1 a.m. Cover varies. All major cards.

The Copa
21 Scollard St.
• 922-6500

A huge barn of a place, the Copa rocks at such a powerful decibel level that local residents regularly complain about the noise. The club turns down the volume for a while, then up it goes again and the phones start ringing again. It's a local ritual turned tradition. All the fuss is over some pretty bland, squeaky-clean

rock music pounding out over the good-sized dance floor to the obvious enjoyment of the university-age, squeaky-clean patrons. But there is another side to The Copa. Hidden behind the steady beat of The Stones that easily bring in the rent money for this place are the heady rhythms of Reggae bands—live. The Copa has given us some of the best practitioners of the art of Reggae: The Wailers, Ziggy Marley, Shinehead, Dennis Bown and Jimmy Cliff. Skip the middle-of-the-road squeaky stuff and head for the buffet and the Reggae. This is one club who's split identity is a boon for both management and patrons.
Open Mon.-Fri. 8 p.m.-2 a.m., Sat. 8 p.m.-4 p.m. Showtimes & covers vary. Cards: AE, MC. V.

The Lizard Lounge
66 Gerrard St. East, Downtown
• 340-9558

A haven for the alternatives in personality, music, dancing, clothing and lifestyles, this dark, steamy, little cavern is trying to clean up its image to appeal to a less alternative crowd. The denizens of the lounge don't and won't notice unless, of course, the minimal lighting is turned up on the low-ceilinged dance floor: the main attraction of the room. Known for a wide variety of fetish nights catering to select clienteles, the Lizard is most popular with a stylish, monied, punk-type patronage that indulges freely in straight shots of tequila. Not a spot for casual sightseeing.
Open Tues.-Sat. 9 p.m.-1 a.m. Cover varies. No cards.

RPM
132 Queen's Quay East, Downtown
• 869-1462

This is one of the few Toronto clubs that openly recognizes and caters to regulars. The doorman has his whims: tonight it's first come, first served; tomorrow he may decide it's regulars only. There is no discernable pattern to the fluctuating admission policy, so we stand in line with the rest of the mob and take our chances. Once inside, we remember why we put up with all this attitude: The dance floor goes on for miles, and the music is just what we need after a hard day behind the counter with all the other ribbon clerks. But then, there are no regulars here tonight. They're waiting for Psychedelic Monday, the night regularly given over to the *in* clique, those who make the trends and discard them before we can get used to them. This is the place to be for the truly hip and those who aspire to that status. The go-go dancers flailing away on the open scaffolding may be a holdover from the 1960s but they fit right in with the smoky warehouse dance/bar atmosphere RPM emulates better than any other Toronto club. Attitude or not, for those who know, this is the club to frequent.
Open Mon.-Tues. & Thurs. 8 p.m.-2 a.m., Wed. 7:30 p.m.-2 a.m., Fri.-Sat. 7 p.m.-3 a.m., Sun. 6 p.m.-midnight. Cover Mon.-Thurs. Can$5, Fri.-Sun. Can$8. All major cards.

NIGHTLIFE Jazz & Blues

Spectrum Restaurant and Disco
2714 Danforth Ave., Danforth
• 699-9913

In a white-and-gold ballroom surrounded by mirrors, white wrought iron railings and fake marble pillars, the bank clerks and stenos nightly sport their lamé gowns and silk shirts that they wear more like costumes. The glitzy decor and studied look aside, the Spectrum has the best permanent light show of any Toronto dance club. The music is a steady mix of the latest danceable material available, and the house deejay has a real rapport with his audience, whether he's doing an ad-lib stand-up routine or leading a disco cheer. For a great night of retro disco dancing without the attitude that pervades at some hotter places, the Spectrum is our choice. No jeans, T-shirts or sneakers on Saturdays.
Open nightly Wed.-Sun. 8 p.m.-2 a.m. Cover varies. Cards: AE, MC, V.

JAZZ & BLUES

Albert's Hall
481 Bloor St. West, Bloor-Yorkville
• 964-2242

Best described as a raucous, friendly, time-worn shrine to the blues, Albert's Hall is one of the top clubs on the North American blues circuit. The legends of the genre—Etta James, Albert Collins, Buddy Guy—have played here and will play again, as well as those who will be legends soon. The crowd is in good voice as we lip-synch our order to the waiter, and the music rolls on. Table-thumping, cheering and clapping are standard behavior here, fitting right in with the shabby decor that remains untouched and untainted by the hands of a decorator. The art of blues is treated as a group experience in a rambunctious beer hall such as this. Jump right in, the music is fine.
Open nightly Mon.-Sat. 9 p.m.-1 a.m. Cover varies. Cards: AE, V.

Café des Copains
48 Wellington St. East, Downtown
• 869-0148

A open-brick, vaulted cellar provides near-perfect acoustics for unamplified solo jazz sets. The tiny room, made even smaller by the stand-up bar located on a raised level, is dominated by a full-size grand piano. The ambience is low-key, soft-spoken and quietly elegant. The music is provided by an international roster of the top names in jazz piano. This is the bar where local jazz practitioners come to hear other artists play. But on nights when the room is crowded, any loud conversation will drown out the fragile compositions. We usually leave when this happens, opting to come back another night. The Loud Crowd doesn't feel

NIGHTLIFE   Jazz & Blues

welcome here, and its members don't make a habit of lingering. *Open Tues.-Fri. noon-1 a.m., Sat. 5:30 p.m.-1 a.m., Sun. 5 p.m.-10 p.m. Cover Tues-Fri. Can$5, Sat.-Sun. Can$6. Shows Tues.-Fri. & Sun. 8:30 p.m., Sat. 8:30 p.m., 9:40p.m., 10:50 p.m. & midnight. All major cards.*

George's Spaghetti House
290 Dundas St. East, Downtown
• 923-9887

This room has a reputation—as Toronto's most enduring jazz club—that it substantiates by having survived in one continuous line since 1956. Check out the autographed photos of the jazz greats who have passed this way, then forget the ragged-edge decor left over from the 1950s and give yourself over to the music. The quality of the sound, and the music, ranks among the finest in the city. The ambience is relaxed and easy. Moe Hoffman, the club's music director, engages artists that run the spectrum from Phil Dwyer to Time Warp. Local musicians and a regular schedule of weekly guest artists serve up hot and cool jazz the way it is meant to be heard. For a moment, we became so lost in the music, it was difficult to remember whether we were in New York, New Orleans or Toronto. The place has that timeless quality about it that dedicated jazz buffs search out and cherish.
Open Mon.-Thurs. 6:30 p.m.-12:30 p.m., Fri.-Sat. 6:30 p.m.-1 a.m. Shows Mon.-Fri. 8:30 p.m., Sat. 9 p.m. Cover varies. All major cards.

Top of the Senator
253 Victoria St., Downtown
• 364-7517

From the moment we walk into the club above the Senator Restaurant, there is no doubt we're in the right place. The room has been tastefully and restrainedly decorated as a recreation of one of those evocative, blue-lit jazz clubs of the 1920s and 1930s. The place oozes atmosphere. We settle in comfortably with high expectations of a great evening of jazz. Tonight's combo more than fulfills our high expectations, and the lineup for the next few months—Harry Connick Jr., Herb Ellis, Betty Carter—indicates a commitment on the part of management to high quality performers for a knowledgable clientele.
Open nightly 8 p.m.-1 a.m. Shows nightly 9:30 & 11 p.m. Cover varies. All major cards.

LOUNGES

Aquarius 51 Lounge
55 Bloor St. West,
Bloor-Yorkville
• 967-5225

From the 51st floor of the Manulife Centre, the floor-to-ceiling windows on both sides of the room give the illusion of floating over the city, which is spread out for miles in all directions below us. The muted decor and low lights add to that intimate, in-flight atmosphere. There is nothing quite so romantic as watching the moon rise over the lake down there by the CN Tower and the SkyDome unless, of course, we count snuggling on the decadently comfy sofas and sipping smart cocktails with that special someone. As a romantic hideaway, this is it.
Open Mon.-Fri. noon-1 a.m., Sat. 5 p.m.-1 a.m., Sun. 5 p.m.-11 p.m. Cover Can$3 after 8:30 p.m. All major cards.

The Imperial Room
Royal York Hotel,
100 Front St. West,
Harbourfront
• 368-2511

The last of the big hotel rooms in the grand style of The Plaza or The Carlyle, the Imperial Room has new policies. The cabaret stage now is home to a dance band and the patrons now come for the nostalgia, not the names. A lovely evening of dining and dancing to a live band playing songs to which we know the lyrics. As the setting for a romantic interlude, this elegant hotel ballroom, glittering with crystal chandeliers, is tops. For gentlemen: a jacket and tie are required.
Open Mon.-Sat. 5:30 p.m.-11:30 p.m. Cover varies. All major cards.

Sparkles Nightclub
CN Tower,
301 Front St. West,
Harbourfront
• 362-5411

Dancing amid the stars is about as romantic as it gets when our special date is 1,100 feet (350 meters) above street level in the CN Tower's lounge. The decor is strictly by the book: nothing extravagant, nothing threatening. The clientele is mostly tourists, young couples out to impress their dates or older, married couples celebrating with a predictable night on the town in a predictable atmosphere. The view is the biggest thrill this set can cope with, other than an impromptu dip during the slow numbers or the debatable cachet of sipping your Champagne three-fifths of the way up the tallest free-standing structure in the world. No bluejeans or sneakers are allowed on Saturdays, hardly a necessary regulation for this dressy crowd.
Open Mon.-Sat. 11 a.m.-7 p.m. & 8:30 p.m.-1 a.m. Sun. 8 p.m.-midnight. Cover Can$10. All major cards.

NIGHTLIFE Music Clubs

MUSIC CLUBS

As much fun as dancing is in Toronto, live music remains another popular alternative when looking for a night out on the town. The same wide variety of styles and venues in which we strut our stuff applies here. On any night, we can hear raw rock-and-roll in a dimly-lit dungeon, slinky soul on a smoky stage, live folk or hip-hop in a dingy cellar tavern or country-western in a noisy beer hall with sawdust on the floor.

The Bamboo Club
312 Queen St. West, Downtown
• 593-5771

This tropical oasis on Queen West has nightly lineups that begin around 8 p.m. It's a hot club with hot music and hot food—literally. The rich blend of live calypso, reggae, salsa and Tex-Mex jive matches the menu and draws an eclectic crowd of tourists and locals. The Bay Street types happily rub shoulders with Queen West artists and jam the dance floor to sport the hottest new styles and fads. The live bands are hard to see, the sight lines in this room are, at best, impossible, but hearing is never a problem. The party atmosphere is augmented by the relaxed standing-room policy and constantly shifting crowds. The room gets stuffy so we wander, actually squeeze, through the milling mob, out onto the open terrace for a break. The cool night air offers a welcome respite and the music is piped out here from the madness inside. The city seems far away, the music drowning out the noisy Queen Street traffic, as we relax under the potted, lush, tropical foliage.
Open Mon.-Sat. noon-1 a.m. Showtimes & covers vary. All major cards.

The Cameron Public House
408 Queen St. West, Downtown
• 364-0811

What Albert's Hall is to the blues, the Cameron is to the musically outrageous of Queen Street West. Here the scene is dark and dirty. The gritty decor and the rag-tag youths in black feel at home in this haven for the newest bands with the newest original sound. We don't come here to hear cover music. This is music on the raw edge and the experience can be exciting if the band is hot and has talent. It happens, though, that we find little talent amid the crush and the noise.
Open Mon.-Sat. noon-1 a.m. Showtimes vary. Cover Can$10. Cards: V.

NIGHTLIFE Music Clubs

Clinton's Tavern
693 Bloor St. West,
The Annex
• 535-9541

Clinton's is a three-stage hit for the senses. The front bar is a bogus, varnished-log rendering of an art director's idea of a typical Canadian beverage room. We pass up the dubious pleasures of lingering here and go straight through to the show room. The miniature dance floor infringes on the limited stage space for no discernable purpose, but we came to listen, not to dance. The rocking band is in fine form and can be seen from any spot in the house. The regulars from The Annex, as the area around here is called, are getting into the crescendo of music and the joint is really jumping. This is the best bar in Toronto to hear guitar greats, the famous and the not-yet-but-hopefully-soon-to-be famous, working out and stretching musical muscles. Downstairs, the standard gamut of lounge games and a big-screen television offer a momentary diversion but the guitarist on stage upstairs just played an impossible riff, so we head back to the show room for more of what Clinton's does best.
Open daily 3 p.m.-1 a.m. Cover varies. No cards.

The Horseshoe Tavern
370 Queen St. West,
Downtown
• 598-4753

Rising like the phoenix from an mixed and often-unsavory-and-best-forgotten past, the Horseshoe is the home of country rock or, if you will, rockin' country music in Metro. In any survey of oh-so-sophisticated Toronto nightlifers, not many admit to downing a few brews and stomping the dust out of the cracks with a mean two-step at the 'Shoe. If we can get them to admit that much, a hearty endorsement as the premier bar for letting down hair and inhibitions quickly follows. Most any night, the stiffly starched, squeaky-clean Bay Street boys and the university preppies can be found strutting around the bar in Stetsons, bejewelled collar tips, string ties and boots. They've come for a rest from all that pretense, to swing to country music from such luminaries of the art as k.d. lang, Blue Rodeo, Cowboy Junkies, Prairie Oyster and the Razorbacks. The nightly crowds range in age, taste and degree of sophistication and dedication to pub-crawling. But when the lights go up on stage, the differences melt into the shadows and everyone is just a rockin' cowboy or cowgirl at heart. Long lines are common on weekends, but seating is at a premium any night so we advise an early arrival to snag a seat close to the stage and the dance floor.
Open Mon.-Sat. noon-2 a.m. Shows Mon.-Sat. 10 p.m. & midnight. Cover (Thurs.-Sat. only) varies. Cards: V.

Lee's Palace
529 Bloor St. West,
Toronto
• 532-7383

The definitive Toronto avant-garde showcase, this room has a long-standing reputation as a supporter of local talent. In fact, Lee's presents more local acts than any other Toronto nightspot. The oddly troubling, always-insolent mural that pinpoints

Lee's on Bloor Street West is the creation of a local artist who signs himself Runt. Not heeding the warning signs—the mural is only a hint of what awaits us on the inside—we take our place at what seems to be a three-ring circus involving musicians and audience. Gone are the hushed, reverent audiences at concerts. This music is interactive and the crowds of youths in tattered denim with girls in black, and a biker and a hippie throwback who have wandered in off the street drawn by the violence of the noise, flail the air with limbs and jet-black hair in time to the steady beat of the current attraction. There are three acts showcased most nights and true devotees sit through it all—from rockabilly to jazz to punk bands—and claim to have had a great night out. This is not a musical venue for the casually curious but rather a testing ground and showcase for music from the edge that is making it's not-so-cautious way toward the mainstream. Any evening at Lee's is a musical adventure.

Open daily 11 a.m.-1 a.m. Shows nightly 10 p.m., 11 p.m. & midnight. Cover varies. No cards.

The Legendary Club Bluenote

128 Pears Ave., Toronto
• 920-1230

A wild, hot, slinky house band, fronted by the best of the best, Toronto's finest soul vocalists, delivers the best live R&B this side of Motown. The club caters to a specific need in the city's club scene: a place to get down, boogie and hear classic soul music with a loud, brassy horn section. These cats play the kind of fine and mellow music we miss but rarely even admit to remembering these days. But in this crowded, dimly lit club, the vocalist is still the feature act, standing under a smoky-blue spotlight, moaning low about all those lovers that got away and threatening to create a heatwave in that sequined tube masquerading as a gown. The crowd is mixed but the attentions are not. When the singer takes a break, the lounge lizards declare open season just as they did in the 1960s. If we're not in a time warp, we must be in the Bluenote shaking our bootie. Weekend lineups are a frequent hazard.

Open Tues.-Thurs. 8 p.m.-1 a.m., Fri.-Sat. 8 p.m.-4 a.m. Showtimes & covers vary. Cards: AE, MC, V.

SHOPS

ANTIQUES	148
BEAUTY	149
BOOKS & NEWSSTANDS	150
CHILDREN	153
CLOTHES & JEWELRY	155
DEPARTMENT STORES & SHOPPING CENTERS	166
FOOD	168
GIFTS & HOUSEWARES	168
LEATHER & LUGGAGE	171

ANTIQUES

Atelier Art and Antiques
588 Markham St.,
Bloor-Yorkville
• 532-9244

This is *the* place in Toronto for native folk art, including crude-beautiful wooden statues, hunting decoys, primitive paintings and other aged, native handiworks.
Days & hours vary.

Estate Collection
21 Avenue Rd.,
Bloor-Yorkville
• 921-6443

As befits the tony neighborhood (this shop is in the Four Seasons Hotel), the antique jewelry, glassware and silver collectibles are on the pricey side, but the quality and authenticity are first-rate, justifying those tariffs. You'll find some beautiful tabletop items here.
Open Mon.-Sat. 10 a.m.-6 p.m.

Harbourfront Antique Market
390 Queen's Quay West,
Harbourfront
• 340-8377

Toronto abounds with antique and flea marketplaces, and this is one of the most voluminous: up to 200 vendors sell their wares here at any one time, and you'll find just about anything you may be looking for—including some things you never even thought existed—furniture, dolls, jewelry, various collectibles and all and sundry manner of vintage thingumabobs.
Open Tues.-Fri. 11 a.m.-6 p.m., Sat. 10 a.m.-5 p.m., Sun. 8 a.m.-6 p.m.

Journey's End Antiques
612 Markham St.,
The Annex
• 536-2226

If you're into memorabilia, vintage postcards, and fine forms of silver, this is a must. For those who collect on a grander scale, there's some terrific antique furniture, as well.
Open Mon.-Sat. 10:30 a.m.-6 p.m., Sun. noon-5 p.m.

Louis Wine
848-A Yonge St.,
Downtown
• 929-9333

This beautiful shop carries a stunning selection of flatware and hollowware from the British Isles, dating to the eighteenth and nineteenth centuries, as well as some beautiful Victorian jewelry. The staff is very friendly and knowledgable.
Open Mon.-Sat. 10:30 a.m.-6 p.m.

Michel Taschereau
176 Cumberland St.,
Bloor-Yorkville
• 923-3020

Keep this one on your antique list for its fine selection of nineteenth- and twentieth-century antique furniture. Items of importance will run you from Can$1,500 to Can$10,000, so bring your checkbook along with that inheritance.
Open Mon. 10 a.m.-5:30 p.m., Tues.-Sat. 10 a.m.-6 p.m.

SHOPS Beauty

Stanley Wagman Antiques and Gifts
33 Avenue Rd.,
Bloor-Yorkville
• 964-1047

Yorkville is chockablock with respected and renowned antique shops, and Stanley Wagman is one of the most venerable and reputable. This shop is not for the faint of heart (or pocketbook); Bigger Is Better is the byword here, and you'll find breathtaking mantels, beds, opulent light fixtures and armoires as big as the Ritz.
Open Mon.-Sat. 10 a.m.-6 p.m.

St. Lawrence Market
92 Front St. East,
Downtown
• 392, 2718, 483-6471

This indoor mart that turns into an antique-and-craft show on Sundays has quite a bit of dross, though there are inexpensive treasures to be unearthed. Lots of vintage toys, glassware, jewelry and native crafts; there's also a snack bar where you can to refresh yourself in between bouts of rummaging.
Open Sun. 10 a.m.-5 p.m.

BEAUTY

The Body Shop
397 Queen St. West,
Downtown
• 348-8903

Unless you've been living in a cave, you're probably familiar with The Body Shop. This British-based company was a pioneer of ecological, gentle personal-care products, and its outlets are hugely popular all over the world. We first discovered this line in Hong Kong, and have been converts ever since. Anita Roddick, The Body Shop's owner, plows part of her profits into Earth-saving causes, and the company does not test on animals or use any harmful or artificial ingredients. The result is a line of fresh, fabulous hair, skin and bath products, as well as cosmetics. Plus, the staff is as user-friendly as the goods they sell.
Open Mon.-Sat. 10 a.m.-8 p.m.

Bretton's
Manulife Centre,
55 Bloor St. West,
Bloor-Yorkville
• 975-9097

This trendy compendium of boutiques carries the British Molton Brown line of cosmetics and skin care, products reputedly favored by members of the royal family and celebrities alike. And for good reason: the products are made of natural ingredients with no artificial fragrance or preservatives added. Biodegradable and not tested on animals, Molton Brown's line of makeup comes in fabulous colors (the lipsticks have a particularly smooth texture), as well as skin, hair and bath goods are no less attractive.
Open Mon.-Wed. & Sat. 10 a.m.-6 p.m., Thurs.-Fri. 10 a.m.-9 p.m.

SHOPS Books & Newsstands

H₂0
Hazelton Lanes,
87 Avenue Rd.,
Bloor-Yorkville
• 925-7080

H₂0 takes its cue from the supernal British Body Shop. Like its mentor's products, H₂0's are based on botanicals and something called "hydrogel." The shop itself is kicky and modern, as is the packaging. You'll find necessary luxuries such as shower gel infused with gold dust, casaba-melon bath powder and cherry bath gel.
Open Mon.-Sat. 10 a.m.-6 p.m.

Mira Linder
108 Avenue Rd.,
Bloor-Yorkville
• 961-6900

A wonderful mini-spa guaranteed to pamper, whether you go for a full day of indulgence, for a facial, manicure and pedicure, scalp treatment, makeover and hair styling, or any single one of these services. A visit here is quite a treat—especially after a long week. Just make sure you call ahead for an appointment.
Open Mon.-Sat. 9 a.m.-6 p.m.

BOOKS & NEWSSTANDS

NEW

Albert Britnell Book Shop
765 Yonge St.,
Bloor-Yorkville
• 924-3321

A browser's paradise. A bibliophile can truly lose her/himself here, in this venerable old place that opened its doors nearly a century ago—and some of the staff members have been here nearly a third of that time. The folks who work here are of that breed that is rare nowadays in new-book shops: those who are actually knowledgeable about what they are selling, which is a large general-interest selection of all-new books.
Open Mon.-Sat. 10 a.m.-6 p.m.

The Book Cellar
142 Yorkville Ave.,
Bloor-Yorkville
• 925-9955

A terrific general-interest bookstore, with a special bent toward travel and art books, as well as an impressive slew of international periodicals.
Open Mon.-Sat. 10 a.m.-6 p.m.

Lichtman's
144 Yonge St.,
Downtown
• 368-7390

The real claim to fame here is the world-class assortment of international magazines and newspapers, which are absolutely up-to-date. If you're feeling homesick, or just like to keep up with what's going on all over the globe, you'll have a field day here—there are racks upon racks of mags from utter tabloid trash to erudite intellectual journals. Lichtman's also stocks a general range of books, both nonfiction and fiction, with a decent section on business and computer literature.
Open Mon.-Sat. 9 a.m.-9 p.m., Sun. 9 a.m.-7 p.m.

SPECIALTY

Bakka Science Fiction Book Shoppe
282 Queen St. West,
Downtown
• 596-8161

Canada's largest science-fiction bookshop will make any devotee of the genre very happy. This shop is a real magnet for fantasy/sci-fi fans from all over the world, who revel in Bakka's encyclopedic selection of books and magazines, both new and used.
Open Mon.-Sat. 10 a.m.-6 p.m.

Ballenford Architectural Books
98 Scollard St.,
Bloor-Yorkville
• 960-0055

Canada's foremost bookstore specializing in architecture and design books, Ballenford is designed for the architectural fanatic. You'll find an international selection here, including many obscure and hard-to-find titles on interior and exterior design, landscape and architecture, both on fact and on theory.
Open Mon.-Sat. 10 a.m.-6 p.m.

Children's Bookstore
604 Markham St.,
Bloor-Yorkville
• 535-7011

Located in shop-clogged Mirvish Village (one man's physical embodiment of all that is wonderful about retail—take a bow, Ed Mirvish!), the Children's Bookstore remains one of the largest such shops in North America, housed in an absolutely charming Victorian edifice. Both children and adults will be captivated for hours here.
Open Mon.-Sat. 10 a.m.-6 p.m., Sun. 11 a.m.-6 p.m.

The Cookbook Store
850 Yonge St.,
Bloor-Yorkville
• 920-COOK

The Cookbook Store exudes absolute warmth and friendliness—and we'd be hard-put to name a book dealing with the culinary arts that can't be found here. Book signings by renowned cookbook writers and chefs are a regular occurrence here; and a good selection of food magazines and videotapes is also on hand.
Open Mon.-Sat. 10 a.m.-6 p.m.

Edward's Books & Art
356 Queen St. West,
Downtown
• 593-0126

387 Bloor St. East,
Bloor-Yorkville
• 961-2428

2179 Queen St. East,
Cabbagetown
• 698-1442

A minichain known mainly for its art books, but with an impressive selection of general-interest hardcover and paperback books as well. There are some amazing sales on remaindered books at Edward's, as well as a fine stock of out-of-print titles. A socially relevant note here: Edward's owner is locally famed for his fight to keep his shop open on Sundays, which he battled for successfully, setting a precedent for many Torontonian retailers.
Open daily 10 a.m.-6 p.m.

SHOPS   Books & Newsstands

Gulliver's Travel Bookshop
609 Bloor St. West,
Bloor-Yorkville
• 537-7700

How exactly do you say "Where is the best restaurant in the city?" in Turkish? This is the spot to answer that and even more arcane questions about traveling the world. There are guides and more guides, but don't forget the full range of travel gadgetry as well.
Open Mon.-Fri. 10 a.m.-8 p.m., Sat. 10 a.m.-6 p.m.

International News
370 Yonge St.,
Downtown
• 340-7283

Sample this small store's enormous collection of periodicals, especially if the music biz is your bailiwick. International News offers music magazines from all over the world, from the pop bible, *Billboard* magazine, to obscure thrash metal rags.
Open daily 10 a.m.-midnight.

Mabel's Fables
662 Mt. Pleasant Rd.,
Rosedale
• 322-0438

As adorable as its name, this sweet children's book shop, named after the kitty who resides here, looks simply lovely—and it carries a wonderful array of books and related goodies for kids both small and large.
Mon.-Sat. 10 a.m.-6 p.m.

Open Air Books & Maps
25 Toronto St.,
Downtown
• 363-0719

We've all been bitten by the ecology bug, and this is the right spot to load up on travel books with an eco-slant. Also manuals on the great outdoors, including natural history.
Open Mon.-Fri. 10 a.m.-6 p.m., Sat. 10 a.m.-5:30 p.m.

This Ain't the Rosedale Library
483 Church St.,
Downtown
• 929-9912

As can be evidenced from the irreverent name, this store features an eclectic selection of mostly new books, ranging from politics to jazz to photography to boxing. For sports fans and rock-and-roll buffs, there are collections of both new and used books, including more books on baseball than you've ever seen outside of Cooperstown.
Open Mon.-Sat. 10 a.m.-7 p.m.

Ulysses
101 Yorkville Ave.,
Bloor-Yorkville
• 323-3609

Whether your an accidental tourist–type or a peripatetic traveler, Ulysses contains just about every travel book you can imagine, covering practically every corner of the earth. The staff is quite friendly and knowledgeable—if you can't find something, they'll do their best to get it for you.
Open Mon.-Sat. 10 a.m.-6 p.m.

USED

Abbey Bookshop
89 Harbord St.,
Toronto
• 960-9076

Shouldn't we start calling used books "pre-owned," the same way that salespeople do with automobiles and houses? Pre-owned or not, the collection of books here makes for delicious browsing, especially for collectors of rare editions and those who enjoy the weightier subjects. Abbey stocks a fine collection of philosophy, poetry and theater-related literature.
Open Mon.-Thurs. 11 a.m.-10 p.m., Fri.-Sat. 11 a.m.-midnight, Sun. noon-8 p.m.

Abelard Books
519 Queen St. West,
Downtown
• 366-0021

The choosey come here to marvel at the rare, the first edition, the hard-to-find. It's also a cozy haven in which to lose yourself for the afternoon, in one of the roomy armchairs scattered about the place.
Open Mon.-Wed. & Sat. 10 a.m.-6 p.m., Thurs.-Fri. 10 a.m.-9 p.m., Sun. noon-5 p.m.

CHILDREN

CLOTHES

Bally
Eaton Centre,
290 Yonge St.,
Downtown
• 971-5455

You'll probably blanch when you see the price tags here, unless you happen to be the prince of a rich emirate, but you'll absolutely swoon over the kiddie togs here. Bally is the famous Swiss monger of fine shoes and casual clothing, and the children's line of clothes, shoes, accessories and backpacks is to die for. Fittingly, the bills you'll rack up are to die from. Check the phone book for other locations.
Open Mon.-Fri. 10 a.m.-9 p.m., Sat. 9 a.m.-6 p.m., Sun. noon-5 p.m.

Cotton Basics
162 McCaul St.,
Downtown
• 977-1959

Cotton Basics carries great, everyday, easy-to-care-for kids' clothes that are both inexpensive and fashionable. Made of 100 percent cotton, you'll find sweats, tees, jammies, playsuits and leggings for newborns on up—even for the little ones' parents.
Open Mon.-Sat. 10 a.m.-6 p.m.

SHOPS Children

Dr. Denton
130 Cumberland St.,
Bloor-Yorkville
• 924-0666

Yes, this is the Dr. Denton of drop-seat-pajama fame. Although the good doctor passed on long ago, his legacy remains in this shop for the little ones. Truth be told, the merchandise is a little disappointing—and much more expensive than reason would suggest. There are some cute things here, though, and there is the not inconsiderable nostalgic cachet of the Dr. Denton label.
Open Mon.-Sat. 10 a.m.-6 p.m.

Laura Ashley
18 Hazelton Ave.,
Bloor-Yorkville
• 922-7761

Trying to outfit your kids in an updated Victoriana mode? Laura Ashley, long renowned for its line of women's clothing, bedding and home furnishings, also offers a beautiful line of raiments for little girls, from simple calico frocks to sumptous velvet party dresses with lacy collars.
Open Mon.-Sat. 10 a.m.-6 p.m.

Marci Lipman
231 Avenue Rd.,
Bloor-Yorkville
• 922-7061

Hazelton Lanes,
87 Avenue Rd.,
Bloor-Yorkville
• 921-1998

Here's a real find, featuring adorable cotton sweats, T-shirts, leggings and pajamas for the little ones, with darling, hand-painted animal designs. Prices are reasonable for such original togs, and the quality is quite good.
Open Mon.-Sat. 10 a.m.-6 p.m.

Moving Forward
101 Bloor St. West,
Bloor-Yorkville
• 960-0274

Moving Forward, with its friendly staff and peppy atmosphere, sells an impressive selection of kids and teens Esprit-wear, including trendy casual clothes and accessories. The Esprit credo is stylish duds at popular prices, and that's what you'll find here.
Open Mon.-Sat. 10 a.m.-6 p.m.

FURNITURE

Storkland
3291 Yonge St.,
North Toronto
• 488-1141

A veritable supermarket of kids' home furnishings, decorative goodies, strollers and baby-carriers, as well as toys and clothing. One can spend many hours browsing—and buying—here.
Open Mon.-Sat. 10 a.m.-7 p.m.

TOYS

Kidstuff
738 Bathurst St.,
The Annex
• 535-2212

A kinder, gentler kids' toystore where everything says "soft and squishy"—no heavy metal or artillery allowed. The emphasis is on wonderful stuffed, plush toys, as well as European wooden pull toys, puzzles and lots and lots of art supplies. The staff is terrific here—they truly love kids.
Open Mon.-Sat. 10 a.m.-6 p.m.

Science City, Jr.
50 Bloor St. West,
Bloor-Yorkville
• 968-2627

The grownups have their own branch of Science City across the way from this shop; this one really gives brainy, deductive-reasoning-type juveniles a run for their mind. Heck, you don't even have to be a science nerd to have a blast here—there are lots of games, kites, model sets and all manner of dinosaur stuff among the science and chemistry kits here.
Open Mon.-Sat. 10 a.m.-6 p.m.

The Toy Shop
62 Cumberland St.,
Bloor-Yorkville
• 961-4870

One of Toronto's most venerable toy stores, this double-decker shop features a jaw-dropping selection of Madame Alexander historical dolls, educational toys, gorgeously detailed doll houses, stuffed animals of every stripe, color and breed, and row upon row of just toys, toys, toys.
Open Mon.-Sat. 10 a.m.-6 p.m.

CLOTHES & JEWELRY

ACCESSORIES

Accessity
136 Cumberland St.,
Bloor-Yorkville
• 972-1855

This cool, hip shop has a fabulous selection of men's and women's accessories ranging from slouchy hats and nutty neckties to belts, purses, scarves, crazy socks, hand-wrought jewelry by Lisa Jenks and lots of goodies with which to artfully bind ones hair. There are also sunglasses by chic accessories mongers such as Persol and Jean-Paul Gaultier, among others, and the staff is bubbly, friendly and helpful.
Open Mon.-Wed. & Sat. 10 a.m.-6 p.m., Thurs.-Fri. 10 a.m.-7 p.m.

Eddie Bauer
50 Bloor St.,
Bloor-Yorkville
• 961-2525

The stalwart Eddie Bauer shops stays absolutely in tune with the more austere, utilitarian times we're in; now that it's positively de trop to parade one's riches around on one's back, and with *Twin Peaks*-inspired Northwest chic all the rage, the outdoorsy items sold at Eddie Bauer look just right. You'll find everything from porkpie hats to compasses to jackknives, heavy socks and down vests. This is the kind of store that inspires you to venture out on a camping or hiking trip, even if you've never been outside of a climate-controlled building before.
Open Mon.-Sat. 10 a.m.-7 p.m.

SHOPS Clothes & Jewelry

The General Store
Hazelton Lanes,
87 Avenue Rd.,
Bloor-Yorkville
• 323-1527

This ain't your granddad's general store, no siree. This shop's a sort of consumer's digest of all that's cool and superfluous for the home and office: a digital grill for indoor barbecuing, desktop high-tech toys, ultra-expensive, ultra-trendy Alessi kitchenware, Mont Blanc and Porsche pens—the true power tools of the modern executive—and various other let-them-eat-cake gadgets for those with money to burn—even in these tough times.
Open Mon.-Sat. 10 a.m.-6 p.m.

Hermès
Hazelton Lanes,
87 Avenue Rd.,
Bloor-Yorkville
• 968-8626

The tony, French House of Hermès has recently received a shot in the arm, by hiring new designers, waging a spectacular ad campaign, and offering a younger sensibility to it's former line. Hermès's costly clothing, accessories and gardening wares are some of the hottest status-symbols one can own these days: more expensive than Chanel and supremely more desirable than has-been Gucci (despite the current attempt at an image overhaul), with the added cachet of being nuttily over-the-top with its campy, horsey designs. The men's ties and women's scarves are true classics, and this shop has scads of these silken strips.
Open Mon.-Sat. 10 a.m.-6 p.m.

Karir
2 Bloor St. West,
Bloor-Yorkville
• 975-0536

This beautiful, chic eyeglass/optician's shop done up in sleek marble looks small, yet carries a well-selected stock of stylish rims for those who need their visual acuity assisted. There are frames by Armani, Alain Mikli, Gianni Versace and others; Frank Nacci is the personable optician on the premises.
Open Mon.-Sat. 10 a.m.-6 p.m.

The Yorkviller
75 Yorkville Ave.,
Bloor-Yorkville
• 921-9229

This rather eccentric yet wonderful spot carries men's sportswear and swimwear, but the real deal is the amazingly exotically simple imported underwear offered. Lines carried here are Hom, Kirtos, and Eminence. But the best stuff for bottoms here is made by Scheisser—underwear with an almost fetishistic, Germanic edge to it. If Albert Speer had designed unmentionables, these would be the result.
Open Mon.-Sat. 10 a.m.-6 p.m.

JEWELRY

Beni Sung
Creeds Department Store,
45 Bloor St. West,
Bloor-Yorkville
• 923-1000

The jewels designed by Beni Sung are quite original and beautifully crafted, and for the most part, quite expensive. Pearls and semiprecious stones are what these desings are based on; if you admire and collect the unique in bijoux, this designer is for you.
Open Mon.-Sat. 10 a.m.-6 p.m.

SHOPS Clothes & Jewelry

Cartier
111 Bloor St. West,
Bloor-Yorkville
• 967-0700

For many of those who collect serious pieces, there is Cartier and only Cartier. This fabulous jeweler carries the weight of its illustrious history proudly and with great aplomb—after all, the House of Cartier has created jewels for royalty both on the throne and in exile, for women who collect world-class jewels, and for men who collect world-class women. Granted, the classic triple-band rolling ring can be had for under Can$400, and the simple tank watch is a classic, but is that really what we peer into Cartier's windows for? Whether you're a browser or a buyer, there's something almost mystical about the flawless creations wrought of platinum, gold, emeralds, diamonds and rubies here—something almost atavistic. It's all part of the Cartier gestalt. The staff here is remarkably free of snobby attitudes—they seem happy to have you as a customer whether you're purchasing a trifling piece of leather for Can$75 or a chorus-girl bracelet for Can$250,000.
Open Mon.-Sat. 10 a.m.-5:30 p.m.

18 Karat
71 McCaul St.,
Bloor-Yorkville
• 593-1648

Got a design in your head and money in your pocket? The craftsfolks here will probably be able to take your creation from an idea to a finished work.
Open Mon.-Wed. & Sat. 10 a.m.-6 p.m., Thurs.-Fri. 10 a.m.-9 p.m.

European Jewellery
111 Bloor St. West,
Bloor-Yorkville
• 967-7201

European Jewellery (sic) carries original designs utilizing precious and semiprecious stones, pearls—you name it. They have models you can choose from an already-existing portfolio, or you can design your own pricey baubles. There is also a good selection of expensive watches, including Cartier, Baume et Mercier and Rolex.
Open Mon.-Sat. 10 a.m.-6 p.m.

Fabrice
Hazelton Lanes,
87 Avenue Rd.,
Bloor-Yorkville
• 967-6590

Have a yen for fun jewelry? enter Fabrice, a real candy-shop for gem lovers. The designs are original and well-executed; there is costume stuff as well as pieces crafted of silver, gold and semi-precious stones. Wonderfully creative, and the prices aren't bad.
Open Mon.-Sat. 10 a.m.-6 p.m.

KSP Jewellery
Hazelton Lanes,
87 Avenue Rd.,
Bloor-Yorkville
• 922-4100

What was the sincerest form of flattery, did you say? KSP carries terrifically fabulous fakes, starting at prices as low as Can$25. Designs range from fairly simple to rather opulent, yet it is all quite fashionable and well-made.
Open Mon.-Sat. 10 a.m.-6 p.m.

SHOPS Clothes & Jewelry

Lumière
559 1/2 Queen St. West,
Downtown
• 360-6550

Lumière offers absolutely original jewelry crafted from stained glass. Though not to everyone's taste, these beautifully-crafted earrings, necklaces, bracelets and accessories are quite remarkable, the colorful glass accented with brass, silverplate and/or copper. The pieces are amazingly inexpensive—and these are things you won't see adorning every other person on the street.
Open Mon.-Sat. 10:30 a.m.-6:30 p.m.

Staccato
290A Queen St. West,
Downtown
• 971-5215

Fun, avant-garde jewelry designs, at reasonble prices. Lots of glass beads, gold and silver plate rendered into earrings, rings, bracelets and necklaces.
Open Mon.-Sat. 10:30 a.m.-6:30 p.m.

MENSWEAR

Alan Goouch
89 Bloor St. West,
Bloor-Yorkville
• 964-8395

If you're a gent that looks for forward fashion, but not so forward that you're out of style by the time you wear a new garment for the first time, you're the perfect customer for Alan Goouch's wonderful selection of very handsome, modern clothes by Europe's top menswear designers. The lines carried here include Byblos, Kenzo, Paul Smith and Hugo Boss, as well as accessories (socks, ties and the like) from the whimsical/retro Modules line.
Open Mon.-Sat. 10 a.m.-6 p.m.

Boomer
309 Queen St. West,
Downtown
• 598-0013

Despite this store's rather obnoxious name, it carries an impressive selection of au courant men's clothing, by designers both local and international. Some of the labels seen here are Thalie, the very excellent Hoax, Couture and Babel, as well as accessories by Gaultier.
Open Mon.-Sat. 10:30 a.m.-7 p.m., Sun. 1 p.m.-5 p.m.

Club Monaco
403 Queen St. West,
Downtown
• 979-5633

Though Club Monaco also sells women's and children's clothing, we think the most successful goods here are in the men's line. Now a successful chain with branches worldwide, this company is the brainchild of celebrated local designer Alfred Sung; the workable theory here seems to be to design Polo-style sportswear and sell it at Esprit prices. Lots of outerwear, polo and rugby shirts, cotton sweaters and chinos, as well as leather accessories.
Open Mon.-Wed. 10 a.m.-7 p.m., Thurs.-Fri. 10 a.m.-9 p.m., Sat. 10 a.m.-6 p.m., Sun. noon-5 p.m.

SHOPS   Clothes & Jewelry

Emporio Armani
80 Bloor St. West,
Bloor-Yorkville
• 920-0657

This sleek, chic and very classy store is home to Giorgio Armani's more youthful, lower-priced Emporio line. While there's much in the way of suits, topcoats and even tuxes here, the focus is on sportswear: great jeans, sweatshirts, tees, and casual jackets and shirts, as well as underwear, bodycare products, and household tchochkes. This may be Armani's tertiary line (Mani is the secondary men's collection), but this doesn't necessarily mean the clothes come particularly cheap here: expect to pay about Can$100 for a pair of jeans. The styles are terrific, though, as is the staff.
Open Mon.-Sat. 10 a.m.-6 p.m., Sun. noon-6 p.m.

Harry Rosen
82 Bloor St. West,
Bloor-Yorkville
• 972-0556

A Toronto tradition for men, Harry Rosen's first-rate shop has been clothing gentlemen in sartorial splendor since 1954 out of this, his flagship store (there are other branches around town). The cozy, men's-clubby feel here is quite attractive, as are the Ralph Lauren, Armani, and Hugo Boss clothes Rosen carries. There's also a good selection of casual, sporty things, as well as shoes, underwear and haberdashery.
Open Mon.-Sat. 10 a.m.-9 p.m

Hoax
450 Queen St. West,
Downtown
• 864-9855

This fabulous, Gothic-Moderne boutique features original designs by owners Jim Searle and Chris Tyrell; if you're into beautifully made, forward-looking clothes, Hoax is a must. You won't see these clothes coming and going on everyone in the street; everything is made in a limited edition. Fabrics are sumptuous, the workmanship divine, and the designs are different without being too way-out. The shop itself is a haven of minimalist luxury; it reflects the clothing sold here.
Open Sat.-Wed. 11 a.m.-7 p.m., Thurs.-Fri. 11 a.m.-9 p.m.

Kimina
448 Queen St. West,
Downtown
• 362-1081

Minimalist Japanese, Comme des Garçons–like clothing, with soft, draping lines. The menswear here is very easy fitting, with the emphasis on dark colors and wonderful fabrics.
Open Mon.-Sat. 10:30 a.m.-5 p.m.

Mari Boutique
110 Yorkville Ave.,
Bloor-Yorkville
• 961-1302

This is a roundup of the usual stars of the Japanese clothing world: Mari carries a good selection of Issey Miyake, Yoshi Yamamoto and Commes des Garçons for men.
Open Mon.-Sat. 10:30 a.m.-6 p.m.

Polo/Ralph Lauren
Hazelton Lanes,
87 Avenue Rd.,
Bloor-Yorkville
• 968-8686

A Polo shop is a Polo shop is Polo shop, but the staff's friendlier here than at most of the others we've ever visited. And this is the largest Polo shop in Canada. Ralph Lauren has made quite a cottage industry of co-opting the moneyed WASP look, and although we think you don't quite get value for money where his goods are concerned (for the prices charged, we think that

SHOPS Clothes & Jewelry

the clothing in particular should be better made, and out of finer fabrics), but who are we to argue with billion-dollar success? The full line of menswear is carried here, from socks to loafers to braces and hacking jackets, and the shirts are undeniably handsome.
Open Mon.-Sat. 10 a.m.-6 p.m.

Studio 267
55 Bloor St. West,
Bloor-Yorkville
• 366-4452

If you prefer your menswear on the conservative side, you can't miss at Studio 267. The more sedate models by Armani, Hugo Boss, Valentino and Bugatti can be found here, and the staff is most helpful at putting things together for you.
Open Mon.-Sat. 9:30 a.m.-6 p.m.

Yukata
687 Yonge St.,
Downtown
• 972-0943

As stark and arresting architecturally as a Frank Lloyd Wright concrete-block house, Yukata, owned by a pair of brothers, Stephen and Thomas Chan, stuns—a classically modern boutique with classically modern clothes from Japan. The main designer here is Homme Comme des Dansens, and while the clothes here are not for the insecure, neither are they too crazy-looking. The store itself has a wonderful atmosphere, and the folks who work here are quite helpful.
Open Mon.-Wed. & Sat. 11 a.m.-7 p.m., Thurs.-Fri. 11 a.m.-9 p.m.

Yushi
162 Cumberland St.,
Renaissance Court,
Bloor-Yorkville
• 923-9874

This is a cool kinda store for cool kinda guys (and women, too): the best of the avant-garde in menswear, almost exclusively Japanese can be found at Yushi, including duds by Matsuda, Issey Miyake, Plantation (Miyake's less expensive line), Tokio Kumagai and Windcoat.
Open Mon.-Wed. & Sat. 10 a.m.- 6 p.m., Thurs.-Fri. 10 a.m.-8 p.m.

WOMENSWEAR

Bodywear
25 Bellair St.,
Bloor-Yorkville
• 968-2277

As the name implies, Bodywear specializes in exercise togs—although these days, workout garb does double-duty as daywear. Lots of leggings, leotards, lycra T-shirts, skirts and other casual wear by Dance France, Danskin, as well as a large number of Betsey Johnson's youthful, body-hugging designs for day and evening.
Open Mon.-Sat. 10 a.m.-6 p.m.

SHOPS Clothes & Jewelry

Bretton's
Manulife Centre,
55 Bloor St. West,
Bloor-Yorkville
• 975-9097

This newish store is notable mainly for its excellent selection of Canadian designer wares. While you'll find conservative American and European lines such as Liz Claiborne, Carole Little, Albert Nipon and Mondi, there are lots of items by locals such as Alfred Sung, Debora Kuchme, Tu Ly and Wayne Clark. There's an area devoted to some beautiful evening wear, and Bretton's is also the exclusive Canadian outlet for the excellent line of Molton Brown cosmetics and skincare products.
Open Mon.-Sat. 10 a.m.-6 p.m.

Chanel
131 Bloor St. West,
Bloor-Yorkville
• 925-2577

Here's one of the friendliest Chanel Boutiques we've encountered, and we've shopped or browsed in virtually all of them. Madame Coco's imprimatur infuses the shop—all fawn-colored suede, chrome and black lacquer—and there's a fabulous selection of handbags, shoes, jewelry, belts and other iconic Chanel accessories, as well as the full line of ready-to-wear. The array of merchandise here is impressive, and so is the friendly staff.
Open Mon.-Sat. 10 a.m.-6 p.m.

Donna Elena
162 Cumberland St.,
Bloor-Yorkville
• 962-6860

A chic shop, located in the chic-est of neighborhoods, which has a hushed elegance, yet the staff is extremely helpful and friendly. You'll find the big name European designers here, including Armani, Luisa via Roma and Erreuno, with styles running to the more conservative end of the spectrum. Donna Elena carries everything from casual (yet classy-casual) wear to evening togs, with an emphasis on beautiful day dresses and suits.
Open Mon.-Sat. 10 a.m.-6 p.m.

Emily Zarb
278 Queen St. West,
Downtown
• 979-8938

Original designs are the name of the game here, most with a touch of the romantic. The focus is on natural fabrics, and you'll find everything from daywear to very fancy evening frocks.
Open Mon.-Sat. 10 a.m.-6 p.m.

Emporio Armani
80 Bloor St. West,
Bloor-Yorkville
• 920-0657

This cool, Milanese-style place, two-level shop offers Signore Armani's youthful, lower-priced line, Emporio. While these clothes are by no means cheap, jackets here run from Can$300 to Can$400, as opposed to Can$1,200 to Can$1,500 in the Black Label couture line. The staff is infectiously friendly, and this is really a soup-to-nuts shop: jeans, sportswear, eveningwear, underwear, outerwear, toiletries, shoes, accessories, candles and various desk-top tchotchkes. Don't forget to commemorate your visit by purhasing one of the signature Emporio T-shirts, an oversize, cotton number emblazoned with an arty photo in the front, and the city name and date printed on the back. They change yearly, and one can make a rather

SHOPS Clothes & Jewelry

globe-trotting hobby of collecting these from the various Emporio locations.
Open Mon.-Sat. 10 a.m.-6 p.m., Sun. noon-6 p.m.

Fab
274 Queen St. West,
Downtown
• 979-7813

Cute, youthful separates and dresses by local designers, very well-priced.
Open Mon.-Sat. 10 a.m.-6 p.m.

Ferragamo
131 Bloor St. West,
Bloor-Yorkville
• 964-9561

Though Ferragamo's exquisitely made Italian designs are a bit too staid for us, the clothing styles have loosened up a bit over the past few years, and of course, the shoes and accessories have been classics for years. This shop features the full panoply of Ferragamo designs—clothes, shoes, bags and other accessories.
Open Mon.-Sat. 10 a.m.-6 p.m.

Georges Rech
Hazelton Lanes,
87 Avenue Rd.,
Bloor-Yorkville
• 969-9034

Hazelton Lanes suggests kind of an enclosed version of Beverly Hills' Rodeo Drive, populated with lots of chic, expensive stores. One of the nicest is Georges Rech, which features beautifully-made knockoffs of clothes by designers such as Genny and Armani, and while expensive, they're still cheaper than the above labels. Service is extremely friendly and knowledgable.
Open Mon.-Wed. & Fri.-Sat. 10 a.m.-6 p.m., Thurs. 10 a.m.-8 p.m.

Giorgio
153 Cumberland St.,
Bloor-Yorkville
• 963-5052

We'd like to sing the praises of Toronto's Giorgio. This shop is all sleek concrete, wood and glass, hushed and tiptoe-y, except for the moderne music issuing forth from hidden speakers. As befits a temple of avant-garde clothing, the staff is hoplessly more svelte and better-dressed than most human beings you've ever known, but somehow they're not intimidating. The labels read like a Who's Who of forward fashion: Jean-Paul Gaultier, Moschino, Kenzo, Rifat Ozbek, as well as more classic masters like Armani and Gianfranco Ferrè. And if you're lucky enough to happen upon a sale here, you'll be well rewarded: we found a fabulous, mustard-colored Gaultier riding jacket (of a fabric not found in nature—on any planet) that had retailed for Can$850, marked down to Can$250. Quel bargain!
Open Mon.-Wed. & Sat. 9:30 a.m.-6 p.m., Thurs.-Fri. 9:30 a.m.-9 p.m.

Hoax
456 Queen St. West,
Downtown
• 864-9855

We fervently hope that the magnificent clothes at Hoax find their way south of the Canadian border soon; we've become addicts. The shop itself looks small, done in neo-Gothic Moderne, and the staff is so friendly and chatty, you kind of want to hang out here for hours. But let's get down to the nitty-gritty:

SHOPS Clothes & Jewelry

the clothes are fantastic. All are original designs by the shop's owners, Jim Searle and Chris Tyrell, a talented pair of gents who know their way around a dress form. The styles run to fitted jackets, slim, short skirts and tiny dresses that could probably fit into a minaudière, as well as trousers and suits. These clothes are beautifully made out of luxurious fabrics; all garments are fully lined and finished with intricate handwork. You don't find too many garments made like this anymore, unless you happen to frequent the Parisian ateliers of *trés-haute* couturiers. For the quality and style you'll find here, prices are quite reasonable (average jacket: Can$500); there are also some terrific T-shirts and accessories. Hoax is a real find, and a true original.
Open Mon.-Wed. & Sat. 11 a.m.-7 p.m., Thurs.-Fri. 11 a.m.-9 p.m.

Josaly
559 Queen St. West,
Downtown
• 594-1447

If *Breakfast at Tiffany* is your favorite film, and Audrey Hepburn your role model, you'll find the wardrobe for the movie in your mind at Josaly. The shop itself is very unprepossessing, but don't let that turn you off. The designs here are original, very kicky, very French, very sixties (with some Depression-era styles thrown in for good measure). Just get a little black dress here, wrap a chiffon scarf round your tousled hair, complete with a pair of black sunglasses, and voila! Bardot redux!
Open Mon.-Sat. 10:30 a.m.-6:30 a.m.

Max Mara
131 Bloor St. West,
Bloor-Yorkville
• 927-9975

The compleat Max Mara can be found here; fans of this midpriced Italian designer will have a field day in this shop, featuring Mara's conservative-yet-youthful styles, with the emphasis on separates and daywear. There are also lot of accessories here, and the shop also carries Mara's less expensive, younger Pennybank line.
Open Mon.-Wed. & Fri.-Sat. 10 a.m.-6 p.m., Thurs. 10 a.m.-8 p.m.

Pam Chorley Fashion Crimes
395 Queen St. West,
Downtown
• 592-9001

If you're young, hip and have a well-exercised bod, Fashion Crimes carries lots of cute, kicky, figure-conscious styles by Betsey Johnson, as well as a slew of original designs, executed here. Prices are quite reasonable, too.
Open daily 9 a.m.-4:30 p.m.

Parade
557 Queen St. West,
Downtown
• 868-6789

It's a groove thang at Parade—young, cute clothes for young, cute people. Local designers are well-represented here, as are international lines like Street Life, In Wear and Big Fish. Lots of cottons, washed silk and stretchy stuff, all reasonably priced.
Open Mon.-Sat. 10:30 a.m.-6 p.m., Sun. 1 p.m.-6 p.m.

SHOPS Clothes & Jewelry

Pink House
81 Yorkville Ave.,
Bloor-Yorkville
• 921-6821

Pink House, a small boutique, features original versions of sleek, avant-garde clothes—very Japanese in concept. However, the styles don't really get too outre, and prices are quite fair.
Open Mon.-Sat. 10 a.m.-6 p.m.

Price Roman
267 Queen St. West,
Downtown
• 979-7363

To what do we attribute the recent rage for Sixties' fashions? Is it the uptight-yet-something's-abrewing political climate? Is it models such as Claudia Schiffer, all dolled up in those Guess? Jeans ads? Whatever the cause may be, the Sixties and Seventies are the decades being cannibalized, style-wise right now (oh oh—the years are gaining on us; are we going to have to reach all the way back to medieval influences next?), and there are lots of shops in Toronto to service those who are acolytes of The Look. Price Roman is one of them, offering some very cute clothes and low prices.
Open Mon.-Sat. 10:30 a.m.-7 p.m., Sun. noon-6 p.m. (Call first; opening time can vary).

Sportables
55 Bloor St. West,
Bloor-Yorkville
• 967-4122

As the name of the store implies, Sportables carries all that's breezy and stylish for outdoorsy girls or simply women on the go. If you cherish that casual, understated, haute-WASP look, this shop carries scads of Ralph Lauren, Calvin Klein and J.G. Hook separates.
Open daily 10 a.m.-6 p.m.

290 Ion
290 Queen St. West,
Downtown
• 596-7296

290 Ion features adorably hip separates by local designers, those great, floppy, forties-style washed silk shirts by Equipment, and some of the most glamorously nutty costume jewelry we've seen in a long time.
Open Mon.-Sat. 10 a.m.-7 p.m.

Vivian Shyu
104 Yorkville Ave.,
Bloor-Yorkville
• 967-4878

We'd love to see Vivian Shyu's wares in the States; we entered the shop in search of refuge from the rain and walked out with several bagfuls of goodies. The staff is simply wonderful, and so are the clothes: Ms. Shyu takes her cues from the world's top forward-fashion designers, such as Azzedine Alaïa, Romeo Gigli, Issey Miyake and Jean-Paul Gaultier, yet adds her own original twists. All the clothes here are made in limited editions in Canada, out of custom-made fabrics from Italy. When the fabric runs out, so does that particular run. The clothes are very well made, and the materials are truly sumptuous. We particularly fell in love with the jackets, and the pair of silky, cut-velvet black leggings we bought have received more wear—and compliments—than any item of clothing we currently own. This shop is a must, and the prices are very reasonable.
Open Mon.-Sat. 10 a.m.-6 p.m.

SHOPS Clothes & Jewelry

Yushi
162 Cumberland St.,
Renaissance Court,
Bloor-Yorkville
• 923-9874

Yushi's the place for those who adore modern Japanese fashion. The designers represented here are Issey Miyake (both his Miyake and Plantation lines), Hiroko Koshano, Matsuda and Tokio Kumagai.
Open Mon.-Wed. & Sat. 11 a.m.-6 p.m., Thurs.-Fri. 10 a.m.-8 p.m.

SHOES

Bally
50 Bloor St. West,
Bloor-Yorkville
• 924-4772

Bally shoes need no introduction; obviously, this isn't the place for those into winkle-pickers or Doc Martens. As everyone into footwear knows, the Swiss styles here for men and women reflect the character of their country of origin: practical, sturdy and simply styled. Oh, and expensive.
Open Mon.-Sat. 10 a.m.-6 p.m.

Capezio
70 Bloor St. West,
Bloor-Yorkville
• 920-1006

For years and years, Capezio has been the footwear of choice among dancers and the genteely hip; it still is. Famous for their soft leather shoes and tote bags, Capezio goods are well-priced and well made.
Open Mon.-Sat. 10 a.m.-6 p.m.

David's
66 Bloor St. West,
Bloor-Yorkville
• 920-1000

David's remains widely regarded as the premiere bootery in Toronto, and we have no reason to dispute this premise. This lovely shop features imported footwear by the biggest names in shoedom, like Andrea Pfister, Maud Frizon, Walter Steiger, Bruno Magli, Charles Jourdan and Anne Klein. There's also a huge selection of boots, private label shoes, and a terrific offering of men's shoes, too.
Open Mon.-Wed. & Fri.-Sat. 9 a.m.-6 p.m., Thurs. 9 a.m.-9 p.m.

Ferragamo
131 Bloor St. West,
Bloor-Yorkville
• 964-9561

This shop carries Salvatore Ferragamo's (well, his successor's, in any case) women's clothes, too, but the shoes are the real draw here. If you're addicted to sheathing your tootsies in his smart, conservative shoes with their trademark grosgrain bows, you can really go to town in this well-stocked shop.
Open Mon.-Sat. 10 a.m.-6 p.m.

Specchio
77 Bloor St. West,
Bloor-Yorkville
• 961-7989

Specchio offers cute, trendy Italian shoes, mostly knockoffs of big-name, expensive labels. Also carried here are some very fashionable purses.
Open Mon.-Sat. 10 a.m.-7 p.m.

DEPARTMENT STORES & SHOPPING CENTERS

The Bay
Bay St. & Bloor St. West,
Bloor-Yorkville
• 928-3407

The Bay is the most low-rent of the Torontonian department stores; it's akin to Alexander's on the East Coast of the States, and the May Co. on the West Coast. There are several branches, and this downtown flagship store is the main one. You'll find everything from housewares to clothing to gadgets and cosmetics—the usual gang of department-store suspects. This isn't the place to find cutting-edge or finely made clothes, but if you're looking for kid's stuff, inexpensive gifts or items for the home, you do have a lot to choose from here.
Open Mon.-Wed. 10 a.m.-7 p.m., Thurs.-Fri. 10 a.m.-9 p.m., Sat. 10 a.m.-6 p.m., Sun. noon-5 p.m.

Eaton's
Eaton Centre,
290 Yonge St.,
Downtown
• 343-2111

Located in the gargantuan Eaton Centre, and part of an enormous Canadian chain, this is the Eaton's flagship store—what else could it be with over one million square feet of necessary luxuries and luxurious necessities? Comparable to Bloomingdale's, Eaton's offers just about everything of quality for just about everyone with money.
Open Mon.-Fri. 10 a.m.-9 p.m., Sat. 9:30 a.m.-7 p.m., Sun. noon-5 p.m.

Eaton Centre
Yonge & Dundas Sts.,
Downtown

This immense shopping mall remains quite daunting—it's one of those places that is disorienting in its hugeness, where you feel as though you could spend days and still not be able to find the exit. Eaton Centre is Toronto's largest tourist attraction, and that's understandable; there are some very good shops here, and the mall radiates with a commercial energy, appealing to men, women, children and probably even space aliens. Among the more than 300 shops here are Club Monaco, Rodier, Marks & Spencer and Bennetton. The glass-atrium look makes Eaton Centre a very pleasant zillion acres to shop in, and while you're resting in between sprees, take special note of the wonderful Michael Snow fiberglass sculpture of graceful Canadian geese that soars above.
Open daily 10 a.m.-9 p.m.

SHOPS Department Stores & Shopping Centers

Hazelton Lanes
Avenue & Yorkville Rds.,
Bloor-Yorkville

Hazelton Lanes can be called the Rodeo Drive–cum–Madison Avenue of Toronto, albeit an enclosed one. We love the stores here, but we find there's something oppressive about the architecture; is it because there's not enough openness? Not enough light? In any case, Hazelton is an upscale shopper's dream: Aquascutum, Alfred Sung, Basile, Cerruti 1881, Chez Catherine, Club Monaco, Crabtree & Evelyn, Fogal, Gianni Versace, Joan & David, Polo/Ralph Lauren, Teuscher, Turnbull & Asser, Valentino, Yves St. Laurent and much, much more.
Open daily 10 a.m.-9 p.m.

Holt Renfrew
50 Bloor St. West,
Bloor-Yorkville
• 922-2333

Holt Renfrew, the crème-de-la-crème of Toronto's department stores; for that matter, it would be a ultra-first-class emporium no matter where it the world it was located. The spiritual kin of Neiman-Marcus and Bergdorf Goodman (Holt was actually owned by the same company that owns the aforementioned stores until fairly recently), Holt Renfrew carries the absolute best on each of its four floors; its absolute Nirvana for the discerning shopper. The selection of costume jewelry here is superb; so are the men's departments, especially the exquisite nook dedicated to sumptuous Turnbull & Asser shirts. For women, every top name in fashion is represented: Christian Lacroix, Isaac Mizrahi, Calvin Klein, Michael Kors, Donna Karan, Jean-Paul Gaultier, Yves St. Laurent, and Moschino. Plus, there's a complete-separate-but-attached Giorgio Armani boutique. There's also an Alfred Sung boutique, and a wonderful tablewear department on the top floor, nestled next to Holt's terrific café. For dedicated followers of fashion who love to be pampered, Holt Renfrew is a must-go destination.

Remember when shopping that prices are in Canadian dollars, and therefore slightly lower, in U.S. dollars, than they appear. At press time, the rate was roughly Can$1 to U.S.90 cents.

Open Mon.-Wed. & Sat. 10 a.m.-6 p.m., Thurs. & Fri. 10 a.m.-9 p.m.

Simpson's
Queen & Yonge Sts.,
Downtown
• 861-9111

A notch up in quality from Eaton's, Simpson's (also located in Eaton Centre) does offer a pretty good sampling of trendy designer clothes, such as Ozbek and Moschino.
Open Mon.-Tues. 10 a.m.-7 p.m., Wed., Thurs. & Fri. 10 a.m.-9 p.m., Sat. 9:30 a.m.-6 p.m., Sun. noon-5 p.m.

FOOD

Dufflet Pastries
77 Queen St. West,
Downtown
• 368-1812

If you've eaten a "bussed-in" cake or tarte at any of Toronto's restaurants, chances are that it sprang to life right here. The best-seller remains the chocolate-rasberry truffle. Those who love cake as an art form need look no further.
Open Tues.-Thurs. & Sat. 10 a.m.-6 p.m., Fri. 10 a.m.-8 p.m.

Kensington Market
Baldwin, Kensington
& Augusta Aves.
• No phone

Here's a real Toronto happening, where you can find all sorts of ethnic food goodies as you stroll the chockablock streets. Stalls full of specialties are mostly Jewish, Portuguese and Asian, with a dash of Mexican.
Open daily 9 a.m.-9 p.m.

Ten Ren Tea
454 Dundas St. West,
Chinatown
• 598-7872

Did someone say "Tea Time?" A trip down to this neat shop in Chinatown will wow you with the assortment of teas. But hold on to your wallet, you could spend as much as Can$160 per box! You can also buy something to brew it in.
Open daily 10:30 a.m.-7 p.m.

GIFTS & HOUSEWARES

At My Table
Queen's Quay
Terminal,
207 Queen's Quay
West,
Harbourfront
• 861-1750

This lovely shop sells—guess what?—all manner of goodies with which to set a beautiful table. But aside from tablecloths, dinnerware, glassware and flatware, you'll also find some gorgeous bedding, dried floral arrangements and gift baskets.
Open daily 10 a.m.-6 p.m.

Canadiana Shoppe
Eaton Centre,
290 Yonge St.,
Downtown
• 977-6547

Want to bring home examples of local crafts, art and other gift items? You'll find lots of Indian crafts, sculptures, prints and dolls here, and prices are reasonable.
Open Mon.-Fri. 10 a.m.-9 p.m., Sat. 9:30 a.m.-6 p.m., Sun. noon-5 p.m.

SHOPS   Gifts & Housewares

Le Caprice de Marie-Claude
Renaissance Plaza,
150 Bloor St. West,
Bloor-Yorkville
• 921-5119

This wonderful little bed-and-bath shop sells luxurious bedding, towels and robes, mostly by Frette and Descamps—the kind that make you want to lounge around in bed with a box of Godiva bonbons for the rest of your life.
Open Mon.-Sat. 9:30 a.m.-6 p.m.

Chris & Frog Emporium
College Park,
444 Yonge St.,
Downtown
• 595-7266

This absolutely enchanting shop delights both kids and adults; we were initially attracted to it by its window display, consisting of piles and piles of little stuffed pink pigs, along with lots of festive balloons. Inside, you'll find lots of other toys, stuffed and otherwise, cards, and other wonderful gift items.
Open Mon.-Fri. 10 a.m.-6 p.m.

Du Verre
307 Queen St. West,
Downtown
• 593-0182

Du Verre offers the best, newest and trendiest in glassware—no fuddy-duddy cut crystal here! Their specialty is sandblasted glass items, and they will also custom-sandblast designs into glass for you. There are some beautiful and whimsical ceramic plates, bowls and vases here, as well.
Open Mon.-Sat. 10 a.m.-6 p.m.

Geomania
50 Bloor St. West,
Bloor-Yorkville
• 920-1420

Geomania, as one may surmise, really rocks: this is a virtual treasure trove of jewelry and gift items composed of rocks, crystal, geodes, and various fossilized stuff. Kids love this place, too.
Open Mon.-Wed. & Sat. 10 a.m.-6 p.m., Thurs.-Fri. 10 a.m.-9 p.m.

Georg Jensen
95-A Bloor St. West,
Bloor-Yorkville
• 924-7707

We love Georg Jensen's clean, elegant and beautifully detailed designs; when we grow up and get rich, we want to buy his magnificent "Cactus" pattern flatware—which sells for a cool grand a place-setting. And the Flora Danica dinnerware is a collection to be reckoned with. If you cherish Scandinavian design, Jensen's has the best of it; his brushed silver mesh watch is a classic. You'll find enough furniture, jewelry and tableware to leave you gasping with desire for a while; the gentle, helpful staff understands.
Open Mon.-Sat. 10 a.m.-6 p.m.

SHOPS Gifts & Housewares

Irish Shop
110 Bloor St. West,
Bloor-Yorkville
• 922-9400

If you're lured by the call of Caledonia, and are a Celt at heart, the Irish Shop will make you weep with joy. The goods are first-class here, including beautiful linens (including linen shirts for men), handcrafted sweaters, and books which pertain to all that is Irish.
Open Mon.-Wed. & Sat. 10 a.m.-6 p.m., Thurs.-Fri. 10 a.m.-7 p.m.

Kensington Silver Studio
502 Queen St. West,
Kensington Market
• 862-7306

You'll be dazzled by the well-chosen selection of gift items and jewelry, handmade by local artisans, of sterling silver and semi-precious stones.
Open Mon.-Sat. 10 a.m.-6 p.m.

Museum + Design
161 Cumberland St.,
Bloor-Yorkville
• 969-9360

The sleek, functional high-tech items at Museum + Design are akin to what you'll find at the Museum of Modern Art's shops, or at the California chain, By Design. Goods are well-priced here, making this a great place to buy gifts for your more groovy friends.
Open Mon.-Sat. 10 a.m.-6 p.m., Sun. noon-6 p.m.

Richardson's Tartan Shop
546 Yonge St.,
Downtown
• 922-3141

This shop could be subtitled, "Death By Plaid"; we absolutely fell in love with it, and we've never particularly thought of ourselves as Scotsophiles. This shop is so friendly and homey, though, you'll surely be seduced. What you'll find on the cozy shelves and nooks here are kilts, books, clan-crested jewelry, coffee mugs, zillions of tartans, bagpipe accessories (you have to special-order the pipes themselves), sporrans, ties, Balmoral caps and all manner of Scottish sweetmeats, books, tapes, and so on—until you're tipsy from too much Scotch!
Open Mon.-Sat. 9:30 a.m.-6 p.m.

William Ashley
50 Bloor St. West,
Bloor-Yorkville
• 964-2900

Call Ashley's the Geary's of Toronto, offering huge selections of china, flatware and decorative pieces at discount prices. They claim to sell the largest choice of Wedgwood in Canada—over 100 patterns. They also carry various breakables by Lladro, Lalique, Royal Doulton, Alessi, Christofle, Waterford and Scheizer. Be forwarned that things can get pretty hectic and crowded here, so you may have to be a little patient.
Open Mon.-Wed. 10 a.m.-6 p.m., Thurs.-Fri. 10 a.m.-7:30 p.m., Sat. 9:30 a.m.-5:30 p.m.

LEATHER & LUGGAGE

Lanzi of Italy
123 Yorkville Ave.,
Bloor-Yorkville
• 964-2582

Lanzi sells quietly beautiful, sleeky classy leather accessories, such as wallets and that ilk. Especially nice, though, are the desk sets here.
Open Mon.-Fri. 10 a.m.-6 p.m., Sat. 10 a.m.-5:30 p.m.

Judith Teller
York Square,
148 Yorkville Ave.,
Bloor-Yorkville
• 963-9884

Judith Teller is a major name here for chic-if-somewhat-glitzy leather purses and clutch bags, along the lines of Judith Lieber (can you only go into the specialized little-leather-bag biz if your name is Judith? Just asking). You'll find goodies here for both sexes, though, including wallets, briefcases and luggage.
Open Mon.-Sat. 10 a.m.-6 p.m.

Louis Vuitton
110 Bloor St. West,
Bloor-Yorkville
• 968-3993

Somehow, Vuitton is an acquired taste—or perhaps the desire for its *LV*-riddled pieces of luggage is passed on genetically. We can't deny that Vuitton does make some beautiful things: we like their black-and-tan Marco Polo line, and if someone gave us an LV steamer trunk, we'd certainly use it.
Open Mon.-Sat. 10 a.m.-6 p.m.

SIGHTS

AMUSEMENTS	174
BEACHES & PARKS	176
EXCURSIONS	179
LANDMARKS	181
NEIGHBORHOODS	184
SPORTS	186
TOURS	187

Because the city is not yet very well known, visitors are often surprised to discover that Toronto has a fascinating, ever-changing treasure trove of things to see and do. Historic sites and amusement parks, zoos and tennis courts nestle like jewels in the multicultural mosaic setting the city provides.

AMUSEMENTS

Canada's Wonderland
9580 Jane St.,
Maple,
North York
• 832-7000, ext. 392 (collect)

A major commercial theme park with standard theme-park attractions such as musical revues, novelty restaurants, souvenir and craft boutiques and more than 30 rides. The park is a 30-minute drive north of the city and a visit here takes up most of the day. It is fun for children but adults will become jaded within a couple of hours. However, the musical revues are top-notch and well worth the journey.
July 1-Labor Day: open weekdays 10 a.m.-8 p.m., weekends 10 a.m.-10 p.m. Labor Day-June 30: open weekends 10 a.m.-10 p.m. Adults Can$22.95, children 3-6 Can$10.95.

McLaughlin Planetarium
100 Queen's Park,
Scarborough
• 586-5736

The Star Theatre features a frequently changing program of celestial goings-on. Seasonal programs track the yearly movements of the stars and planets. Special event programming allows for detailed examination of unusual phenomena such as eclipses, solar spots and planetary conjunctions. As well, an ongoing entertainment program links the music of popular rock groups with laser images projected onto the dome. These programs are popular with younger audiences. The Astrocenter features interactive and three-dimensional displays of space exploration and discoveries.
Open daily 10 a.m. Exhibits only. Showtimes vary. Phone for details. Advance tickets only: adults Can$4.50; seniors, students & children Can$2.50.

Metro Toronto Zoo
Meadowvale Rd.,
West Hill, Scarborough
• 392-5900

This 710-acre park is a popular spot for a day's outing year round. With more than four thousand animals housed in natural settings and a minimum of fenced enclosures, this zoo ranks with the world's best. Although about three hundred species are housed inside in eight tropical pavilions, many "exotic" animals can also be seen romping in enclosures deep with snow. If the prospect of walking through 710 acres of park seems too daunting, the zoo can be seen from an efficient, enclosed, electric monorail system. In winter, there are three cross-country ski trails through the African, Canadian and Eurasian animal domains offering the fitness-oriented a closer look at the beasts.

A full public-education program includes tours for the physically and mentally disadvantaged, photography workshops and an outreach service.
Open daily year-round (except Christmas Day) 9 a.m.-7:30 p.m. Adults Can$8, children 5-11 Can$3.

Ontario Place
955 Lakeshore Blvd. West, Harbourfront
• 965-7711

Rising out of the waters of Lake Ontario on three artificial islands, this educational and entertainment complex at the bottom of Bathurst Street is an easy getaway from the exhausting heat of a Toronto summer day. Cool lake breezes rustle the poplars and pines in the hilly park as music from the strolling musicians, huskers and revue entertainers on the Waterfall Stage and restaurants takes up the aural slack. The Cinesphere features daily programs of chillingly realistic IMAX films, plus an evening program of regular films on a 40-foot-high screen. The Wilderness Ride and Children's Village are popular with the young set. The Forum, located at the heart of the complex, presents a regularly-scheduled season of live music and dance performances.
Open Mon.-Sat. 10 a.m.-1 a.m., Sun. 10 a.m.-11 p.m. Adults Can$7, seniors Can$3. Admission daily after 11 p.m. Can$2; free Wed.

Ontario Science Centre
770 Don Mills Rd., North York
• 429-4100

It may be a window on the future, but it's a window we can reach through. This huge, permanent exhibition of technology and science becomes a playground for all ages with more than 800 hands-on displays and simulations. Live demonstrations, films, lectures and changing exhibits of updated technology, almost before it happens, keep this educational attraction at the top of the list for visitors and Torontonians who never tire of the fun to be had when they can really get their hands on that gizmo and make it work.
Open Mon.-Thurs. & Sat. 10 a.m.-6 p.m., Fri. 10 a.m.-9 p.m., Sun., noon-6 p.m. Adults Can$5.50, students 13-17 Can$4.50, children Can$2, seniors free. Admission free Fri. after 5 p.m.

Riverdale Farm
201 Winchester St., Cabbagetown
• 392-6794

In the heart of Cabbagetown, one of the oldest neighborhoods in Toronto, the city operates a working farm as part of its educational- and recreational-resource programs. The standard farm animals, maintained as purebred stock, provide a unique inner-city resource for observational research. Located on the slopes of the Don Valley Ravine, the year-round programs at the farm involve the entire community from spring births to seasonal festivals, celebrated in a traditional pioneer style using materials grown on the farm. This is not a petting zoo. Rather

it is a step back into Toronto's heritage and a gentle reminder of the way life used to be.
Open daily 9 a.m.-5 p.m. Admission free.

Tour of the Universe
301 Front St. West, Harbourfront
• 364-3134

To call Tour of the Universe a ride denies the educational aspects involved. To say it's educational belies the sheer fun, or terror, of the chance to explore a fully functional space port of the 21st century before fastening the seat belts for a simulated trip to Jupiter. This is a terrific group experience for the whole family to enjoy. The educational aspects are peripheral for most space travelers, but the bumpy ride into outer space aboard the Hermes space shuttle provides hours of happy memories and a great story for the folks back home.
Open Mon.-Thurs. 10 a.m.-7 p.m., Fri.-Sat. 10 a.m.-10 p.m., Sun. 11 a.m.-7 p.m. Adults Can$11.95, seniors Can$7.95, children under 12 Can$4.

BEACHES & PARKS

BEACHES

As in almost every great city in the world, metropolitan Toronto has a major problem with pollution. The air is getting harder to breath and the water is certainly not the pristine element it once was. While tap water is safe to drink, bathing at any of the beaches dotted along the city's sprawling waterfront is a day-to-day decision. Don't make any definite plans to swim until checking with the people at the **Beach Hotline** (392-7161), operating mid-June to Labor Day. Boating continues to be a popular pastime and the marinas are a hive of activity all season. Just don't fall overboard. If you do, don't swallow the water.

Ashbridge's Bay Park
South from Lakeshore Blvd. East opposite Coxwell Ave., Beaches

A great spot for family picnics and wind surfing. Excellent facilities for boat launching and mooring. The boardwalk is well maintained and provides quiet relaxation and a rest from all that exhausting sunbathing on the immense flat boulders lining the harbor.

SIGHTS Beaches & Parks

Bluffer's Park
South from Kingston Rd. on Brimley Rd. South, Scarborough

At the base of the towering Scarborough Bluffs, a natural erosion, Bluffer's Park has spacious picnic and beach facilities, an active marina, boat launching and day-mooring facilities. Climbing the bluffs is not advised but join the ever-present impromptu gallery to cheer on the few who inevitably dare the heights and the law. Bring a camera to capture one of the spectacular sunsets.

Centre Island
Toronto Islands (access only by ferry from the foot of Bay St.)
• 392-8193 (ferry schedules), 360-1430 (mooring information)

One of a collection of small islands formed in the Toronto harbor by a freak storm in 1857, Centre Island features broad, sandy beaches, a fully-equipped marina, a children's amusement park and petting zoo, miles of groomed park land, nature trails and cycling paths. A formal dining room provides an alternative to picnics and hot-dog stands.

Cherry Street Beach
South from Lakeshore Blvd. East on Cherry St., Toronto

A small, intimate beach with treed picnic facilities and some boat launching facilities. A real haven away from the crowds at the other beaches, especially on weekdays.

Hanlon's Point
West end of Centre Island, Toronto Islands (access only by ferry from the foot of Bay St.)
• 392-8193 (ferry schedules)

Adjacent to the Toronto Island Airport and a bird sanctuary, this stony beach, named for rower Ned Hanlon, offers secluded nature trails, cove-like beaches and peaceful solitude. Take along a good book and plenty of sun tan lotion. Public tennis courts are a popular attraction for the more energetic sun worshipers. The city's large gay community has long thought of Hanlon's Point as its own, though the area certainly isn't exclusive.

Kew Beach & Balmy Beach
South of Queen St. East, on Woodbine St. to Neville Park, Toronto

The last two of the four original beaches that gave the surrounding neighborhood its name, this wide expanse of sand sprawls down from the boardwalk and grassy park above it to provide a playground suitable for sunbathing, playing volleyball, building sand castles and dabbling in the waves along the shore. Tennis courts and hot-dog stands are popular favorites. The boardwalk remains the focal point of the area and offers a year-long changing panorama for inveterate strollers. Early-morning joggers, romantic couples at sunset and dog-walkers after dark know no season and enjoy the spectacular view year-round in any weather.

SIGHTS Beaches & Parks

Marie Curtis Park
South from Lakeshore Blvd. West on 42nd St., Toronto

Excellent picnic facilities, a playground and wide sandy, beaches make this park a family favorite. Boat-launching ramps and ample parking, even on weekends, add to its appeal.

Sunnyside Beach
Lakeshore Blvd. West, west of Parkside Dr., Toronto

An immense white stucco, rococo bathing pavilion, a restored relic from the turn of the century when this popular bathing spot was fondly known as the poor man's Riviera, dominates the wide, gently sloping beach. A small grassy park adjacent to the pavilion, which is now purely decorative in function, has a children's playground and an outdoor swimming pool, popular with inner-city residents in summer.

Ward's Island
East end of Centre Island, Toronto Islands (access only by ferry from the foot of Bay St.)
• 392-8193 (ferry schedules)

A boardwalk and a clean, broad beach open to Lake Ontario make this spot a perennial favorite with sunbathers, wind surfers and operators of small sailing craft.

PARKS

Allan Gardens
Carlton & Sherbourne Sts., Cabbagetown

In the center of the city is this oasis of beauty and rest for smog-clogged eyes and noses. The oldest botanical garden in Toronto boasts lush lawns, sparkling fountains and a tropical garden housed in the glass conservatory.

Edwards Gardens
Lawrence Ave. East & Leslie St., North York

In a park setting, complete with rustic bridges and gravel paths through the flower beds, Torontonians love to rest and contemplate nature as they stroll through the 34 acres of grassy greenery in this primly manicured garden.

High Park
Bloor St. West & Keele St., Toronto

The largest wooded area in Toronto, High Park's 399 acres are mainly unmanicured. Its wild, tangled natural forests and woods contrast well with the highly organized formal rose garden near the food pavilion. In summer, the ravine is home to the free Shakespeare productions and, in winter, Grenadier Pond becomes a community skating rink.

James Gardens
Edgehill Rd. & Edenbridge Dr., Etobicoke

Another manicured, formal park with well-defined walkways and flower beds, all neatly labeled. If you don't like nature sullied by wild disorganization, this park is for you.

SIGHTS   Excursions

Toronto Islands
Access only by ferry from the foot of Bay St.
• 392-8193 (ferry schedules)

Popular all year, these islands, created in the Toronto harbor by a violent storm in 1857, provide sunny beaches, wooded park land, formal gardens, inland canals for small pleasure boats, biking trails and an unparalleled and surprising view of the city's skyline.

EXCURSIONS

There is a wide variety of things to see and do on day trips out of metropolitan Toronto. From the Bard on the boards to lions in their lair, it's all within a couple of hours' drive from the city.

African Lion Safari
Hwy. 401 west to Hwy. 6 south, right on Safari Rd. exit, RR1, Cambridge
• (519) 623-2620

What better way to spend a day out of the summer heat of Toronto than hunting African big game—with a camera? An hour's drive west from Toronto, the African Lion Safari provides a full day of adventure. The daily package includes a drive through the game reserve in your own car. The animals are used to visitors, and they like to approach vehicles to get a closer look at the strangers in their midst. A small rail line and an African river boat take the less adventurous on a tour through the animals' domain. Demonstrations of hunting birds and pet tricks are standard fare in the Animal Amphitheatre.
Open Apr. 27-Oct. 27 Mon.-Fri. 10 a.m.-4 p.m., Sat.-Sun. 10 a.m.-5 p.m. Adults Can$11.95, seniors & teenagers Can$9.95, children 3-12 Can$7.95, children under 2 free.

Farmer's Market
Cities of Kitchener & Waterloo

The picturesque markets in these twin cities an hour north of Metropolitan Toronto draw curious and avid gastronomes alike for farm-fresh produce, meat and poultry, home baking and preserves. In the heart of the Mennonite settlement district, the food is definitely worth the drive, even if it's just for lunch.
Jan.-Apr.: open Sat. 5 a.m.-2 p.m. May-Dec.: open Wed. 7 a.m.-2 p.m. & Sat. 5 a.m.-2 p.m.

Kortright Centre for Conservation
Pine Valley Dr., Kleinburg
• 661-6600

Discover nature as it should be in the best of all possible worlds. Guided nature walks, film presentations, demonstrations and exhibits in the midst of a lush natural forest setting provide essential information in pleasant doses. This is a terrific day trip away from the hectic crush of the city to commune with Mother Nature on intimate terms.
Open daily 10 a.m.-4 p.m. Adults Mon.-Fri. Can$3.25, Sat.-Sun. Can$3.50; students, seniors & children Can$1.75.

SIGHTS Excursions

McMichael Canadian Art Collection
Islington Ave., Kleinburg
• 893-1121

An intensive look at an extensive collection of art by Canadian artists, in a setting that simply takes the breath away. Lush pine forests and hand-hewn log buildings frame a collection that includes works by members of the Group of Seven, plus those by Emily Carr, David Milne and Clarence Gagnon.

Jan.-Apr.: open Mon.-Sat. 11 a.m.-5 p.m., Sun. 11 a.m.-6:30 p.m. May-Dec.: open Tues.-Sun. 11:30 a.m.-4:30 p.m. Adults Can$2.50, students Can$1, children under 5 free, seniors Can$1.50 (free on Wed.), families Can$6. Group rates can be arranged.

Niagara Falls
Niagara Parks Commission, Box 150, Niagara Falls L2E 6T2 (access off the Queen Elizabeth Hwy. south of Toronto)
• 356-2241

One of Earth's natural wonders, Niagara Falls is a tourist and honeymoon destination known around the world. The falls are illuminated at night and, in winter, the waters take on an aura of the fantastic due to the whimsical ice formations created by the frozen spray. The town itself is a midway of souvenir shops, fast-food restaurants and tourist gimmicks, but a couple of our favorite stops are: the Rainbow Tower Carillon's free summer concerts in Rainbow Gardens; a ride on the Maid of the Mist which travels right into the heart of the pounding waters; Table Rock Scenic Tunnels which offer a unique view from behind the falls. The hooded raincoats provided are not a gimmick. It gets very wet on these trips. *See also* pages 202 to 207.

Falls: open year-round. Carillon: concerts daily June 15-Labor Day. Maid Of The Mist: open May 15-Oct. 15. Tunnels: open year-round except Christmas.

> *Be aware that many of Ontario's sights and attractions have limited hours during the winter months, so call ahead before visiting.*

Niagara-on-the-Lake
Access north on Hwy. 55 off the Queen Elizabeth Hwy., south of Toronto

At the mouth of the Niagara River, this prettily preserved town emulates the lifestyle when it was the first capital of Upper Canada, 1791–1796. Quaint inns and restaurants—reproductions, not restorations—abound. The place oozes with colonial charm, a veneer that wears thin quickly. The Shaw Festival Theatre, located here, presents a summer season of plays by George Bernard Shaw and his contemporaries. *See also* pages 207 to 212.

Open year-round.

LANDMARKS

ARCHITECTURAL

Casa Loma
1 Austin Terrace,
The Annex
• 923-1171

A 98-room medieval-style castle in the heart of Toronto. Originally built as a private residence in 1911, it has secret staircases within the walls, an underground tunnel to the stables (which have walls lined with Spanish mahogany) and two tower fortifications. Abandoned and abused after the 1930s, its restoration, room by room, is the work of a local service club. A self-guided audio tour is provided.
Open daily 10 a.m.-4 p.m. Adults Can$7, seniors & children Can$4.

CN Tower
301 Front St. West,
Harbourfront
• 360-8500

Situated on the lakefront between Spadina and University avenues, this 553.3-meter (1,815-foot) monolith is the tallest free-standing structure in the world. (Yes, it has a good 110 meters on Chicago's famed Sears Tower, which is officially the world's tallest *building*.) The elevator-ride to the top is the best way to reach the two observation decks, although the world's longest metal staircase—2,570 steps, to be exact—provides an exhausting alternative. A revolving restaurant and lounge (Sparkles Nightclub, see page 143) are located on the first observation level. A guided audio tour is offered.
Open Sun.-Thurs. 10 a.m.-10 p.m., Fri.-Sat. 10 a.m.-11 p.m. Elevator ride: Adults Can$10, seniors & children under 16 Can$3.

Eaton Centre
Yonge & Dundas Sts.,
Downtown
• 598-2322

A born-to-shop shopper's dream come true, with more than 360 stores, boutiques and restaurants under one roof in the heart of the city. The enclosed atrium above the mall is home to business offices, and features a mobile sculpture depicting a flock of Canada geese taking flight. The soaring glass-domed roof, stretching along two city blocks, and the building's unusual construction are key attractions in this architectural wonder.
Open daily 6 a.m.-2 a.m.

Maple Leaf Gardens
60 Carlton St.
• 977-1641

There are no tours of this famous sports landmark a block off Yonge Street, but interested fans can look around inside when there are no events scheduled for that day. It's the permanent home of the Toronto Maple Leafs Hockey Club with plenty of

SIGHTS   Landmarks

seasonal National League action augmented by ice shows, rock concerts, wrestling and circuses.
Open year-round on event dates.

SkyDome
300 The Esplanade West, Harbourfront
• 341-3663

Home of the Toronto Blue Jays Baseball Club and the Toronto Argonaut Football Club, the Dome is a multipurpose facility with a retractable roof. Rock concerts and opera productions vie for space with trade shows, gala business meetings and product launches in the off-season. The seating capacity of 63,000 allows for a true round of applause. Walking tours of the facility are available, but call ahead for schedules.
Open year-round on event dates. Tours: adults Can$7, seniors & children Can$5.

Underground City
Access from Union Station on Front St. West or Eaton Centre, 220 Yonge St., Downtown

A network of underground malls provides more than five square city blocks of restaurants, shopping and services in climate-controlled comfort. The exotic gardens flourish under the skylights in even the severest winter's freezing rain.
Open year-round during regular business hours.

HISTORIC

Black Creek Pioneer Village
1000 Murray Ross Pkwy., North York
• 736-1733

A heritage project of the metropolitan Toronto and Region Conservation Authority, the historically correct restorations are peopled with actors in period costumes going about the daily life of a nineteenth century frontier village.
Open Mon.-Fri. 9:30 a.m.-5 p.m., weekends & holidays 10 a.m.-6 p.m. Adults Can$5.50, seniors Can$3.50, students & children Can$2.50.

Elgin and Winter Garden Theatre Centre
189 Yonge St., Downtown
• 594-0755

Canada's largest theater restoration, the Elgin Theatre reopened in 1989, 76 years to the day it originally opened as a vaudeville house. Above it, the Winter Garden Theatre, with a unique outdoor decor, was closed from 1928 until 1989. Both theaters present a variety of live theater and concerts on a continuing basis. Tours can be arranged by phoning in advance.
Open year-round on performance dates.

Fort York
Garrison Rd. off Fleet St. near Bathurst St., Harbourfront
• 392-6907

A restored military fort from the War of 1812, it houses exhibits of historic and military interest, craft demonstrations and the Fort York Guard. The regiment, in period uniform, re-enacts the battles of the war, within the walls of the fort (daily during

SIGHTS Landmarks

summer). This is one of Toronto's most important historic sights.
Open daily 9:30 a.m.-5 p.m. Adults Can$4, seniors & children Can$2.

Massey Hall
178 Victoria St., Downtown
• 363-7301

A true concert hall, rather than a theater, this one-hundred-year-old veteran is a favorite of performers. Lily Pons, Enrico Caruso, Luciano Pavarotti and Maria Callas have claimed the hall's acoustics to be among the finest in the world. They should know. There are few theater productions here, because the backstage space is too limited, but a vocal concert is one of our favorite ways to enjoy the pure colors of music.
Open year-round on performance dates.

Old City Hall
Bay St. & Queen St. West, Downtown
• 392-7341

The new Toronto City Hall, fronted by Nathan Philips Square on Queen Street West, is a wonder of modern architecture. But it can't hold a candle to the Old City Hall, which stands just east of it. The Gothic design and hewn-stone construction, as well as the fantastic artistry of the individually carved gargoyles which surround the upper floors, give the building an elegance that's so clearly so obviously missing from its counterpart next door. Free guided tours daily but phone ahead for times.
Open Mon.-Fri. 9 a.m.-5 p.m.

Ontario Parliament Buildings
111 Wellesley St. West, Toronto
• 965-4028

See the provincial government in operation when Parliament is in session, and also view the art and geological exhibitions. The architecture is stunning, set off beautifully by its Queen's Park setting. Group tours can be arranged.
Open Mon.-Fri. 9 a.m.-4:30 p.m.

Pantages Theatre
244 Victoria St. & 263 Yonge St., Downtown
• 362-3218

As a project of the Toronto Historical Board, the opulence of the 2,117-seat theater has been restored after much abuse and neglect. What used to be a seedy movie theater is once again an elegant legitimate theater, just as it was when it opened in 1920. Tours can be arranged by calling in advance.
Open year-round on performance dates.

Royal Alexandra Theatre
260 King St. West, Downtown
• 593-4211

Yet another theatrical restoration from the turn of the century, this 1,500-seat beauty is home to top-notch touring productions and musicals.
Open year-round on performance dates.

SIGHTS   Neighborhoods

St. Lawrence Market
95 Front St. East, Downtown
• 392-7219

The most authentic farmer's market within the city limits, this splendid architectural dinosaur sprawls steel and glass over a full city block. The front facade still contains the original structure around which the market is built: Toronto's City Hall circa 1845. The Market Gallery upstairs is the repository for the City of Toronto Archives.
Open Tues.-Fri. 8 a.m.-6 p.m., Sat. 5 a.m.-6 p.m., Sun. 10 a.m.-5 p.m.

NEIGHBORHOODS

The Annex
Bloor St. West between Bathurst & Spadina Sts.

An urban village in the true sense of the phrase, this neighborhood is a favorite of university students, artists and rock bands. The elegant houses built along narrow, Victorian streets provide the perfect setting for youthful and/or artistic impoverishment. Terrific markets with great prices abound.

The Beaches
Queen St. East from Woodbine Ave. to Neville Park.

Trendy yuppies have unofficially claimed this area as their own. Restored older houses line narrow streets that slope steeply down to the shores of Lake Ontario at Kew and Balmy beaches. The chic boutiques, antique stores and hip restaurants that crowd each other along Queen Street East mirror the neighborhood resident's tastes.

Cabbagetown
Area around Parliament & Carlton Sts.

Another yuppie haven of restored older houses and trendy, expensive restaurants. The division of the have and have-nots is embarrassingly evident here: the east side of Parliament Street is the sight of extensive and costly renovations, but the west side is home to the poverty-stricken and the homeless. The fabulous houses on the tree-lined streets of the east side are beautiful but cannot erase the sting of created by the sharply divided economic status.

Chinatown
Area around Dundas West & Spadina Sts.

A tribute to the ethnic mosaic of Metropolitan Toronto, the community is nestled in between Kensington Market to the west and Queen Street West to the south, the Annex to the north and the Eaton Centre to the east. As with all the city's ethnic communities, fresh produce and authentic restaurants abound.

SIGHTS Neighborhoods

Church and Wellesley
Church & Wellesley Sts.

Sometimes known locally as The Ghetto, the city's large gay community calls this twelve-city block neighborhood home. Apartment blocks and condos crowd out the few single-family houses. The restaurants, bars and shops in the area cater to a mostly gay clientele. The 519 Community Centre is the focus of community life and, of course, Gay Pride Day celebrations.

The Danforth
Danforth Ave. between Broadview & Pape Sts.

The Greek community calls this neighborhood home and provides the rest of Toronto with the best Greek food and entertainment west of Athens. Lots of pastries, fresh meat and produce available in the tiny, family-run shops.

Harbourfront
Queen's Quay West from Yonge St. to Bathurst St.

A vibrant community on the city's lakefront, designed with an eye to a "total living environment." A planned community, it incorporates shops, theaters, parks, apartments and water sports into the daily life of the large business community that has settled here. Rather than rely on new construction alone, many of the abandoned warehouses are renovated for office space, creating successful architectural contrasts.

Kensington Market
Baldwin, Kensington & Augusta Aves., west of Spadina Ave.

An open-air European-style market that hums with activity from 5 in the morning to far past midnight. A fresh-food-lover's delight, its aromas and sounds spill over into the narrow streets, along with the produce and live poultry, to create a motorist's nightmare. You'll find everything from Portuguese breads and sausages to Jewsih smoked fish to Middle Eastern spices.

Little Italy
St. Clair West & Dufferin Sts.

The city's vast Italian community gathers here to eat, drink, shop, argue and enjoy life. Fabulous shopping for fresh pasta, cheese and meat.

Queen Street West
Queen St. West between University Ave. & Roncesvalles Ave.

A show place and a home for Toronto's avant garde. The galleries, boutiques, restaurants and studios elbow each other for space in an area where the newest sensation is old hat within hours. A fast-paced, artistic neighborhood dedicated to youthful imaginations and enjoying life to the max.

Roncesvalles
Between Howard Park Ave. & Queen St. West

A Polish-influenced neighborhood with great restaurants and fresh produce not found in other parts of the city. The sounds of Slavic music and languages fill the air in tiny coffee shops and markets.

Rosedale
Yonge St. & Crescent Rd.

Old money calls this residential area home. Grand mansions on winding tree-lined streets have park-sized lawns in front and chauffeurs out back, giving the neighborhood a decidedly staid, elegant aura. A great spot for long walks.

Yorkville
Bay St. & Bloor St. West

Formerly the home of the hippies in the 1960s, the area has cleaned up to become the center of high fashion in Toronto and Canada. The chic-est of the chic gather here to see and be seen in the trendy bars and restaurants that have taken over from the smoky coffeehouses and jazz joints of the earlier decade.

SPORTS

Torontonians are greater spectators than doers when it comes to sports, as evidenced by the vast numbers that turn out to watch live sporting events. That said, Toronto does have its fitness-happy contingent, whose members dutifully go to aerobics classes or gyms to get fit themselves. The city has provided the **Martin Goodman Fitness Trail**, fifteen kilometers (nine miles), which winds through the wooded ravines that rake the city core and across the lakefront from the Humber River in the west to Neville Park in the Beaches. This designated trail is great for cycling, jogging or walking. There is a series of free-access, public tennis courts provided throughout the city, many of them downtown, which are used by enthusiasts.

BASEBALL

Toronto Blue Jays Baseball
• 341-3663

A full season of American League baseball is played in the SkyDome, Harbourfront, April to October.

FOOTBALL

Toronto Argonaut Football
• 595-1131

A full season of Canadian League football is played by the "Argos" in the SkyDome, Harbourfront, July to November.

SIGHTS Tours

GOLF

Glen Abbey Golf
Rural Rte. 2, Oakville
• 844-1800

The course, designed by Jack Nicklaus, is host to the Canadian Open tournament every year. At other times, the championship course is available for private tournaments and individual play.
Open during summer.

HOCKEY

Toronto Maple Leafs Hockey
• 977-1641

A full season of National League hockey is played in Maple Leaf Gardens, Downtown, October to May.

HORSE RACING

Greenwood Race Track
1669 Queen St. East, Toronto
• 698-3131

Harness racing at its finest with plenty of parking or easy access to public transit. Betting facilities provided.
Open Mon., Tues. & Thurs.-Sat. 7:30 p.m. Clubhouse seat Can$6.50, grandstand Can$3.25.

Woodbine Race Track
550 Rexdale Blvd. at Hwy. 27, Rexdale
• 675-6110

Thoroughbred horse racing in a suburban setting out by the International Airport. It's a long way to drive to lose money on the ponies, but a great day's outing if you don't take the wagers too seriously. Known as one of North America's great thoroughbred race tracks, Woodbine is host to the Queen's Plate. Betting facilities available.
Open Wed. 4 p.m., Thurs.-Sat. 1:30 p.m. Admission Can$3.25.

TOURS

Canadian Helicopters
Buttonville Airport, Hangar 11, Markham, Ontario
• 477-7203

Chartered tours available with advance reservation.
Tours year-round. Cost Can$25 per person, one-hour minimum.

SIGHTS Tours

Gray Line Boat Tours
5 Queen's Quay West, Harbourfront
• 364-2412

A tour of the Toronto harbor, islands and lagoons in a glass-domed excursion boat, with colorful commentary. Tours leave from docks at foot of Yonge Street.
Open daily noon-7 p.m. Tours hourly. Adults Can$8.95, seniors & students Can$6.95, children Can$4.95.

Gray Line Bus Tours
610 Bay St., Downtown
• 393-7911

Two-hour bus tours of the Toronto area, with a guide's commentary. If you have limited time, it's a great way to hit the high spots without getting out of your seat.
Tours daily. Call for times. Adults Can$15.

Vintage Streetcar Tour
150 Dundas St. West, Downtown
• 393-7911

A narrated tour on one of Toronto's famous Red Rocket streetcars. The 90-minute circuit gives a leisurely look at the varied attractions in the downtown core.
Open daily. Call for times and pickup locations. Adults Can$16, children Can$9.

ARTS

DANCE	190
GALLERIES	191
MUSEUMS	193
MUSIC	195
THEATER	197

Metropolitan Toronto sizzles as the acknowledged cultural hub of Canada in that every Canadian who is anybody in the arts—visual, performing, graphic or fine—has been a part of the constant flow of talent through the city. A veritable roundhouse for the movement, gathering and distribution of talent, the city is also home base for many of the world's great talents in all areas of the arts.

DANCE

Dancemakers
927 Dupont St., Toronto
• 535-8880

A modern dance company with a strong repertory season. Eight energetic, innovative, youthful dancers ensure a high energy level at each performance, supported by intensive training in all facets of the art.
Regularly scheduled performances Oct.-Mar. in the Premier Dance Theatre, 207 Queen's Quay West, Harbourfront.

DanceWorks
1087 Queen St. West, Toronto
• 534-1523

As presenters of independent artists and companies working in contemporary dance, DanceWorks's main season is performed in the Betty Oliphant Theatre. This is a daring group that takes high risks by composing its season of more than 80 percent world premieres.
Regularly scheduled performances Oct.-Apr. in the Betty Oliphant Theatre, 404 Jarvis St., Cabbagetown.

Danny Grossman Dance Co.
511 Bloor St. West, Bloor-Yorkville
• 531-8350

With wit and style, this energetic company of twelve dancers uses an astounding physical sense to get across its message of belief in compassion and strength to improve the human condition.
Regularly scheduled performances Nov.-May in the Betty Oliphant Theatre, 404 Jarvis St., Cabbagetown & the Premier Dance Theatre, 207 Queen's Quay West, Harbourfront.

Desrossiers Dance Theatre
• 463-5341

A modern dance troupe of thirteen dancers noted locally for its almost nonexistent home season. More a touring company based in Toronto, Desrossiers tours regularly to major U.S. and Canadian centers as well as Europe and Asia, acting as artistic ambassadors for Canada and the Toronto arts community. When it does perform at home, the reviews are always raves.
Regularly scheduled performances in the Premier Dance Theatre, 207 Queen's Quay West, Harbourfront.

ARTS Galleries

National Ballet of Canada
157 King St. East,
Downtown
• 362-1041

A small, efficient and elegant company of dancers present classical and contemporary works to local audiences as well as carrying on an extensive touring schedule throughout the year. This is the flagship classical dance company for the country.
Regularly scheduled performances Nov.-May in the O'Keefe Centre, 1 Front St. East, Downtown.

Toronto Dance Theatre
80 Winchester St.,
Cabbagetown
• 967-1365

A modern dance company and school which focuses on training and company performance. This in no way limits the resident choreographers nor the audience enjoyment, rather it enhances the works. The company's approach makes the unfamiliar more accessible for the nonadventurous modern-dance patron.
Regularly scheduled performances Oct.-May in the Premier Dance Theatre, 207 Queen's Quay West, Harbourfront.

GALLERIES

Art Gallery of Ontario
317 Dundas St. West,
Downtown
• 977-0414

A permanent collection of more than eleven thousand works is on display in the wide, sunny galleries, along with regularly rotating exhibitions of contemporary and traditional art. There is a whole wing devoted to the sculpture of Henry Moore, which works he donated to the people of Toronto.
Tues. & Thurs.-Sun. 11 a.m.-5:30 p.m., Wed. 11 a.m.-9 p.m. Adults $4.50, seniors & students $2.50. Admission free Wed.

The Power Plant
213 Queen's Quay
West,
Harbourfront
• 973-4949

Changing exhibits of contemporary art featuring local and international artists in design and graphic arts, sculpture and painting. It is the largest noncollecting contemporary art gallery in Canada.
Open Tues.-Fri. noon-8 p.m., Sat.-Sun. noon-6 p.m. Admission free.

COMMERCIAL GALLERIES

Metropolitan Toronto's established art galleries are only the tip of the iceberg. The alternative and commercial galleries, not always one and the same, play a large role in the active season of exhibitions that runs year-round. The City has brought art out into the streets with an enthusiastic and forceful program of outdoor sculpture installations on street corners in the downtown business core. If the old-guard venues uphold the tradition, it is the commercial galleries that feed the market. In Toronto, some of the commercial galleries have earned international reputations over the years, daring to challenge the Establishment view of what is art with innovative exhibitions. The most successful and enduring of these are: **Carmen Lamanna Gallery** (788 King St. West, Downtown; 363-8787; open Tues.-Fri. 10 a.m.-6 p.m., Sat. 11 a.m.-6 p.m.), **Gallery Moos** (136 Yorkville Ave., Bloor-Yorkville; 922-0627; open Tues.-Sat. 11 a.m.-6 p.m.), **Mercer Union Gallery** (333 Adelaide St. West, Downtown; 977-1412; open Tues.-Sat. 11 a.m.-6 p.m.), **Mira Godard Gallery** (22 Hazelton Ave., Bloor-Yorkville; 964-8197; open Tues.-Sat. 10 a.m.-5:30 p.m.).

ALTERNATIVE GALLERIES

Young artists can have problems getting recognized by the commercial galleries as viable risks. Traditionally, the Establishment ignores them. Toronto's wide-ranging alternative-gallery network provides them with a venue for their creativity and invention, and gives us a view of the freshest, not-yet-dry-to-touch, provocative contemporary art.

A Space
183 Bathurst St., Ste. 301, Toronto
• 364-3227

This is a multidisciplinary, artist-run center which provides a forum for new and alternative art, with the accent on artists and communities under-represented in major art galleries and venues.
Open Tues.-Fri. 10 a.m.-5 p.m., Sat. noon-5 p.m. Admission free.

Craft Studio at Harbourfront
York Quay Centre, 235 Queen's Quay West, Harbourfront
• 973-4963

Working on the resident-artist concept, the studios provide space and equipment for artisans working with glass, ceramics, metal, wood or textiles, with the aim of helping them establish a professional career. The open-access policy to the studios gives the public a perfect opportunity to watch craftspeople at work. Discussion and exchange is encouraged, but don't get too involved or you may find yourself on the other end of an anvil or a loom. There is a shop on the premises selling the pieces created in the studios.
Open daily 10 a.m.-6 p.m. Admission free.

Del Bello Gallery
363 Queen St. West, Downtown
• 593-0884

A forum for contemporary art and artists, this small alternative gallery has gained an international reputation by sponsoring an annual show and sale of miniature and small format art. The event attracts more than three thousand submissions from artists around the world each November.
Open Mon.-Sat. 10 a.m.-6 p.m. Admission free.

ARTS Museums

Toronto Sculpture Garden
King & Church Sts.
opposite St. James Cathedral,
Downtown
• 485-9658

A small park, set like a jewel in the midst of the business district, is the setting for rotating exhibitions of sculpture and large outdoor installation pieces.
Open year-round during daylight hours. Admission free.

YYZ Artist's Outlet
1087 Queen St. West,
Downtown
• 531-7869

This gallery space has a mandate to show contemporary art works in all media: video, performance, installation, you name it, they show it. Part of the underground establishment now, YYZ can be counted on for the best of what's innovative and exciting in every discipline.
Open Tues.-Fri. 10 a.m.-5 p.m. Admission free.

MUSEUMS

Torontonians don't like their rich heritage preserved and embalmed in stuffy vaults and served up in glass cases. They view the past as a living history lesson and instill in their children a sense of living their history every day. In more than 40 unique and varied heritage centers and museums throughout the city, they live with their history as they create it.

MAJOR MUSEUMS

George R. Gardiner Museum of Ceramic Art
111 Queen's Park Rd.,
Bloor-Yorkville
• 586-8080

This museum is dedicated to the display, research and study of ceramics with collections owned by the Gardiner family. Included are pieces of pre-Columbian, Italian Maiolica, English Delftware and English and continental porcelain from the eighteenth century. This extensive collection is one of the finest research projects on the subject in North America.
Open Tues.-Sun. 10 a.m.-5 p.m. Adults $5, seniors & students $3.

Marine Museum of Upper Canada
Exhibition Place,
Toronto
• 392-6827

A detailed history of the Toronto harbor and its multifarious activities, from fur trade to warships, is augmented with detailed ship models, maps, artifacts and a superb audio-visual presentation. The museum is housed in the former officer's quarters of historic Stanley Barracks, dating from 1841.
Open Mon.-Sat. 9:30 a.m.-5 p.m., Sun. & holidays noon-5 p.m. Adults $2.50, seniors & children $1.50, families $7.

ARTS Museums

Royal Ontario Museum
100 Queen's Park Crescent, Toronto
• 586-5549

Famous for its extensive Chinese collections, the ROM also houses displays of prehistoric animals in their natural habitat, the intriguing and seductive sights and sounds of a traditional Islam market, the magnificent splendor that was ancient Greece and Rome. Children will appreciate the Discovery Gallery with its many accessible displays and a hands-on policy.
Open Mon., Wed. & Fri.-Sun. 10 a.m.-6 p.m., Tues. & Thurs. 10 a.m.-8 p.m. Adults $5; seniors, students & children $3; families $12. Admission free Thurs. after 4:30 p.m.

OTHER MUSEUMS

A true variety of Toronto history can be found in the smaller, offbeat museums. Offering yet another way of looking at things, they also provide insights into the commercial and sometimes quirky daily life of the city's ancestors.

Hockey Hall of Fame and Museum
Exhibition Place, Toronto
• 595-1345

The venue here examines and chronicles the sport from its earliest beginnings to the present. The Stanley Cup is permanently housed here, surrounded by historic equipment such as sweaters, sticks and pucks that figure prominently in the history of the sport. Minor trophies, plus a collection of historic photos that can be purchased in reproduction, are augmented with historic film footage of landmark plays.
Open Mon. 10 a.m.-5 p.m., Tues.-Sun. 10 a.m.-7 p.m. Adults $3, seniors & students $2.

Market Gallery (City of Toronto Archives)
95 Front St. East, Downtown
• 392-7604

As keepers of the vital records of the municipal government dating from 1834 when the city was incorporated, the archivist and staff oversee more than 1,200 paintings of personalities and events, one million photographs and a wide selection of surveyor's maps, commemorative gifts to the city and historic artifacts.
Open Wed.-Fri. 10 a.m.-4 p.m., Sat. 9 a.m.-4 p.m., Sun. noon-4 p.m. Admission free.

Museum for Textiles
55 Centre Ave., Toronto
• 599-5515

Intentionally devoted to nonwestern cultures, the museum exhibits fifteen thousand examples of hand-made materials from around the world. A rotating schedule of shows includes items from the fifth century B.C., African commemorative cloaks and rich embroideries from the Ottoman Empire.
Open Tues.-Fri. 11 a.m.-5 p.m. Admission $2.

ARTS Music

Museum of the History of Medicine
288 Bloor St. West, Bloor-Yorkville
• 922-0564

The exhibit here cover five thousand years of health care and feature a three-thousand-year-old autopsied Egyptian mummy with slides of skin tissue and blood samples. Other highlights include seventeenth-century Oriental artifacts and medical tools. The museum hosts an active exhibition program as well, that addresses current health-care and preventative issues.
Open Mon.-Fri. 9:30 a.m.-4 p.m. Adults $4, seniors & students $2.50.

Redpath Sugar Museum
95 Queen's Quay East, Downtown
• 366-3561

Housed in the lakefront plant that produces two million pounds of refined sugar daily, the venue traces the development of the sugar industry in Canada through the lives of the people who have figured prominently in it. Their detailed diaries, photographs and personal artifacts give an intimate glimpse into life in Canada in the mid-1800s.
Open Mon.-Fri. 10 a.m.-noon & 1 p.m.-3:30 p.m. Admission free.

Toronto's First Post Office
260 Adelaide St. East, Downtown
• 865-1833

The growth of the city is inextricably linked to the growth of the Canadian postal service in this historic setting. There is lots of documentation as well as artifacts to be read and looked at, but the most fun, for children and adults alike, is the opportunity to write a letter with a quill pen and seal it with be-ribboned hot wax. Philatelists will cherish the unique, on-site, hand cancellation.
Open daily 10 a.m.-4 p.m. Admission free.

MUSIC

Music in all its forms and disguises plays a big part in Toronto's daily life. Street buskers vie with opera students for air space on campuses and around rehearsal spaces. Music resounds in plush theaters and plays alone on benches in café back rooms. In whatever guise, Torontonians support music and musicians.

Canadian Opera Company
• 363-6671

A large company with a full orchestra, presenting a broad repertoire from the classics to contemporary works on a grand scale. The soaring sets and elegant costumes are shown off at their best in the barnlike O'Keefe Centre where the company performs. Guest artists from the world of grand opera perform roles regularly throughout the season.
Regularly scheduled performances Sept.-June in the O'Keefe Centre, 1 Front St. East, Downtown.

ARTS Music

Toronto Mendelssohn Choir
• 598-0422

A one-hundred-voice mixed choir with a strict classical repertoire, this group performs its own subscription season as well as an integrated season with the Toronto Symphony Orchestra.
Regularly scheduled performances in Roy Thomson Hall, 60 Simcoe St., Downtown.

Toronto Symphony Orchestra
• 593-4828

A full season of subscription concerts, highlighted by an energetic pops series and frequent appearances by renowned guest artists and conductors. The symphony tries to squeeze in a little something for every taste—and it succeeds. There is no room here for a watered-down season; first-rate performances at all times.
Regularly scheduled performances Oct.-June in Roy Thomson Hall, 60 Simcoe St., Downtown.

OTHER MUSIC

Schola Cantorum Concerts
60 Aldwych Ave.
• 465-9596

One of the best of the small musical groups in the city, Schola Cantorum is a concert group dedicated to the presentation of talented young male singers by providing an ongoing venue for gifted boy sopranos who are recruited from the male choirs in Toronto churches. With a varied program of classics from which to choose, the group provides several evenings each year of professional music from another time.
Irregular season of performances at venues throughout the city. Phone for details.

Toronto Boys' Choir
123 Colin Ave.
• 920-7664

Formed in 1976, this large choir is broken down into three sections by age and voice. The senior boys' choir has no virgin, unchanged voices, but it provides a beautiful counterpoint to the ranges of the junior men's and men's choirs. As well as a regular subscription series, the choir performs with the Toronto Symphony Orchestra, Toronto Pops Orchestra and Toronto Mendelssohn Choir.
Regularly scheduled performances in St. Andrews Presbyterian Church, 75 Simcoe St., Downtown.

Toronto Pops Orchestra
178 Victoria St.,
Downtown
• 365-7677

A full subscription season of light classics, operetta, show tunes, jazz and popular music. Guest artists perform regularly. The venue, Massey Hall, is the perfect place for these performances. Its acoustics have been lauded by the likes of Enrico Caruso and Lily Pons. This is music heard as it was meant to be heard: live and crystal clear.
Regularly scheduled performances Oct.-June in Massey Hall, 178 Victoria St., Downtown.

THEATER

The large theater community in metropolitan Toronto provides an ever-changing spectrum of the art for natives. In any given week, Torontonians can see everything from Shakespeare done both classically and in punk drag to Harold Pinter to mime and puppet troupes. The variety is staggering, but what a wealth of talent is there.

Alumnae Theatre Company
70 Berkeley St., Cabbagetown
• 364-4170

A group of women graduates from the University of Toronto who wanted to continue staging plays after graduation formed this acting community in 1918. In 1990, the group expanded its horizons somewhat to professional status. It focuses on works by, for and about women from playwrights it feels don't get a fair representation in even the alternative theaters around town. The Alumnae also stages its share of Harold Pinter and Samuel Beckett.
Regularly scheduled performances Oct.-May.

Canadian Stage Company
• 367-8243

This group has a mandate to present and promote Canadian artists and theater people in a repertory of classical, international and Canadian plays. It does just that and does it expertly. The main-stage productions in the Bluma Appel Theatre are the meat and potatoes of the company, while the two stages, Upstairs and Downstairs, on Berkeley Street offer a wider variety of contemporary works and provide more opportunity for both actors and audiences to take risks.
Regularly scheduled performances Oct.-May in three venues: Bluma Appel Theatre, 27 Front St. East, Downtown; Upstairs & Downstairs, 26 Berkeley St., Cabbagetown.

Factory Theatre
125 Bathurst St., Downtown
• 864-9971

A professional company presenting a season of original Canadian works.
Regularly scheduled performances Sept.-June.

Shaw Festival
Niagara-on-the-Lake, Ontario
• 468-2172

A full summer season of works by George Bernard Shaw and his contemporaries in the Royal George Theatre and the Festival Theatre. The setting is a picturesque town restored to the era of the 1900s, just a short drive southwest from Toronto.
Regularly scheduled performances played in repertory May-Oct. Phone for details.

ARTS Theater

Stratford Festival
Stratford, Ontario
• (519) 273-1600 or toll free from Toronto (800) 363-4471

Hear the Bard in traditional presentations on the Festival Theatre stage, then wander along the Avon River to The Third Stage to see more contemporary creations in an avant-garde setting. The Avon Theatre, in the center of town, offers classical and other non-Shakespearean fare in a sumptuously restored vaudeville house. The city of Stratford is just an hour's drive west of Toronto.
Regularly scheduled performances played in repertory May-Oct.

Tarragon Theatre
30 Bridgman Ave., The Annex
• 531-1827

On two different stages, this company fulfills its original mandate to develop brand new Canadian plays. One stage, the Mainspace, presents a subscription season of fully developed works, while the other, the Extraspace, presents smaller, more risky works.
Regularly scheduled subscription performances Sept.-June.

Theatre Passe Muraille
16 Ryerson Ave., Toronto
• 363-8988

This small, regional company presents an experimental, works-in-progress repertoire of original Canadian plays. Always professional but sometimes *too* original for our taste, the company does have a loyal following. Don't let the name fool you: it rarely presents plays in the French language.
Regularly scheduled performances Oct.-May.

Toronto Truck Theatre
94 Belmont St., Bloor-Yorkville
• 922-0084

Now in its fourteenth year of continuous production of Agatha Christie's classic play, *The Mousetrap*, this company of young performers provides a lot of work for the Toronto theater community and a fun night out for tourists and locals alike. The production has become an institution on the Toronto theater scene.
Performances Tues.-Fri. 8 p.m., Sat. 6:30 p.m. & 9:30 p.m. Adults $16, seniors & students under 16 $14, Fri.-Sat. all seats $18.

Young People's Theatre
165 Front St. East, Downtown
• 864-9732

A theater for children, about children, by adults. It incorporates an intensive training program for young actors and encourages new works and adaptations of classic children's literature for the stage
Regularly scheduled performances Oct.-June.

ALTERNATIVE THEATER

Buddies in Bad Times Theatre
142 George St.,
• 863-9455

A open-concept forum for new and established works for the stage, by gay and lesbian artists about the gay experience. Always controversial, seldom professional, the company is in its fourteenth year of continuous production. The loyal following it has

ARTS Theater

earned appreciates all the works all the time..
Regularly scheduled performances in a variety of local theaters on a subscription season Oct.-May. Admission free.

Equity Showcase Theatre
221 Dufferin St., Ste. 308-A,
Toronto
• 533-6100

This is a venue specifically designed to showcase the talents of members of the Canadian Actors' Equity Association, the theatrical union, for their peers and interested producers and directors. The works performed provide a stretch for the actors involved so they can try out roles in a nonpressured, peer-group situation. The productions are open to the public but are geared to an audience of the theater community.
Regularly scheduled performances Sept.-May in the Studio Theatre, York Quay Centre, 235 Queen's Quay West, Harbourfront. Admission free.

Factory Theatre Studio Café
125 Bathurst St.,
Toronto
• 864-9971

A venue for smaller, off-the-wall theater productions that would have trouble getting space or audiences elsewhere. Factory Theatre is recognized as a leader in this field of artistic promotion and support. The midnight shows on weekends have a cult following.
Irregularly scheduled performances all year. Phone for details.

Native Earth Performing Arts
37 Spadina Rd.,
Toronto
• 944-1988

Another special-interest group, Native Earth presents plays about the experience of Native Canadians. The company produces a subscription series of plays by Native writers, using Native actors.
Regularly scheduled performances Nov.-May, Native Canadian Centre of Toronto, 16 Spadina Rd., Harbourfront.

The Puppet Centre
171 Avondale Ave.,
North York
• 222-9029

Using a three-pronged approach, the center faces the challenge of promoting the history and joys of puppetry head on. As a museum, the only one of its kind in Canada, it displays hundreds of examples of puppets from around the world. As an educator, it carries out an effective and popular program in conjunction with the local school boards. As a theater, it provides a perfect venue—a permanent puppet theater—with proper lighting and facilities for local and international professional puppeteers.
Regularly scheduled performances Oct.-June.

ARTS Theater

Théatre Français de Toronto
219 Dufferin St., Ste. 303,
Toronto
• 534-7303

Toronto's only professional French-language theater company produces classical and contemporary works in conjunction with the Canadian Stage Company. The subscription season includes plays by Franco-Ontarian writers, when any can be found, as well as French and Franco-Canadian playwrights.
Regularly scheduled performances Oct.-May in the Bluma Appel Theatre, 27 Front St. East, Downtown.

OUT OF TORONTO

NIAGARA FALLS	202
NIAGARA-ON-THE-LAKE	207
KLEINBURG	212
CAMBRIDGE	216
COTTAGE COUNTRY	217
STRATFORD	224

NIAGARA FALLS

RESTAURANTS	204
QUICK BITES	205
SIGHTS	205

Just as Paris is not France and New York City is not the state of the same name, Toronto is not Ontario—although most people in those three major world centers would have you believe it is so.

Toronto sits on the northern shore of **Lake Ontario** at one tip of the so-called "Golden Horseshoe" with the Niagara region completing the semicircle. One may travel in any direction and discover a different Ontario awaiting your visit: North to the lake district, resorts and cottage country; west to the farming counties and cities of **Hamilton**, the heart of the country's steel industry, the German founded twin cities of **Kitchener-Waterloo** and stately, conservative **London**; east to historic **Kingston** and the beauty of the **Thousand Islands** cruises through the **St. Lawrence** (and further on to Canada's capital of **Ottawa**.)

If you are a sailor, you can even travel south from Toronto harbor along the coastline of **Lake Erie** or across the waters to the United States. The most popular tourist route, however, is around the horseshoe drive of Lake Ontario to the region of **Niagara**, with its miles of beautifully landscaped parkland, its bountiful grape and wine industry, the preserved small-town charm of **Niagara-on-the-Lake** and the summer theater at the **Shaw Festival** and, of course, one of the major tourist attractions in the world, **Niagara Falls**.

Simply known as "the Falls," this is one of the seven natural wonders of the world and attracts upward of fourteen million visitors a year. It used to be known as the "Honeymoon Capital of the World" and though honeymoons may not be as popular as they once were, the waterfall still is.

The first-known honeymooners to visit the Falls was Napoleon's brother, Jérôme Bonaparte, and his wife Elizabeth, who traveled together by stagecoach all the way from New Orleans to see this wonder of nature. It was not mentioned how long the journey took but it is safe to say this may have been the longest honeymoon trip on record. It took some time for the craze to catch on but honeymooners did indeed begin to flock to the Falls to watch as 34 million gallons of water per minute crashed over the slowly eroding limestone cliffs, from Lake Erie into **Niagara Gorge** below.

And a tourism industry was born—along with many offsprings some nine months after various honeymoons. As a result of the increasing popularity of the Falls, hotels and motels seemed to spring up overnight, alongside museums and galleries, parklands and golf courses, restaurants and fast-food stands and countless tacky souvenir shops full of "made in Hong Kong" kitsch, kitsch that unbelievably sells so fast they can't keep enough stock in the stores. (It's a toss-up whether Niagara Falls or the Poconnos in upper New York state produced the first heart-shaped bed. They can be found in both honeymoon havens.)

But though it is easy—and fun—to knock the commercialism of silly museums along the **Clifton Hill** strip (**House of Frankenstein, Movieland Wax Museum** and so on), one cannot criticize the natural majesty of the ten-thousand-year-old Falls of Niagara. Even the most jaded tourist displays initial wide-eyed wonderment at this spectacle. The **American Falls** (on the New York side) are some 320 meters wide (more than 1,000 feet) and come crashing down into the Niagara Gorge. This will likely be your first sight of the Falls, but that spectacle will pale in comparison to the **Horseshoe Falls** (or, **Canadian Falls**) just a little further down the parkway. The Horseshoe Falls is an 800-meter (2,600-foot) semicircle of awesome rushing power; at one point you can actually stand a few feet from the edge where the blue water turns white on its 51-meter (161-foot) downward plunge. This may not seem as high as you thought, but the sheer force of the Falls creates the impression that's it's higher than even the CN Tower.

On a particularly crowded summer day, you will be well advised to park your vehicle somewhere and just stroll along the walkway above the gorge; depending on the breeze that day, you can usually feel the fine mist from the plunging, pluming water. (On some days, the weather will be sunny and clear elsewhere, but raining along the walkway; within a matter of feet you can step out of the constant rainshower into the bright sunshine and onto dry pavement. When you visit Niagara, just plan on getting wet at some point during your stay.)

If you have limited time, you can certainly view the Falls and return to Toronto in one day—the drive itself is about an hour and a half—but there is actually a great deal to see and do in the area if your'e so disposed. Take a helicopter ride above the mighty Niagara Gorge; wander through some of the local vineyards and wineries; visit the baby whales at **Marineland** or slide down a monster slide at the **White Water Wave Pool**; touring the tacky museums of Clifton Hill; or meander through the colorful horticultural gardens along the Niagara escarpment. (Lineups for some of these activities can mean a wait of several hours on a hot summer weekend.)

The single most popular and exciting event is the boat ride on the Maid of the Mist; if there is time for only one adventure, this is the one to take. Prepare to line up and wait, secure in the knowledge that the boat trip into the white water will be worth it. You'll be suited up in a rain slicker as you board the little boat and chug your way into the base of the Falls. Rainbows follow you as you charge into the white maelstrom, until the boat, seemingly exhausted, is forced to turn back to the safety of the dockside. Another tour worth the lineup is the walk along the **Scenic Tunnels,** quite a different view of the waters of Niagara. Your group can actually descend by elevator to a linkup of tunnels immediately behind the Horseshoe Falls, where tons of white water come cascading down in front of you.

OUT OF TORONTO Niagara Falls

The best view of the Falls, certainly on a clear sunny day, is from the 50-story-tall **Skylon Tower**, which gives you a birds-eye perspective of the Horseshoe Falls and the mist that perpetually hangs in the air high above the water. The restaurant and bar area of the Tower revolves slowly to allow patrons a 360-degree view of the Falls and town of Niagara. This is an ideal point from which to snap some photos. You can also get a dramatic aerial view of the Falls and **Niagara River** on a **Niagara Helicopters** ride. Or, further along the **Niagara Parkway**, near the huge Floral Clock display, you can glide over the whirlpool torrent of the Niagara River in the **Spanish Aerocar**. Again, on a busy weekend, expect to wait your turn.

The best way to avoid the seasonal crowds is to visit the area during the week—not Fridays, Saturdays or Sundays—and try to get there around mid-morning. Other than that, there are many who feel the only time to visit the Falls is during the winter months, from December to early March. For one thing, there are no crowds (mind you, many of the activities close on Canadian Thanksgiving Weekend, the second weekend of October.). What was once summer mist is suspended as winter ice; everything near the Falls—trees, guardrails, buildings—dons a coat of several inches of transparent frozen water. This is truly an awesome sight and without the crowds, it's strangely peaceful on a clear sunlit day. As well, the winter season **Festival of Lights** dazzles your senses with reds, blues, greens and blinding white as the raging water is lit up every night with high-powered beams of brilliant color. It's a perfect time to visit Niagara; there are no crowds or busloads of tourists, you can easily get a dinner reservation without any problem and lovers of tacky souvenirs can still return home with some true finds to add to their collections from around the world.

RESTAURANTS

Skylon Tower
5200 Robinson St.,
Niagara Falls
• 356-2651
CONTINENTAL

10/20

Probably the most popular tourist restaurant in Niagara Falls, not because of the the quality of food, but because of the spectacular view of Niagara Falls, Skylon sits on top of it all, so to speak. The restaurant's perched some 236 meters (775 feet) above the Horseshoe Falls and slowly revolves 360 degrees per hour-and-ten-minute period to allow the 275 patrons a good look at the entire area; there is also seating for another 165 in the Summit Suite dining lounge.

The Niagara region produces a rich vegetable and fruit harvest, which is reflected in seasonal salads, fruit starters and desserts. Meat and seafood dishes fine, maybe a tad above other revolving restaurants. The ticket here is to keep it simple and enjoy the view. The wines come mainly from the local area and your waiter will be more than willing to explain the types of Ontario wines and grape varietals. Open year-round and reservations, especially during summer, are a must. About Can$70 dinner for two, including wine and gratuity. All cards accepted. *Open daily 7 a.m.-1 a.m. All major cards.*

Table Rock Restaurant

Queen Victoria Park, Niagara Falls
• 354-3631
AMERICAN

9/20

Horseshoe Falls's only full-service restaurant stays crowded all day, with people fighting to get the coveted window tables of the second story eatery. The only ones to get reservations are bus tours and large groups. Get the picture? Seating capacity is only 225, and the restuarant naturally tries for fast service and a large turnover of clientele. As a result, food is not fancy, tending more toward steaks, burgers, soups and sandwiches. Don't expect any gastronomic miracles, here, where the food is merely passable for most meals. It's best to avoid peak dining hours, especially during the day, although things are more relaxed in the evening. About Can$45 for two at dinner, with wine.

Open daily 7:30 a.m.-10 p.m., reduced hours in winter. All major cards.

QUICK BITES

Victoria Park Cafeteria

Queen Victoria Park, Niagara Falls
• 356-2217

It's fast food at the brink of the Horseshoe Falls, all located on the ground floor of the Table Rock Restaurant. Grab burgers, fries and chicken fingers to go on one side of the building, and souvenirs on the other. In other words, this is a crowded place. The food is fine for take-out fare. There are picnic tables outside, as well as acres of green grass and trees, where you can munch your burger or sip your soda and take a snooze before checking the Falls again to make certain the water is still running. Count on Can$20 for two with soft drinks.

Open Mon.-Fri. 9 a.m.-5 p.m., Sat.-Sun. 9 a.m.-7 p.m. All major cards.

SIGHTS

Maid of the Mist

5920 River Rd., Niagara Falls
• 358-5781

From mid-May to Labor Day in September, these two little boats chug valiantly against the current of the Niagara Gorge, bucking and rocking past the American Falls and the Cave of the Winds, directly into the center of the spectacular Horseshoe (or Canadian) Falls. The little ships were named after the Indian legend of the tribal maiden who was sacrificed as a bride to appease the god of the river. The 30-minute trip, which begins at the base of Clifton Hill directly across from the American Falls, leaves every fifteen minutes. The trip starts with a ride down the incline railway to the water's edge. Raincoats are provided. Possibly a two-hour wait during peak summer hours but worth it.

Open May 15-June 30 & Sept. 1-Oct. 15 Sat.-Sun. 9 a.m.-9 p.m. Adults Can$7, children 6-12 Can$4.

Marineland
7657 Portage Rd.,
Niagara Falls
• 356-2142

The main attraction here is the King Waldorf Marine Show, featuring killer whales Kandu and Nootka as well as sea lions and dolphins that provide a watery romp six times a day during the summer months (four marine shows during the winter). There is also a zoo with buffalo, bear, elk and other North American wildlife, a huge aquarium and circus rides for the family, as well as the world's largest roller coaster.
Summer (June 16-Sept. 15): open daily 9 a.m.-dusk. Sept. 16-June 15: open daily 10 a.m.-dusk. Summer: adults Can$16.95, children Can$13.95; Sept. 16-June 15: adults Can$7.50, children Can$ 5.75.

Niagara Falls Museum
5651 River Rd.,
Niagara Falls
• 356-2151

The oldest museum in North America (est. 1827) is the one to visit while in the area, if only for the history detailing the daredevils who have attempted (some successfully) to conquer Niagara. You'll see original newspaper photos of highwire artist Blondin as he walked across the gorge, some of the barrels used over the years, and the lifejacket of a 10-year-old boy who lived after being swept over the edge.
Open Feb.-Dec., daily 9 a.m.-dusk. Adults Can$3, children 7-12 Can$1.25.

Niagara Helicopters
3731 Victoria Ave.,
Niagara Falls
• 357-5672

A helicopter flight with this company, which is located just north of the Falls near the Whirlpool Rapids, provides a unique view as you soar along the Niagara River over both the Horseshoe and American falls. A must for photo buffs.
Open Feb.-Dec. 9 a.m.-dusk. Adults Can$50 (or two for Can$80), children 2-11 Can$15.

Niagara Spanish Aero Car
Niagara Parks Commission,
P.O. Box 150,
Niagara Falls
• 356-2241,
(800) 263-2558

Located about five kilometers (three miles) north of the Falls along the Niagara Parkway, this aerial car glides high across the Niagara Gorge, where the river twists and turns into the dangerous whirlpool rapids. The cable car travels across the gorge between two points of the Canadian shoreline.
Open April 1-Oct. 15, daily 10 a.m.-8 p.m. Adults Can$3.50, children 6-12 Can$1.75.

Skylon Tower
5200 Robinson St.,
Niagara Falls
• 356-2651

There are three "yellow bug" elevators that crawl quickly up the outside of the 236-meter (775-foot) tower and afford a breathtaking view of Niagara as you reach the observation deck. Like the revolving restaurant, it's open year-round. This is the best place in winter to see the nightly illumination of the Festival of Lights on both waterfalls. The lower level contains 40 boutiques, an indoor arcade and rides for the children.
Adults Can$4.95, children 6-12 Can$2.95.

OUT OF TORONTO   Niagara-on-the-Lake

Table Rock Scenic Tunnels
Niagara Parks Commission,
P.O. Box 150,
Niagara Falls
• 356-2241,
(800) 263-2558

Located at the top of the Horseshoe Falls beside the Table Rock Restaurant, you'll take the elevator down 38 meters (125 feet) through the solid rock of Niagara to a labrithyth of tunnels that lets you walk directly behind the rushing waters of the Falls and outside, near the base. Raincoats are provided. You'll need one.
Open July-Aug. 9 a.m.-9 p.m., Sept.-June. 9 a.m.-4 p.m. Adults Can$4.50, children Can$2.50.

Whitewater Water Park
430 Lundy's Ln.,
Niagara Falls
• 357-3380

If, after seeing all the rushing water, you're oversome by an urge to test the waves, just bring your bathing suit to this supervised aqua park, with its five giant waterslides, ten-thousand-square-foot surf wavepool, minislides and hot tubs. There are change rooms, restaurants, picnic areas and plenty of suntanning opportunities.
Open May 15-Sept. 4, daily 10 a.m.-8 p.m. Adults Can$10.95, children 4-7 Can$7.95.

NIAGARA-ON-THE-LAKE

RESTAURANTS	208
QUICK BITES	210
HOTELS	210
SHOPS	210
SIGHTS	211

If you need a break from the crowds and cacophony of the Falls, take the slow and winding drive north along the twenty-mile stretch of **Niagara Parkway**. This is all designated parkland: you will pass picnic areas overlooking the gorge; fruit stands extolling some of Niagara's finest peaches, apples and grapes; and vineyards and little cottage-industry wineries (most of which offer daily tours); all highlighted by some of the prettiest lush countryside you've probably ever seen.

Like the yellow-brick road, all this scenic splendor leads to the little preserved time capsule of **Niagara-on-the-Lake**. "Quaint" is an abused expression; it is, however, the word most often heard from visiting tourists when they describe this little village. In any case, the area remains a living monument to the nineteenth century; the town fathers even have a bylaw stating that any new structure—commercial or not—must conform to the period character of the village.

OUT OF TORONTO — Niagara-on-the-Lake

This was once the capital of Upper Canada (Ontario) back in 1792 when it was known as Newark; one of the local tourist attractions is the historic restored Fort George that was the British outpost during this period. The fort overlooks the American side of the Niagara River, just a musket shot away.

Niagara-on-the-Lake was a sleepy little Ontario village until 1962, when the fledgling **Shaw Festival** appeared on the scene to complement **Shakespeare's Festival Theatre** in Stratford. Since that time, the area has attracted Toronto weekenders and tourist busloads every season. The Shaw Festival, which presents plays of George Bernard Shaw and his contemporaries, literally has put the village on the map of the world theatrical stage. Both Broadway and Hollywood luminaries, from award winning Jessica Tandy, Hume Cronyn, Ian McKellen, Paxton Whitehead, Kate Reid and many others, have appeared here over the years. Attendance usually runs at near capacity and most theatergoers book tickets when the season is announced some six months before the May opening.

Tourists have also discovered the slow pace and enjoy wandering down the six blocks of the main **Queen Street**, basically from the Shaw Festival to the Oban Inn. Park your car. There is no need to drive as you browse through the shops selling Scottish woolens, homemade fudge, oldtime ice cream, midafternoon tea with scones, or crafts from local artisans.

Wait to eat seriously until you're in the village. Most of the inns have their own dining facilities, and they are good; be sure to reserve for lunch or dinner.

Accommodations in Niagara-on-the-Lake are at a premium—the 10,000 residents see over 2.5 million visitors a year. Everyone wants to stay here, yet the town has a mere 769 guest rooms; 619 of these are inns and hotels, the remaining 150 are found in local bed-and-breakfast establishments. As you can guess, during peak season the hotels can charge whatever they wish—and quite often do so. (One actor once described the village as "Niagara-on-the-Take.") But for a weekend escape, although the less crowded mid-week would be better, it can be a wonderfully relaxing stroll into the past.

RESTAURANTS

The Buttery Theatre Restaurant
19 Queen St.,
Niagara-on-the-Lake
• 468-2564
ENGLISH

10/20

The Buttery has the busiest outdoor dining veranda in town just opposite the town clock that seems to sprout like a tree in the middle of Queen Street. It's mainly for the hearty bowls of homemade soup along with a satisfying ploughman's lunch of freshly baked bread with chunks of cheese that people come here. Serving wenches dressed in old-English garb are both friendly and efficient. The afternoon tea with silver tea service features hot scones with local jams and jellies. The Buttery is known for its fun-filled Henry VIII evening feast, a spread of chicken with wine and honey, spicy pâtés, platters of roast pork and lamb and more. You won't be able to attend any perfor-

mances at the Shaw if you partake in this lengthy dinner, but that's okay, because the meal itself is most theatrical and entertaining event. Lunch for two costs about Can$25, with wine.
Open daily 11:30 a.m.-8 p.m. Henry VIII begins at 8 p.m. All major cards.

The Oban Inn Restaurant
160 Front St.,
Niagara-on-the-Lake
• 468-2165
ENGLISH

10/20

This stately old inn, overlooking the lake, was built in 1824 although the amenities are all modern twentieth century. The inn itself has only 23 rooms while dining capacity reaches 160. And it usually is filled beyond capacity. The menu tends toward the "olde English" style—rare roast beef with Yorkshire pudding, roast lamb with homemade mint sauce. The food is uniformly good, but not memorable: nice soup/salad/sandwich selections are available at noon and after the theater.

Avoid the congested lunchtime, for the Oban caters to large bus groups, but do return at night to sit in the English pub to enjoy an impromptu session around the piano or sip a glass of wine on the glassed-in patio. Dinner for two, including wine costs about Can$50.

Open daily 7 a.m.-8 p.m. Bar snacks until midnight. All major cards.

The Pillar and Post Inn Restaurant
King & John Sts.,
Niagara-on-the-Lake
• (416) 468-2123
CONTINENTAL

10/20

Another local inn but built originally as a canning factory in the early 1900s and restored as an inn in 1970. The restaurant has remained true to its roots for it turn out some competent dishes created with local vegetables, fruits and dairy products; homemade soups, pâtés, terrines, crisp summer salads and dessert fruit dishes highlight a menu ranging from thick all-beef hamburgers to filet mignon and lobster. Dinner for two, about Can$50 with wine.

Open daily 7 a.m.-10 p.m. All major cards.

The Prince of Wales Hotel Restaurant
6 Picton St.,
Niagara-on-the-Lake
• 468-3246
CONTINENTAL

11/20

For years, the general rule of thumb was to leave your hotel for a restaurant whose only business was to create and serve food. Not so in general anymore, as hotel food has vastly improved, and certainly not so in this village. The best restaurants are found in the various hotel dining rooms. This one extended the dining facilities along with the hotel (The additions, by the way, have been done so well it is difficult to tell the original structure from the new). The dining areas are elegant and the cuisine has been designed to match. You can order an exquisite rack of lamb from the dinner kitchen or a homemade soup and fresh salad après-theater. Dinner for two, with local wine, is easily Can$80.

Open daily 7 a.m.-10 p.m. All major cards.

QUICK BITES

The Angel Inn Restaurant
224 Regent St., Niagara-on-the-Lake
• 468-3411

Another good après-theater spot, The Angel Inn specializes in light English-style pub grub (toad-in-a-blanket and spotted dick), all highlighted by 26 drafts of the world all on tap. Originally built in 1782, the fun atmosphere of a restored, old-English countryside inn and pub prevails. There's also Continental dining during regular hours. Seating capacity is 150, plus another 30 in the seasonal wine garden, so book early during the busy weekends. Lunch for two with wine will run about Can$20.
Open daily 7 a.m.-10 a.m., 11:30 a.m.-3 p.m. & 5 p.m.-10 p.m. Pub food served until midnight. All major cards.

HOTELS

Gate House Hotel
142 Queen St., Niagara-on-the-Lake
L0S 1J0
• 468-3263
No fax

This restored inn stands out for its elegant, ultramodern interior design, so don't walk in expecting a quaint village inn. There are only nine guest rooms upstairs, all recently zapped up in a striking Italian design. There's plenty of black decor, marble, handsome fixtures and the requisite television. Yes, indeed, sitting right here in the little village is a little touch of Italy.
Doubles: Can$160.

SHOPS

Angie Strauss Gallery
178 Victoria St., Niagara-on-the-Lake
• 468-7788

This restored Victorian home just off the main street doubles as home and studio for this Canadian artist; it's also her shop, where she sells unique, one-of-a-kind clothing, featuring sweaters and women's fashion (as well as her paintings, of course) that feature bold floral prints. You will never have to worry about seeing anyone else in your outfit.
Open June-Sept. daily 9 a.m.-5 p.m. Closed Mon. during winter.

Irish Design
38 Queen St., Niagara-on-the-Lake
• 468-5254

The store is filled—some would say crammed—with designer knitwear, sweaters, coats and capes all imported from the Emerald Isle. There are very distinctive selections of items in linen and lace with clothing for both women and men. The old-world-style products blend with the atmosphere of the village.
Open June-Sept. daily 9 a.m.-6 p.m. Closed Mon. during winter.

Old Towne Antiques
287 Davy St.,
Niagara-on-the-Lake
• 468-5105

If you're an antique hunter, this is the right town to add to your collection. The shop specializes in selected traditional and country furniture (you can often find some solid old early Ontario or Quebec pieces here). There's china and primitive dolls.
Open daily 10 a.m.-6 p.m. Closed Mon. during winter.

SIGHTS

Cobble-Stone Galleries
223 King St.,
Niagara-on-the-Lake
• 687-7088

This gallery, opposite the Prince of Wales Hotel, features some fine examples of Canadian art with such known artists as Linda Kemp (watercolors), Eleanor McComb (oils) and Jack Pischedda. The owners were considering relocating at press time, so be sure to call first.
Open daily 9 a.m.-6 p.m.

Fort George National Historic Site
Box 787,
Niagara-on-the-Lake
• 468-4257

The British built this fort in 1797 and it was their principal military installment on the Niagara frontier to repel any invasion by the Americans. The Yankees did capture it in 1813, however, and burned most of the town of then-Newark before the British recaptured their fort later that same winter. The British then rebuilt and extended the installation and it was eventually abandoned when the two factions made an uneasy alliance. Fort George was restored in 1939 and the original buildings include the soldiers' barracks, carpenters' shops and stone powder magazine.
Open year-round. Tours May-Sept., daily. Adults Can$2, children Can$1.

Inniskillin Winery
Rural Rte. 1,
Niagara Pkwy.,
Niagara-on-the-Lake
• 468-3554

Several wineries operate in the area, each with daily tours and special tastings, but this is perhaps the one that will give you the best look at a small cottage industry. Inniskillin started the recent Canadian trend in microwineries by being the first to blend the native Lambrusco grape with European varietals to give the Canadian wine industry a healthier reputation. This tour demonstrates the latest techniques in wine-making on a smaller scale with an adjacent wine boutique in a restored nineteenth-century barn.
Open daily 10 a.m.-5 p.m. (wine boutique). Tour times vary.

OUT OF TORONTO Kleinburg

Niagara Apothecary Museum
5 Queen St. at King St., Niagara-on-the-Lake
• 468-3845

Originally erected in 1866, the apothecary is now maintained and operated as a museum; instead of dispensing medicine, it sells lollipops. There have been very few changes in the decor over the years and the original walnut and butternut fixtures remain, as well as the crystal gasoliers and a rare collection of apothecary glass. The building is located in the middle of town, just across from the Prince of Wales Hotel.
Open May 15-Sept. 30, daily 9 a.m.-6 p.m. Admission free.

Shaw Festival
Box 774, Niagara-on-the-Lake
• 468-2172

The fledgling theatrical experiment of 1962 has developed into a world-class permanent summer attraction, featuring stage and film luminaries as well as record-breaking box-office-attendance figures. The plays of George Bernard Shaw and his contemporaries are presented on three stages: the 863-seat Festival, the historic (former town hall) 344-seat Court House Theatre and the 351-seat Royal George Theatre. Depending on the annual schedule of productions, the theater is open for evenings, matinees and even lunchtime performances, with the Monday as *the* day to go.
Schedules change according to season; mantinee 2 p.m., evening show 8 p.m. Prices range from Can$19.50-Can$42.

KLEINBURG

RESTAURANTS	213
SIGHTS	215

One of the most popular weekend escapes for Toronto residents is less than an hour's drive north of the city's urban core, to the little village of Kleinburg. There are also some fun diversions along the way. Consider **Black Creek Pioneer Village** and the theme playpark known as **Canada's Wonderland**, for example. The drive, itself, is an easy one. From downtown Toronto, travel west along the Queen Elizabeth Highway, then north on Highway 427, which turns into Highway 27, then watch for the turn off sign to Kleinburg.

This tiny town of 227 residents suddenly appears on the highway, when the road signs caution you to slow down to 50 kilometers an hour (about 30 miles an hour). You may miss it, as it takes up all of four blocks on the highway. It's a town of tiny stores, ice-cream parlors and antique shops, in a quiet rural setting. There's also a

OUT OF TORONTO Kleinburg

secret treasure trove of some of the finest art galleries in Canada. For example, the **McMichael Canadian Art Collection** features a large number of paintings by Canada's Group of Seven. The gallery started inauspiciously enough when Robert and Signe McMichael bought some land in 1952, built a comfortable log cabin and started collecting art by Canadian painters. Soon their collection expanded so much, they would have had to build another structure just for their paintings and native sculptures; so the two decided to share their artworks with the general public.

En route to Kleinburg, not far from **York University**, you'll find **Black Creek Pioneer Village** (416-736-1733), a perfect re-creation of nineteenth-century Ontario's homes, stores, shops and buildings. All of it was gathered from around the province and moved to this site. The **Metro Toronto Conservation Authority**, whose members all dress in period costumes, operates the Village. You can watch the residents grind flour in the old operating mill, shoe horses in the blacksmith shop, sell penny candy at the corner store and even serve you some thick farm-style vegetable soup in the restaurant (which is fully operational). One somewhat sour note for the bargain-hunter: prices belong to the present era and not to the good old days. Horse-drawn wagons—or sleighs in winter—carry guests through the village on a complete tour or they may elect to stop at any of the homes for a visit. There are even schoolchildren, dressed from a century past, who spend the day learn the "three R's" in the one-room schoolhouse.

This is a fun and friendly visit to the past, although it can be a bit of a jolt to look up and find yourself dwarfed by the modern-day apartment buildings and university campus just down the highway.

If you would rather tour the present, then head north from the city, along Highway 400, toward Maple and the theme park, Canada's Wonderland. This is a 370-acre park is based on the cartoon characters of Hanna-Barbera, including the smurfs, who wander throughout the park among children and parents out to enjoy a sunny day. Visiting Canada's Wonderland is a full day's outing, especially if you're with children, so if you don't get a chance to move on, save the Kleinburg trip for another day.

RESTAURANTS

The Doctor's House and Livery
P.O. Box 41
Kleinburg
• 893-1615
CONTINENTAL

11/20

Originally the village doctor's house, dating back to the days of the Confederation, is now a charming little gift shop while the renovated bar, or livery, now serves food that pleases. Old overstuffed couches and wingback chairs fill the comfortable upstairs lounge. This is a relaxed, homey, wood-beamed spot, with a menu—based on a nineteenth-century Canadian cookbook—that features rack of lamb, roast duckling, braised rabbit and fresh country produce. As well, the fresh country baking would do any pioneer wife proud. A relaxed dining experience

OUT OF TORONTO Kleinburg

with nice food and friendly country service. Dinner for two will cost Can$75, including wine.
Open daily 11:30 a.m.-3 P.m. & 5 p.m.-9 p.m. All major cards.

Flowers for My Daughter
10512 Islington Ave., Kleinburg
• 893-2710
MEDITERRANEAN

Run on a shoestring by a couple of escapees from Toronto, this decent restaurant in the middle of town has a Gothic decor, with rigid, high-backed chairs, but the sunshine-inspired cooking makes up for all that.

The kitchen, a one-person high-wire act by chef/co-owner Kenny Brudner, is an offshoot of our collective love-affair with the taste and abandon of the cuisines of the Mediterranean basin. Grilling is the favored technique here, and marinating in spice, a signature procedure. Chicken, pork and tuna make compatible plate mates when they are part of a team of grilled appetizers, served with a homemade, sweet pepper chutney. Grilled tuna also serves as a main course, alongside an anise-flavored pilaf and freshly sautéed vegetables. Nicely grilled lamb chops appear on the menu (naturally), and also calamari, greaselessly fried until they're weightless. Even the vegetarian dishes, especially the eggplant specialties, betray the extra care and unique touches of this chef. A modest wine list of ordinary Italian and Spanish vintages are just the right potions to counterpoint the earthy cooking and wash it down with gusto. Dinner for two, with wine, Can$70.
Open Wed.-Fri. 12:30 p.m.-3 p.m. & 6 p.m.-11 p.m., Sat. noon-11 p.m., Sun. noon-9 p.m. Cards: MC, V.

Going traveling? Look for Gault Millau's other "Best of" guides to Chicago, Florida, France, Hawaii, Hong Kong, Italy, London, Los Angeles, New England, New Orleans, New York, Paris, San Francisco, Washington, D.C. and more to come...

Halfway House Dining Room
Black Creek Pioneer Village,
1000 Murray Ross Pkwy.,
Downsview
• 736-1740
CANADIAN

10/20

This basement dining room at the Black Creek Village site serves some good basic food during the lunchtime hours as well as a special afternoon tea. Hearty, early-Canadian country soups, thick beef stews and bread steaming hot from the baker's original wood-burning ovens taste as bone-sticking as they should. There are also full meals of beef and fish with fresh carrots or beans picked daily from their gardens. And if you are in the area during December, try to reserve a table for their special seasonal turkey dinners, complete with mince pudding and deep-dish apple pie. Canada West Dining Room and Victoria Room available for group dining. Lunch for two runs Can$30 with wine.
Open daily 11:30 a.m.-2:30 p.m. All major cards.

OUT OF TORONTO Kleinburg

SIGHTS

McMichael Canadian Art Collection
• 893-1121

This is the perfect showcase for the Canadian landscape artists known as the Group of Seven; a huge sprawling log cabin with a rough-hewn exterior in a rural setting that perfectly suits the northern wilderness painted by the famous group. There are also examples of native and Eskimo artwork and sculptures—original works carved from stone and bone. Guided tours are available (best to call in advance for the changing times) and souvenir shoppers will enjoy the prints and posters in the art shop. McMichael is especially busy when the lush green of spring or the brilliant colors of autumn highlight the paintings on the walls.
Open Tues.-Sat. 10 a.m.-5 p.m., Sun. noon-5 p.m. Adults Can$3, students & seniors Can$1.50.

Black Creek Pioneer Village
1000 Murray Ross Pkwy., Downsview
• 736-1733

There are more than 30 authentic buildings—including typical homes and shops, a one-room schoolhouse and blacksmith shop, an operating grain mill and a restored restaurant—that make up this nineteenth-century village at the corner of Jane Street and Steeles Ave. West. Visitors are met by costumed residents who explain the mechanics of their "village," while horsedrawn carts trot through the dirt streets and children actually take classes in the schoolhouse. This is one of the best re-creations (all done with authentic structures from around the province) that have been saved to present a typical town of the nineteenth century. Check out the festivities at Thanksgiving and the Christmas Season.
Open daily 10 a.m.-6 p.m. Adults Can$6, students & children 5-15 Can$2.50.

Canada's Wonderland/ Kingswood Music Theatre
P.O. Box 624
Maple
• 832-7000

This theme park, highlighted by Magic Mountain rising mysteriously beside Highway 400, has added new rides and attractions every year to keep up with the demand from an ever-returning public. The rides include seven roller coasters, spins around and through Magic Mountain, waterslides and aquarium shows. There are daily, Broadway-style song-and-dance presentations at the 1,100-seat Canterbury Theatre; band performances and strolling musicians; and huge, fuzzy Smurf characters that wander around the 360 acres park. At night, rock concerts are in the Kingswood Music Theatre.
May 24-Sept. 1: open daily 10 a.m.-10 p.m. Sept. 2 to 2nd week in Oct.: open Sat.-Sun. 10 a.m.-10 p.m. Daily pass Can$22.95, season pass (unlimited use) Can$39.95. Family pass for four persons Can$109.95. Admission to evening performances at Kingswood Music Theatre, Can$7.

CAMBRIDGE

Langdon Hall
Rural Rte. 33
(Intersection of Blair & Langdon Rds.),
Cambridge
• 338-8800,
(519) 740-2100
ENGLISH

Even the pleasures of food can pale against the luxurious prettiness of this grand country inn. You relax immediately upon entering the room, with its polished wood floors and huge windows that overlook the woods. Before Langdon Hall opened last year, the owners were searching for a chef that could complement this setting; they found him in Nigel Didcock, who trained at London's Connaught Hotel before continuing at Troisgros in Roanne, France. Now he balances that training with local produce (sometimes wonderful, sometimes not). Breakfasts and tea are noteworthy: the latter is served in a chintz veranda with a very high grade of ingredients, including a locally made cream with a higher butterfat content than should be legal, and ethereal scones. A generous and fresh breakfast buffet is served in that grand dining room that is transformed by sunshine in the morning.

There is a large herb and vegetable garden outside the kitchen, so at mealtimes, first courses might include a salad of poached beets, celery root and snow peas with a vanilla-oil dressing, or a filet of lake pickerel on a bed of watercress with balsamic vinegar dressing and a tangle of deep-fried root vegetables. Fish dishes are competently done: home-cured Atlantic salmon is glazed with goat cheese and broiled for a first course, or it's baked with yogurt and fresh herbs for a second. Sea scallops are poached and served with a confit of belgian endive, and stir-fried bell peppers in a light ginger sauce. There's not a lot of poultry, but you may see partridge or quail salad with a nut dressing. Depending on the season, meats will get a hearty treatment. Last winter there was rack of Washington State lamb served up with rutabaga, parsnips, carrots and pearl onions and a chiffonade of brussel sprouts with bacon.

Dessert may be an orange mousse glazed with zabaglione or one of the playful compiled plates like the pear grouping of pear sorbet, fresh pear roasted with honey-and-pear frangipane; or the chocolate-lover's dessert that carries nine different chocolate items. The wine list is only moderately interesting, with a small range of Bordeaux and Italian wines in the middle to upper price range, but plans to change it are afoot. Dinner for two will be about Can$140.

Open daily noon-2:30 p.m. & 7 p.m.-10 p.m. Tea Fri.-Sun. 3:30 p.m.-6 p.m. Cards: AE, MC, V.

OUT OF TORONTO Cottage Country

COTTAGE COUNTRY

HOTELS	218
SIGHTS	221

The annual weekend exodus from the urban work-a-day world commences every May 24th (known as Victoria Day, for the former Queen of England) and lasts until Labor Day, the first weekend of September. As if by magic, the city of Toronto's population suddenly drops by half, occasionally seeming empty on weekends, as hundreds of thousands of vacationers point their vehicles north and head for the mecca known as cottage country.

This perennial playground north of Toronto is filled with countless lakes and bays (Ontario has roughly one-half million lakes within its boundaries), little tourist towns, numerous cottages and campgrounds of tents and trailers, as well as hundreds of resorts, inns and motels. There are two primary adjacent areas that make up the area, the **Muskokas** and **Haliburton** regions. The boundaries, roughly, are from the city of **Barrie,** an hour's drive south from downtown Toronto, to **Algonquin Park,** a three-and-a-half-hour drive to the north. The eastern border includes the towns of **Collingwood, Penetanguishene** and **Parry Sound** along the coast of **Georgian Bay,** and the towns of **Bobcaygeon** and **Barrie's Bay** on the western border. Note that although Torontonians consider this area as the northland, the province of Ontario extends another 1,500 miles north of Algonquin Park. Most people drive to the area north from Toronto along Highway 400 and then branch out when they reach the various secondary highway arteries around the town of Barrie: Highway 26 toward the Collingwood area; on Highway 400 toward Penetanguishene; along Highway 69 to Parry Sound. To reach **Gravenhurst, Huntsville** and the Algonquin Park area, just follow Highway 11 from Barrie or take the 118 east cutoff (from Highway 11) to reach the Haliburton Highlands region.

The area is also popular for weekend drives during September's and October's cavalcade of color, when the leaves of the maple trees turn brilliant reds, yellow and orange. The peak color lasts for about two weeks, from the last week of September to Canadian Thanksgiving, the second weekend of October. The lodges and resorts are usually booked with visitors paying homage to the clear, crisp autumn days before the onslaught of the Canadian winter. There are bus tours from Toronto, including both day trips and weekend overnighters, for groups who wish to leave the driving to someone else. In winter, alpine slopes and nordic ski trails call to space-age-suited snowmobilers and dogsled racers. For some, a quiet, crisp walk under snow-covered pines or a convivial evening beside a blazing fireplace in a cozy resort will suffice.

OUT OF TORONTO Cottage Country

The majority of tourists, however, visit during the heat of summer, so here's a friendly word of advice—as a tourist not bound by weekday work patterns, try to avoid a Friday afternoon escape to the north. From Friday noon until late evening, you will only find yourself stuck in Ontario's largest parking lot, since all of the major highways become crowded and jammed as everyone heads out from the city.

Like the legendary story of three blind men describing an elephant—one thought the beast was its waving trunk, another a strong tusk, the third a huge flat surface—cottage country is many things to many people. Some would say it's the raucous resort town of **Wasaga Beach** on Georgian Bay (known to every Toronto teenager), others, a quiet cottage nestled on a sunset lake. Those with with money to spend might characterize the area for its deluxe resorts, or a houseboat cruise through the rivers and locks of the **Trent-Severn** waterways, while others of more modest holiday means would picture a pitched tent in a provincial campground or a mobile home in a little community trailer park.

Whatever the final consensus, there's summer-stock theater and childrens' camps, tennis clinics and antique stores, small-town crafts shops and historic sites. There are even family farm vacations. Swimming and boating, windsurfing and canoeing, suntanning and fishing, sailboats and motorboats are also sporting possibilities.

Everyone has their favorite town or village in Cottage Country; the place where they do their grocery shopping, purchase new bathing suits and suntan lotion, treat themselves to country milkshakes and homemade french fries or while away some shopping time on a rainy afternoon. Names such as Huntsville and Haliburton, Meaford and Minden, Port Elgin and Penetanguishene, Barrie and Bracebridge, Gravenhurst and Glen Orchard. And favorite lakes such as Rosseau, Muskoka, Sturgeon, Buckhorn, Twelve Mile and Scugog. Which one is the best? Easy: The one you like best at the time.

HOTELS

Blue Mountain Inn
Rural Rte. 3,
Collingwood L9Y 3Z2
• (705) 445-0231
Fax (705) 445-8647

Again, here's a winter resort that decided to expand to a four-season operation. The 103-room Inn (as well as the 250 two-and-three bedroom condos that owners make available) provides easy access for guests to the 28 ski runs in winter and the Great Slide Ride in summer. The rooms are pretty much standard fare, but you'll get a nice amenities basket, two double beds and a color TV. There are also fitness and racket facilities in the new recreation complexes, as well as a nearby eighteen-hole golf course. Also, there are cafés and bars aplenty.
Rooms: Can$75-Can$125; condos: Can$150.

Cleveland's House Resort

P.O. Box 60,
Minett POB 1G0
• (705) 765-3171
No fax

This venerable seasonal Muskoka institution entered its 123rd year of operation in 1991, and has played hosts to generations of returning families. Ask for a lake view. Not matter which side of Clevelands House you're on, each room has a refrigerator, TV and a nice bathroom . . . the things that count. The resort features several dozen tennis courts, an extensive childrens' program and vast waterfront playground on the beautiful Lake Rousseau. Even though Clevelands House has a capacity of 500 guests, reservations are necessary due to its continuing reputation. Rates vary, due to accommodation and resort packages, so be sure to ask. Open June 23 to October 30.
Rooms: Can$225-Can$300 (Can$1,400-Can$1,700 per week).

Deerhurst Resort

Rural Rte. 4,
Huntsville POA 1KO
• (705) 789-6411
Fax (705) 789-2431

A few years back, one competitor called this spot "the Cadillac of the resort trade." With the additions, building and expansion of the past decade, it has become the Rolls-Royce Silver Cloud Phantom of Ontario resorts. Deerhurst is no longer a resort, but a community unto itself. Located on Peninsula Lake just east of Huntsville, there are fully equipped cabins with fireplace and Jacuzzi, deluxe condos (for rent or sale), dining facilities, indoor and outdoor pools, lakefront water sports, fly-in fishing, bars, nightclubs, dancing, a Las Vegas Show, sports center, tennis, golf, winter skiing and conference facilities. The list goes on. This is an all-inclusive, year-round resort with a huge (close to 600), friendly staff pays close attention to detail and guest satisfaction. You can, however, expect to pay the big bucks for this fun.
Cabins & condos: Can$200-Can$400.

Domain of Killien

Box 810,
Haliburton K0M 1S0
• (705) 457-1556
No fax

A small resort—nineteen cabins and five rooms in the main lodge—allows the owners of this exclusive retreat to provide personalized service to their clientele. The lodge, hidden away on five thousand acres of lush Haliburton Highlands, is owned by a French Count and his two stepsons, one of whom heads the four-man team of Cordon Bleu chefs. The restaurant at present has not been visited by a Gault Millau reviewer, and, therefore, remains unrated by us. Rooms are simple, but comfortable, and guests seem to be mainly nature lovers, who prefer peace, quiet and good French dining.
Rooms & cabins: Can$200-Can$300 (up to Can$1,800 per week).

OUT OF TORONTO Cottage Country

The Inn and Tennis Club at Manitou
McKellar,
Lake Manitouwabing
P1C0
• (705) 389-2171,
(416) 967-3466 (in winter)
Fax (705) 765-6668

Located north of Parry Sound on Lake Manitouwabing, the Inn & Tennis Club is renowned as one of the best tennis clinics in North America. There are thirteen excellent courts, professional group lessons (a ratio of one pro for three players), individual sessions, available court time all day and night. But not only tennis but superbly appointed rooms (twelve-foot cathedral ceilings, lakefront balconies, Jacuzzis, saunas), swimming pool and sun deck. In fact, the retreat meets (some would say excels) the standards set by its membership in the prestigious Relais et Chateaux. The restaurant at present has not been visited by a Gault Millau reviewer and, therefore, remains unrated by us.
Open mid-May to Oct. Prices vary depending on type of cabin, tennis lessons and instruction, but average weekend for two costs Can$1,00.

The Inn at Horseshoe
P.O. Box 10,
Horseshoe Valley,
Barrie L4M 4Y8
• (705) 835-2790
Fax (705) 835-6352

This is the closest ski spot to Toronto, and in 1987, the Horseshoe Valley ski area finally opened a year-round resort in a major way. The Inn features parlor rooms and loft suites with king-size beds, cherrywood furniture, walk-in showers, Jacuzzis and saunas. Nice. The dining rooms look over the eighteenth hole of a new, professionally designed golf course in the lushness of Horseshoe Valley. Amenities include a piano bar and billiard room, several swimming pools, squash courts, tennis courts and a gym. There are also rental and time-share condominiums.
Rooms: Can$125-Can$200.

Maple Sands Resort
Rural Rte. 1,
Haliburton K0M 1S0
• (705) 754-2800
No fax

Check out this good family resort—if you have a family, that is—with complete childrens' program, water sports, canoeing and boating, tennis courts and volleyball, and healthy heaping portions of country cooking. The resort's open year-round but with limited hours (mainly weekends) in winter to accommodate the cross-country skiiers who tour the 250-miles of linking trails. This is a place where children who are now parents return with their children. There's live "little theater" every Monday evening in summer and a huge television screen for movies during the rainy days.
Rooms: Can$170 (Can$850 per week). Family packages and children's rates available.

Sherwood Inn
Box 400,
Port Carling P0B 1J0
• (705) 765-3131
Fax (705) 765-6668

The epitome of a couples' resort on the quiet section of Lake Joseph (this is not a childrens' camp). Quiet relaxed atmosphere with old-style cabins under towering pine trees just beside the lake. The Sherwood is known for its excellence in food and wine. An intimate getaway weekend for those feeling somewhat stressed out by the city life. Only seventeen cabins (two with whirlpool) and 23 rooms in the main lodge.
Rooms: Can$200.

Sir Sam's Inn
Eagle Lake,
Haliburton K0M 1M0
• (705) 754-2188
Fax (705) 754-4264

Another Haliburton resort, Sir Sam's was originally the country estate of Sir Samuel Hughes, Canada's Minister of Militia during the Second World War. Today it has been totally refurbished into a full-facility lakeside resort. The Inn, thanks to its classic old-world charm, has become known as a couples' hideaway complete with superb dining and romantic Eagle Lake setting hidden away in the lush highlands. There are only 27 units, so book early. Also, just down the road is Sir Sam's Ski Resort, which offers the premier skiing of the Haliburton region.
Rooms: Can$200. Cards: AE, MC, V.

Wigamog Inn
Rural Rte. 2,
Haliburton K0M 1S0
• (705) 457-2000
Fax (705) 457-1962

Located on Lake Kashagawigamog just outside of Haliburton, this family-operated resort provides casual chalets, motel rooms and lodge rooms, with a full range of amenities from tennis courts to shuffleboard, a comfortable stuffed-chair lounge and good, home-cooked dinners. Rooms are simple, and good for what they are. As well, there is a private waterplane service that docks right in front of the lodge.
Rooms: Can$175 (Can$1,000 per week).

SIGHTS

Algonquin Provincial Park
Whitney, Ontario
• (705) 633-5572

Campers alert: this one is the province's most popular park and campground. The main highway, Highway 60, wanders through the southern region of this 7,600-square-kilometer (3,000-square-mile) park that's located on the southern edge of the rocky Canadian Shield. There are over 1,000 miles of canoe routes (you can rent canoes and camping supplies), overnight hiking trails and wilderness camp sites, sandy beaches and excellent fishing streams for lake trout and bass. Much of the park is only accessible by foot or canoe. Check out the exhibits of Pioneer Lodging, as well as the museum featuring the natural history of the park. For those who don't care to "rough it in the bush," there are three lodges—Arowhon Pines, Killarney Lodge and

> *Please note that the prices in this guide reflect what hotels were charging at press time. Also don't hesitate to inquire about packages and off-season rates.*

OUT OF TORONTO   Cottage Country

Bartlett Lodge—where the amenities run from gourmet dining to tennis courts. Cross-country skiing and winter camping in the off-season.

From Toronto it's about a three-and-a-half-hour drive. Begin by traveling north on Highway 400, then continue north on Highway 11 then turn east on Highway 60.

Open year-round; campsite: open June through Labor Day. Admission (in summer) Can$5 per vehicle; campsites Can$10 (without shower) to Can$15 (with shower).

Blue Mountain Slide Rides
Blue Mountain Resort, Rural Rte. 3, Collingwood
• (705) 445-0231

The Great Slide Ride combines a scenic chairlift ride with a breathtaking three-thousand-foot descent by minibobsled through woods and along ski trails—the chairlift and ski trails courtesy of Blue Mountain Ski Resorts. This region is Ontario's premier winter ski area where tens of thousands of skiers pour into the little town of Collingwood every winter. Recently, the folks at Blue Mountain decided to make their resort work year-round for them, adding summer bobsled runs and various water rides down their existing ski hill, where brightly colored ski suits replace bathing gear in the winter months. There is also sunbathing, windsurfing and other water facilities on their nearby sand beach.

Facilities also include the 103-room Blue Mountain Inn, a hotel with all amenities, cafeteria, lounge and gift shop. The ski chalets/condos are available during winter months only.

Open mid-May to Labor Day, daily 10 a.m.-5 p.m. All-day tickets: adults Can$15.50, children Can$12.50.

Houseboat Vacations
129 Carlingview Dr., Rexdale
• (800) 387-3998

Ahoy, landlubbers, this has always been a popular pastime for weekend sailors or for those couples and families who decide to spend a week in summer cruising lazily along the Trent-Severn Waterway. The largest supplier (over one hundred) of rental houseboats is Go Vacations, specialists in managing recreational vehicles throughout North America and yachting holidays in the Caribbean. The staff prepares you with a boating lesson, loads your boat with amenities from bedsheets to silverware (bring your own food) and off you go, cruising the 240 miles of the inland waterway from Port Severn on Georgian Bay to the town of Trenton bordering Lake Ontario. There are countless boats on the waters, from pleasure boats and yachts, to canoes and houseboats, all cruising by the island-dotted lake, quiet rivers, a few small towns and a total of 45 locks. If you run short of supplies, check the marina and stores en route. At night, you can tie up at a town dock, riverbank or stay at one of the little inns along the banks of the waterway. Houseboat prices vary according to number of persons, size of boat and the length of time required for your river excursion. Roughly plan on

Can$125 per day, plus your own food and drink supplies.
Open mid-June to Canadian Thanksgiving. Hours and cruise times vary; phone ahead for schedule.

Sainte-Marie Among the Hurons
P.O. Box 160,
Midland
• (705) 526-7838

They worked hard on this three-acre historic site that details the first settlement by European missionaries in this part of Ontario. It was a mission for Jesuit priests, and today, a shrine to these eight men, who were killed by the Iroquois Indians several centuries ago. An interpretive museum and guided tour of the reconstructed site will give you the low down.

Also nearby is the Martyr's Shrine to commemorate the slain missionaries; the first men in North America to be canonized by the Roman Catholic Church. Midland also boasts a full-scale replica of a typical sixteenth-century village erected by the Huron Indians, complete with longhouses and surrounded by wooden palisades. This shows how the Native Canadians lived before they had any contact with the European explorers.

Open May 20 to Canadian Thanksgiving. Adults Can$5, students Can$3.50.

Segwun Steamship Cruises
P.O. Box 68,
Gravenhurst
• (705) 687-6667

The *RMS Segwun*, a restored 1887 steamship, cruises along the gorgeous setting of the Georgian Bay coastline. The 99-passenger ship (honored recently by the Society of American Travel Writers for its efforts toward "preserving the past for modern-day tourists") has retained its nineteenth-century charm, and the various tours leave from various ports including Honey Harbour, Parry Sound and Penatanguishene, as well as home base of Gravenhurst. Book early, especially for the sunset dinner cruises; the food is good but you may not notice it amidst the stunning sunset scenery of the 30,000 islands.

Prices vary according to the tour route and length of cruise. 2-hour cruise: adults Can$15, children Can$10; Sunset Dinner Cruise: Can$40 (with dinner), Can$20 (without dinner).

Wasaga Landing
• (705) 429-3711

Wasaga Waterworld
• (705) 429-4400
Wasaga Beach

These two water theme parks feature everything from fiberglass flumes that speed riders to splashdown pools, wave pools, paddle boats, mini-golf, thermal whirlpools and a childrens' playground. This beach town is perhaps the most popular weekend resort town in Cottage Country. Its population of five thousand swells to bursting during the summer, with vacationing families and hordes of weekend visitors. There is a stretch of sandy beach running for miles along the coast of Nottawasaga Bay and many city dwellers think nothing of the two hour drive for a day-long or weekend stay.

Both parks open mid-June to Labor Day, daily 10 a.m.-8 p.m. Wasaga Waterworld: adults Can$10, children Can$8. Wasaga Landing: adults Can$13.50, children Can$10.

OUT OF TORONTO Stratford

STRATFORD

RESTAURANTS	226
QUICK BITES	227
HOTELS	228
SIGHTS	229

When Alec Guiness first trod the boards—literally—under a canvas tent erected in a **Stratford** park back in 1953, the sleepy little farming town of nineteen thousand residents would soon find itself transformed into a major theater center known throughout the English-speaking world. In that year, people in Ontario seemed to be starved for culture, and the 1,500-seat tent theater which served up Guiness and Irene Worth in *Richard III* provided just the ticket to calm the hunger pangs. The original five-week season had to be extended to six, and the season marked up an impressive 98 percent occupancy during the summer run. This farming and light-industrial area would never be the same after that summer, as culture mavens began to discover the new, albeit seasonal, artistic mecca.

The idea was the brainchild of local journalist Tom Patterson, who reasoned that since Stratford's namesake village in England was famous for its presentations of Shakespeare's plays, why shouldn't the Canadian counterpart follow suit? Since that first season, award-winning actors, directors and playwrights have flocked to this little town in the middle of Ontario farmland to perform summer works of the Bard, Ibsen, Samuel Beckett, Anton Chekhov, Jean Baptiste Poquelin Molière and Richard Sheridan, to name just a few.

Stratford also became a center for such new Canadian playwrights as James Reaney, Tom Hendry, Michael Ondaatje, Larry Fineberg to premiere their latest works, spawning the country's first theater repertoire company. Douglas Rain, Douglas Campbell, Martha Hendry, Kenneth Welsh, Richard Monette, Nicholas Pennell and others soon became well-known names from coast to coast. As well, the company attracted the visiting talents major stars (Sir John Gielgud, Oscar-winning Maggie Smith, British screen actor Brian Bedford, actor/writer/raconteur Peter Ustinov, among others) and even brought home the talents of others, such as native son Len Cariou, fresh from his Tony Award winning performance as Broadway's *Sweeney Todd*. Theater had finally found a home in Canada.

OUT OF TORONTO Stratford

In 1954, the **Festival Theatre** was designed, under founding artistic director Sir Tyrone Gutherie and designer Tanya Moisewisch, on hilltop parkland overlooking the Avon River. It officially opened in 1957. The duo's concept of a prosenium, or thrust stage, has been copied by at least a dozen major theaters around the world (the concept is based on the classical Greek theater at Epidaurus) with a sweep of 220 degrees. Though the theater holds 2,262 people, no seat is more than 65 feet from the stage. The Festival has since added two other venues, the **Avon Theatre**, an old restored vaudeville house in town, and the **Tom Patterson Theatre** (called until early 1991 the **Third Stage**), which has become synonymous with experimental productions for the **Young Company** of players.

The town, itself, is located about 90 miles (140 kilometers) west of Toronto. You simply drive along Highway 401 West about 60 miles to the **Kitchener-Waterloo** north turnoff, then turn west again on Highways 7 and 8, and follow the road signs right into Stratford. There are also trains, regular bus service and daily theater tours available from Toronto.

As you leave the urban streets of Toronto, you will find that the landscape changes dramatically into lush, green farmland. Fruit and vegetables, dairy products, tobacco and peanuts (yes, there are peanut farms here!) line the road into Stratford.

This is still only a community of 26,000 year-round residents, but over the years millions of people have visited the area during season. Many will drive from Toronto just for dinner and evening performance; others spend a theater weekend, while some take a week long holiday to see six or seven plays, dine in some fine restaurants or just have a picnic lunch along the banks of the Avon River.

The locals realized long ago that tourism was now their lifeblood; new restaurants have appeared over the years, motels flourished and guest houses have proliferated all over town. In fact, anyone with an extra room in their house manages to fill it during the summer months. Though the crowds continue the seasonal migration into the area, taxing its accommodation and dining facilities, the town fathers are very cautious about expansion. For instance, they have turned down applications from various hotel/motel chains, preferring to keep the small-town atmosphere and attitude.

Many tourists prefer Stratford for a relaxing weekend and may not even take in a performance. They stroll the streets, do some souvenir shopping, spend an afternoon lounging or snoozing over a picnic lunch in the park, rent a rowboat and cruise along the waters of the Avon River, visit the art galleries and antique shops or spend hours over dinner at one of the restaurants.

Stratford naturally lends itself to walking; unless your hotel is out on the highway, you will not need your car once you arrive. Just park it for the weekend and enjoy the summer strolls to the theater, restaurants, galleries or shops. Nothing is very far away from wherever you are.

OUT OF TORONTO   Stratford

RESTAURANTS

The Church Restaurant
70 Brunswick St., Stratford
• (519) 273-3424
CONTINENTAL

12/20

At one time the site of an old Anglican church, this restaurant was purchased in the 1970s by restaurateur Joseph Mandel, and refurbished as a stately and grand dining room. One advantage to the church was that you didn't have to wait a month or so to get in, which is the case here. Mandel has since moved on but his standards have been upheld. Appetizers include foie gras salad that tasted light on the oil, and heavy on earthy flavors. On the entrée side, a good bet is the European-style duckling, cooked with the right touch, its meat neither stringy nor dry, the savory tropical highlights of ginger and lime a delight. Lamb dishes remain a consistent draw, and a faithful crowd of regulars still drives into Statford from surrounding towns for the steak tartare, Church's most famous dish. We would probably return for it as well. For dessert, there is the requisite crème brûlée, full of creamy flavor. The atmosphere is more casual upstairs in the 46-seat Belfry Bar, known for its pasta and fish, and if you can book a Sunday buffet brunch, at Can$ 17.50 per person, it is the best dining deal in town. Highly recommended for apres-theater dining. Count on Can$80 for two without wine.
Open Tues.-Sat. 11:30 a.m.-11 p.m. All major cards.

The Old Prune
151 Albert St., Stratford
• (519) 271-5052
CONTINENTAL

12/20

You can easily miss this little restaurant, tucked away in an old house. The Old Prune is operated by two local ladies who love to cook and love to feed you even more. The prix-fixe menu changes daily and offers a half dozen entrées. You might choose from succulent lamb creation, beef tournedoes or crispy quail, all complemented by fresh local vegetables from the market. The soups are lovely, too. If you've never sampled tourtière, the French Canadian meat pie, give it a try here. Seating is limited, so make reservations early. Also lighter fare après-theater. Dinner for two (prix fixe) Can$70, not including wine.
Open daily 11:30 a.m.-3 p.m. & 5 p.m.-10 p.m. All major cards.

Queen's Inn at Stratford Dining Room
161 Ontario St., Stratford
• (519) 271-1400
FRENCH/CONTINENTAL

10/20

A comfortable dining room, elegantly restored to feature its Victorian roots, serves good French and Continental cuisine. The 130-year-old hotel, centrally located, is one of the oldest in the town, and the recent restoration has made it even more popular. Best bets include the meat entrées, for example, steaks, roasts. Also, expect the food to be of the hearty "old-school" preparation style. New to the inn are a piano lounge and lunch menu, as well as Taylor & Bate Ltd., an operating brew-pub on the premises (known as the meeting place for the "Ancient Order of Froth Blowers"). Reservations recommended for the

30-seat dining room, 60-seat lounge and the pub. Dinner for two Can$60 with wine.
Open daily 7 a.m.-10 a.m., 11:30 a.m.-2:30 a.m. & 5 p.m.-10 p.m. All major cards.

Rundles
9 Cobourg St., Stratford
• (519) 271-6442
CONTINENTAL

11/20

A smallish restaurant overlooking the Avon River and always booked due to its reputation for tasty edibles, Rundles specializes in a range of Continental dishes—from liver terrine to lamb with rosemary—and the chef often works magic with the fresh local fruits and vegetables. A nice range of lighter dishes, such as mussels, lobster and white fish, rounds the menu out. The owners will prepare a picnic basket from Can$15 per person for lunch or around Can$30 for dinner, and this will include items from the daily menu, from pasta salad to cold succulent lobster. The whimsical, pastel decor matches the bright summer festival mood of theatergoers. Dinner for two, with wine, is Can$100.
Open May-Nov., daily 11:30 a.m.-2:30 p.m. & 5 p.m.-10 p.m. All major cards.

The Waterlot Restaurant
17 Huron St., New Hamburg
• (519) 662-2020
CONTINENTAL

10/20

Though this restaurant is located about fifteen miles east of Stratford (going back toward Kitchener-Waterloo) it is well worth time out from the theater for a long lunch or dinner to dine in this 1840s country inn. There are four unique dining areas plus a patio in this restored and stately historic house with highlighted decor by local Canadian artists. The cuisine features good, hearty country-style portions of Continental fare. There are also three rooms upstairs for some spacious country accommodation. Dinner for two costs Can$65, not including wine.
Open Tues.-Sun. 11:30 a.m.-3 p.m. & 5 p.m.-10 p.m. All major cards.

QUICK BITES

Bentley's Bar and Restaurant
99 Ontario St., Stratford
• (519) 271-1121

This main street eatery, serving good pub grub as well as full-course dinners, acts as an unofficial watering hole for the cast and crew of the Festival Theatre. You could be standing at the authentic English bar sharing a pint with the lead actor in the production you just saw that afternoon. High back wooden booths add to the pub decor and entrées are reasonably priced, ranging from beef dishes, chicken, fish and pasta. And you can't go wrong with their "olde English–style" fish-and-chips with a pint of imported beer. Outdoor patio at the rear. Dinner for two Can$40 with wine or several pints apiece.
Open Mon.-Sat. 8 a.m.-1 a.m., Sun. 11:30 a.m.-11 p.m. All major cards.

Let Them Eat Cake Dessert Café, Bakery & Take Out
82 Wellington St., Stratford
• (519) 273-4774

Can you tell from the name that this place was designed for lighter eaters and dessert lovers? These two locations specialize in freshly baked dessert and specialty items (designer birthday cakes and more) as well as offering a light menu of soup and sandwiches. They will also pack you a full picnic basket, complete with ice cream and yogurt, for your day by the river. Lunch for two costs around Can$20.
Open 7:30 a.m.-6 p.m., Tues.-Sat. 7:30 a.m.-12:30 a.m., Sun. 10:30 a.m.-6 p.m. Cards: MC, V.

Stratford's Olde English Parlour
101 Wellington St., Stratford
• (519) 271-2772

Here's a popular spot with both locals and canny visitors. The British pub atmosphere offers good hearty fare and friendly service in a homey drop-in ambience. Cuisine ranges from deluxe hamburgers (Can$6.95) to a healthy portion of surf and turf (Can$19.95) as well as some good pub food such as steak and kidney pie. They make their own desserts-check out the Grand Marnier cheesecake or deep-dish Mennonite apple pie—and feature some fine imported beer on draught. Restaurant seating is 140 with an additional 70 on the summer patio. Lighter après-theater menu. Dinner for two Can$50 with several draughts.
Open daily 11:30 a.m.-1 a.m. Cards: MC, V.

HOTELS

Festival Inn
1144 Ontario St., Stratford M5A 6W1
• (519) 273-1150
Fax (519) 273-2111

This sprawling motel complex, located several miles east of town, remains the most popular spot with the seasonal crowd. There are 151 rooms, spacious and well-appointed (every room has a mini-refrigerator) and you can even request a water bed. Their poolside and tennis courts are both popular for Stratford patrons and theater critics who are between plays. The Inn also has a good coffee shop for light pretheater meals and a dining room for more substantial fare.
Singles: Can$79; doubles: Can$110.

Bentley's Inn
99 Ontario St., Stratford M5A 3H1
• (519) 271-1121
No fax

Located on the main street above Bentley's Bar (see page 227), this thirteen-room inn sits close to the theaters, and it's been beautifully decorated with two-tiered living spaces: livingroom and kitchen area on the first level and the loft bedroom above. The inn remains a comfy setting for a romantic weekend getaway. Book early (pre-season with a deposit) for the rooms are in great demand. Locals still refer fondly to the hotel as the Jester Arms, its name until the fall of 1990.
Singles: Can$59; doubles: Can$109.

OUT OF TORONTO Stratford

Queen's Inn at Stratford
161 Ontario St.,
Stratford M5A 3H1
• (519) 271-1400
Fax (519) 271-6272

This 130-year-old building has been restored to its former Victorian grandeur and has once again become a popular spot to stay. There are only 31 rooms, however, so theatergoers should book early. Bright rooms contain all the amenities; Continental breakfast gets you off to a good start.
Rooms: Can$85; superior rooms (two king-size beds): Can$105; suites: Can$120-Can$160.

The Victorian Inn
10 Romeo St.,
Stratford M5A 3H1
• (519) 271-4650
Fax (519) 271-2030

The regular theater crowd loves this place, a large 115-room motel situated on the Avon River, just a few minutes walk across the park to the Festival Theatre. The setting pleases, but the ambience is standard motel. Amenities include a dining room, swimming pool, sauna and a golf course just across the road.
Singles: Can$75; doubles: Can$105; suites: Can$129.

SIGHTS

The Gallery Stratford
54 Romeo St.,
Stratford
• (519) 271-5271

A pleasant little gallery in a parkland setting just through the park from the hilltop Festival Theatre. Their exhibits change every month and range from traditional to contemporary works of art; famous pieces by eighteenth-century English painters; Indian and Eskimo craftwork and bone sculptures; and original watercolors of Festival costumes and stage designs.
Open Tues.-Sun. 10 a.m.-5 p.m. Adults Can$3, children Can$1.

Stratford Festival
Box 520,
Stratford
• (519) 273-1600

World-famous theater company featuring the works of William Shakespeare, Henrik Ibsen, George Bernard Shaw, Anton Chekhov as well as new plays by Canadian playwrights. There are three venues for performances: the famed 2,262 seat Festival Theatre, the renovated 1,107 seat Avon Theatre and the more experimental 500-seat Tom Patterson Theatre (formerly called the Third Stage). The season officially commences on the Long Canadian May weekend every year (although there are prior preview and student performances) and continues into November. The company of players staggers the openings—about three different openings throughout the season—and usually presents upwards of twelve different productions over the six month period. Seminars and lectures are also presented for theater scholars. Try and book mid-week to avoid the inevitable weekend crowds.
Season May 1-Nov. 11. Performances Tues.-Sun. beginning at 8 p.m. Ticket prices range from each theater anywhere from Can$15-Can$45. All major cards.

BASICS

AT YOUR SERVICE	232
GETTING THERE	235
GETTING AROUND	235
GOINGS-ON	237

AT YOUR SERVICE

TELEPHONE NUMBERS

The area code for all Toronto telephone numbers is (416).

EMERGENCY
Assaulted Women's Helpline 863-0511
Canadian Automobile Association Road Service 966-3000
Emergency Dental Service 485-7121
Fire/Medical/Police 911
Kids Help 800-668-6868
Legal Aid 598-0200
Poison Control Centre 598-5900
Rape Crisis Line 597-8808
Suicide Distress Center 598-1121, 486-1456
Travellers Aid Society 366-7788
Veterinary Emergency Clinic 465-3501

INFORMATION
Beach Hotline (from mid-June) 392-7161
Board of Trade of Metropolitan Toronto 366-6811
Bus Terminal 367-8747
Cirrus ATM locations in Canada 1-800-4-CIRRUS
Community Information (social & health services) 392-0505
Directory Information 411
Ferry Schedules 392-8193
Five Star Tickets 596-8211
GO Transit Information 665-0022
Highway Conditions (winter) 235-1110
Metropolitan Reference Library 393-7196
Outdoor Pool Hotline (from mid-June) 392-7838
Postal 973-2433
Ticketron 593-5499
Transit Commission 393-4636
Union Station 366-8411
Visitor Information, Ontario 965-4008, (800) 668-2746
Visitor Information, Toronto 368-9821
Weather 676-3066
Youth Hostel Toronto 368-0207

BASICS At Your Service

CURRENCY EXCHANGE

Banks are generally open 10 a.m. to 3 p.m. Monday to Friday; some also have extended hours and one or two are open Saturday. Foreign currency can be converted at any bank or exchange facility. Many hotels, restaurants and retailers accept U.S. funds but only banks and registered exchange houses guarantee official exchange rates.

Bank of America Canada, 4 King St. West, Downtown, 863-7310 (corporate); 100 Bloor St. West, Bloor-Yorkville, 863-7324 (retail); 120 Adelaide St. West, Downtown, 863-4000.

Thomas Cook Foreign Exchange, 10 King St. East, Downtown, 863-8611; 55 Bloor St. West, Bloor-Yorkville, 961-9822; 60 Bloor St. West, Bloor-Yorkville, 923-6549; 655 Dixon Rd., Skyline Hotel, Rexdale, 247-4600; Yorkdale Shopping Centre, Dufferin St. and Hwy. 401, North York, 789-1827; Square One Shopping Centre, intersection Hwy. 10 & Hwy. 43, Mississauga, 276-3341.

Toronto Currency Exchange, 389 Yonge St., Unit 2; 313 Yonge St.; 391 Yonge St. All locations downtown; 598-3769.

LATE-NIGHT & 24 HOURS

Auto Service

Hi-Tech Auto Service, 175 Ossington Ave., 532-3323. Open 24 hours.

Spotlight Service Centre, 111 Strachan Ave., Toronto; 368-1118. Open daily 24 hours.

Billiards

Billiards Academy, 485 Danforth Ave., Danforth; 466-9696. Open 24 hours.

Bowling Lanes

Thorncliffe Bowlerama, 45 Overlea Blvd., East York; 421-2211. Open 24 hours.

Car Wash

Coin-Op Car Wash, 3385 Dundas St. West, Toronto; 762-3433. Open 24 hours.

Copy Center

Kinko's Copies, 346 Bloor St. West, Toronto; 928-0110. Full range of photocopying services, assisted or self-serve. Open 24 hours.

BASICS At Your Service

Drugstore

Shoppers Drug Mart, 700 Bay St., Downtown; 979-2424. Full-service health-care products and prescriptions. Open Mon.-Sat. 24 hours.

Grocery Stores

Bloor Super Save, 384 Bloor St. West, Toronto; 964-8318. Small neighborhood grocery store. Open 24 hours.

Rabba's Fine Foods, 252 Queen's Quay West, Harbourfront; 979-7496. Full complement of gourmet goodies. Open 24 hours.

Laundromat

24-Hour Coin Laundry, 566 Mount Pleasant Rd., 487-0233. Open 24 hours.

Restaurants & Cafés

Bemelmans, 83 Bloor St. West, Bloor-Yorkville; 960-0306. Popular New York–style bistro. Romantic dining atmosphere and beautiful people four deep at the bar. Open Mon.-Thurs. 11:30 a.m.-1 a.m., Fri. 11:30 a.m.-3 a.m., Sat. 11 a.m.-3 a.m., Sun. 11 a.m.-midnight. Bar closes at 1 a.m. nightly. Cards: AE, MC, V.

Chez Cappuccino, 3 Charles St. East, Bloor-Yorkville; 925-6142. Open 24 hours. All-night haven for actors, musicians, clubgoers, party people. Terrific pastries and munchies. No cards.

Fran's Restaurant, 20 College St., Downtown, 923-9867; 21 St. Clair Ave. West, Toronto North, 925-6336; 2275 Yonge St., Toronto North, 481-1112. Open 24 hours. Standard roadhouse-style cooking and service. Great all-day breakfasts. Cards: AE, DC, MC, V.

Just Desserts, 306 Davenport Rd., Toronto; 922-6824. Open Mon.-Thurs. 11 a.m.-3 a.m., Fri. 11 a.m.-Mon. 3 a.m. No cards.

Pizza Gigi, 189 Harbord St., Toronto; 535-4444. Open 4 p.m.-4 a.m. Delivery only. No cards.

Video Rental

Mr. Video, 1172 Bay St., Downtown; 967-1339. More than 14,000 titles in stock. TV and VCR rentals. Open 24 hours.

BASICS Getting There/Getting Around

GETTING THERE

Lester B. Pearson International Airport serves more than twenty major airlines on regularly scheduled flights. Airport Express, operated by **Gray Coach Bus**, 393-7911, offers daily service every twenty minutes to and from these downtown hotels: Delta Chelsea Inn, Harbour Castle Westin, Holiday Inn Downtown, L'Hôtel, Royal York and Sheraton Centre hotels and frequent service to and from the Islington, Yorkdale and York Mills subway stations.

Some hotels offer shuttle bus service to registered guests to and from the International Airport. Check with the doorman on the arrivals level for the hotels which provide this service.

By car, Pearson International can be reached from highways 401, 427 and 409. Only a taxi with TIA on the license plate is authorized to pick up passengers from Pearson International. The fare from the airport to the Centre of the city is approximately $25 and there is a small fee for additional or excessive baggage and handling. Several limousine services operate to and from the airport at a slightly higher fixed rate. Some provide wake-up calls for early morning travelers. **Air Flight Services**, 445-1999, **Aerofleet**, 678-7077.

Toronto Island Airport, accessible by a ferry at the foot of Bathurst Street, is a small operation by comparison to the international airport. It offers accommodation for private and commuter planes. Landing fees and customs information, 868-6942. **City Express**, 360-7770, has regularly scheduled daily flights to and from Ottawa, Montreal, Hamilton and Peterborough.

City Express offers a regular shuttle bus service to and from major downtown hotels for all its flights. The ferry is accessible from Bathurst Street below Queen's Quay West.

GETTING AROUND

BY BUS

Bus Terminal, 610 Bay St., Downtown, 393-7911. Regularly scheduled service to all points in Canada and U.S. Buses are also available for charter for sight-seeing, private and group tours.

GO Transit, 665-0022, offers regularly scheduled commuter shuttle services to and from the centre of the city for many outlying residential communities.

BASICS   Getting Around

BY CAR

All distance and speed-limit signs are in kilometers. For those unfamiliar with the system, on highways 100 kilometers per hour is equivalent to 60 miles per hour and, in the city, 60 kilometers per hour is equivalent to 35 miles per hour. It is mandatory to wear seat belts in Ontario. A tow-away policy is strictly enforced in Toronto. Prohibited areas and times are clearly indicated on the streets. Public parking facilities operated by **Citipark** (443-1540) and **The Parking Authority of Toronto** (393-7275) are available throughout the city and can be identified by a large green disc with a white "P" in the center. Car-rental facilities are available throughout the city; try **Budget Car Rentals** (676-1240), **Discount Car and Truck Rentals** (961-8006), **Hertz** (620-9620) and **Tilden** (925-4551).

BY PUBLIC TRANSPORTATION

The **Toronto Transit Commission, or TTC,** (393-4636, 393-4000), operates inner-city public transportation utilizing trolley and diesel buses, light-rail transit systems, streetcars and an efficient, clean and safe subway system. Regular service on most routes begins at 5:30 a.m. and ends at 1:45 a.m. The **Blue Night Service** is an all-night continuation of selected major connecting surface routes, but on a greatly reduced schedule. Blue-bus and streetcar stops are clearly identified along the routes. The subway system opens at 9 a.m. Sundays and holidays. Public transportation in Toronto is not generally wheelchair-accessible. The Ride Guide, available free at all subway stations, is a comprehensive map of the entire system and a list of the services provided.

Tickets or tokens (or exact change) are required on buses and streetcars, and can be purchased at subway stations. Monthly, Sunday and holiday passes, good for unlimited travel during the specified time, can be purchased at the subway stations. Students and seniors can purchase reduced fare tickets, which must be used in conjunction with a photo identification card obtainable from the TTC.

BY TAXI

Cabs are plentiful in downtown Toronto and easily hailed from the curb. In the suburbs, it's best to phone and wait to be picked up: **Co-Op Taxi** (364-8161), **Diamond Taxi** (366-6868), **Metro Taxi** (363-5611). Currently, the fare starts at Can$2.20, adding 25 cents every .20 kilometers. Fares to destinations more than five kilometers (eight miles) outside the Metropolitan Toronto area can be negotiated with the driver or in advance with the dispatcher. Most taxis will deliver parcels on a pre-paid fare basis arranged in advance with the dispatcher. To report any altercations with a Metro Toronto taxi driver, phone the **Metro Licensing Commission,** 392-3000.

Limousines provide a more luxurious way to travel around town. **Buckingham Livery Service** (221-4144) will pick you up in a vintage or modern Rolls-Royce, Bentley, Cadillac or Lincoln super-stretch limousines for that added touch of pomp to any circumstance. **Rosedale Livery Limited** (677-9444) provides security-cleared, uniformed chauffeurs operating the largest fleet of luxury limousines in Toronto.

BY TRAIN

Union Station, Bay and Front streets, is the sole point of arrival and departure for rail service in Toronto. **Via Rail** (366-8411), goes to all Canadian destinations; **GO Transit** (665-0022) provides commuter service to outlying towns.

GOINGS-ON

January

- **Metro Home Show**, Jan. 16-20, Metro Toronto Convention Centre, 255 Front St. West, The latest innovations and renovations; 252-7791.
- **Canadian Opera Company**, Jan.-Apr., O'Keefe Centre, 1 Front St. East, presents a full season of first-rate productions of the classics; 363-6671.
- **National Ballet of Canada**, Jan.-May, O'Keefe Centre, 1 Front St. East, in the middle of its current season, performs a mixed repertoire of contemporary and classical ballet; 362-0201. Toronto Maple Leaf Hockey, Jan.-May, Maple Leaf Gardens, 60 Carlton St., participate in National League games; 977-1641.
- **Young People's Theatre**, Jan.-May, 165 Front St. East, presents a subscription season of exciting theater for young audiences and families; 864-9732.
- **Canadian Stage Company**, Jan.-June, Bluma Appel Theatre, 27 Front St. East, and two smaller theaters, 26 Berkeley St., presents both contemporary and classical theater, with top-notch casts, designers and directors; 367-8243.
- **Toronto Pops Orchestra**, Jan.-June, Massey Hall, 178 Victoria St., fills out its season of light classics, jazz and popular music; 365-7677.
- **Toronto Symphony Orchestra**, Jan.-June, Roy Thomson Hall, 60 Simcoe St., plays regularly scheduled concerts with a series of guest artists; 593-4828.
- **Premiere Dance Theatre**, year-round, 207 Queen's Quay West, is host to local and visiting dance companies in Canada's only theater designed specifically for dance with no seat further than 50 feet from the stage; 973-4000.

BASICS Goings-On

February

- **Toronto International Auto Show**, Feb. 14-24, Metro Toronto Convention Centre, 255 Front St. West, presents the newest automotive trends and technologies; 940-2800.

March

- **Festival of Canadian Fashion**, Mar. 10-14, Metro Toronto Convention Centre, 255 Front St. West, presents a look into the future of fashion; 923-3557.
- **Canadian Spring Boat and Cottage Show**, Mar. 28-31, International Centre, 6900 Airport Rd., features the latest in water craft for show and sale; 695-0311.
- **Toronto Sportsmen's Show**, Mar. 15-24, The Coliseum, Exhibition Place, offers everything from log rolling competitions to dog handling to fly fishing; 695-0311.
- **One of a Kind Canadian Craft Show**, Mar. 27-31, Automotive Building, Exhibition Place, Vast array of unique, handcrafted items; 960-3680.

April

- **National Home Show**, Apr. 5-14, The Coliseum, Exhibition Place, celebrates 39 years of presenting dream homes, celebrity rooms, feature gardens and seminars on renovations and residential contracting; 695-0311.
- **Toronto Blue Jays Baseball**, Apr. 8-Oct. 2, SkyDome, open a season of American League baseball; 341-3663.
- **Shaw Festival**, Apr. 19-Nov. 10, Niagara-on-the-Lake, opens a summer season of works by George Bernard Shaw and his contemporaries; 468-2172.
- **Stratford Festival**, Apr. 29-Nov. 10, Stratford, opens its 39th summer season of Shakespearean classics playing in repertory through October; (519) 273-1600 or toll free from Toronto, 363-4471.
- **World Poetry Festival**, York Quay Centre, 235 Queen's Quay West, features 24 poets from five continents in a six-day marathon of readings and panel discussions. Call for dates; 973-4000.

May

- **Canada's Wonderland**, May 12-Sept. 3, 9580 Jane St., Maple, North York, begins its 11th summer season of theme park fun and events; 832-7000.
- **Toronto Antiquarian Book Fair**, May 25-26, Metro Toronto Convention Centre, 255 Front St. West; 537-1852.

BASICS Goings-On

June

- **Metro International Caravan**, June 14-22, celebrates Toronto's unique multicultural mosaic for nine days at more than 40 pavilions representing various facets of the city's heritage; 977-0466.
- **DuMaurier Downtown Jazz Festival**, June 21-30, at a variety of locations around the city, presents more than 500 musicians in a week of concerts of the world's best be-bop, cool, modern and progressive sounds; 979-1120.
- **Benson and Hedges Fireworks**, June 22, 26; July 1, 6 & 10, Ontario, 955 Lakeshore Blvd. West, is a spectacular three-day display of light and a deafening display of noise featuring an international competition of pyrotechnics; 965-6332.
- **Toronto Argonaut Football**, June 29-Nov. 3., SkyDome, open a season of Canadian League football; 595-1131.

July

- **Queen's Plate**, July 7, Woodbine Racetrack, Hwy. 27 at Rexdale Blvd., is Canada's most prestigious thoroughbred race. The Queen Mum usually shows up for this one and can be spotted chatting with the jockeys and checking the racing forms; 675-6110.
- **Molson Indy**, July 19-21, Exhibition Place, is the sixth annual race car event attracting some of the world's top drivers; 598-4639.
- **Caribana**, July 22-Aug. 5., is Metro's week-long celebration of Caribbean rhythms, culture, food and entertainment highlighted by a day-long parade through the city centre; 925-5435.
- **The Dream in High Park**, High Park, Bloor St. West, is Shakespearean comedy outdoors in a natural amphitheater, organized by the Canadian Stage Company. Bring a blanket to sit on, a sweater and a few munchies to help pass the time before the 8 p.m. curtain. No reserved spots on the grass so early arrival is recommended. No alcoholic beverages allowed. Admission is free; 367-8243.

August

- **Women Players Ltd. International Tennis**, Aug. 3-11, National Tennis Centre, York University, 4700 Keele St., has all 10,000 seats jammed as top names on the court circuit compete for a full week as part of the pro tennis tour; 665-9777.
- **Canadian National Exhibition**, Aug. 28-31, Exhibition Place, is midways, exhibits, grandstand shows and international entertainment. The Canadian International Air Show is featured during the last four days of the Ex; 695-0311.

September

- **Festival of Festivals**, Sept. 5-14, is one of the largest, most important film festivals in the world, highlighted by galas, long, endless lines even if you hold a ticket, mad scrambling and juggling of schedules in an attempt to see everything and, of course, some of the finest films from around the world; 967-7371.
- **Toronto Arts Week**, Sept. 21-29, is a nine-day celebration of artistic creativity. More than 200 free events at venues around the city focus on the art around us everyday in design, music, architecture as well as the performing and visual arts. Backstage and studio tours, open rehearsals, trade booths and public performances; 597-8223.
- **Cabbagetown Festival**, Parliament Street south of Wellesley Street, is a neighborhood street festival, now in its fifteenth year, featuring parades, walking tours, house tours, children's activities, food and a cultural festival. Call for dates; 921-0857.

October

- **Toronto Maple Leafs Hockey**, Oct. 10-Mar. 26, Maple Leaf Gardens, 60 Carlton St., opening of a season of National League play; 977-1641.
- **International Festival of Authors**, 235 Queen's Quay West, Harbourfront, an international roster of authors giving readings of their own works; 973-4000.
- **Canadian Stage Company**, Bluma Appel Theatre, 27 Front St. East, and two smaller theaters, 26 Berkeley St., opens its fall season. Call for dates; 366-7723.

November

- **One Of A Kind Canadian Craft Show and Sale**, Nov. 28-Dec. 8, Automotive Building, Exhibition Place. Unique gifts for holiday giving; 960-3680.
- **Royal Agricultural Winter Fair**, Nov. 12-24, The Coliseum, Exhibition Place, is the world's largest indoor agricultural fair highlighted by the horse show and cattle auctions; 393-6400.
- **Santa Claus Parade**, 249-7833, an annual tradition for the past 87 years; 392-9111.

December

- **The Nutcracker**, Dec. 8, O'Keefe Centre, 1 Front St. East, is the National Ballet's annual holiday treat for the city fed up with shopping, gray days and winter in general; 872-2262.
- **New Year's Eve Party**, Dec. 31, Nathan Phillips Square, City Hall, Queen St. West, an annual party the city throws for its citizens. Note: the party is often marred by violence as the huge crowds disperse afterward; 392-9111.
- **Court of Miracles**, Premiere Dance Theatre, 207 Queen's Quay West, a recreation of the medieval Feast of Saint Nicholas by members of the Toronto Dance Theatre. Call for dates; 973-4000.

MAPS

METROPOLITAN TORONTO	242-243
DOWNTOWN TORONTO	244-245
THE TORONTO TRANSIT COMMISSION SYSTEM	246
TORONTO ORIENTATION	247

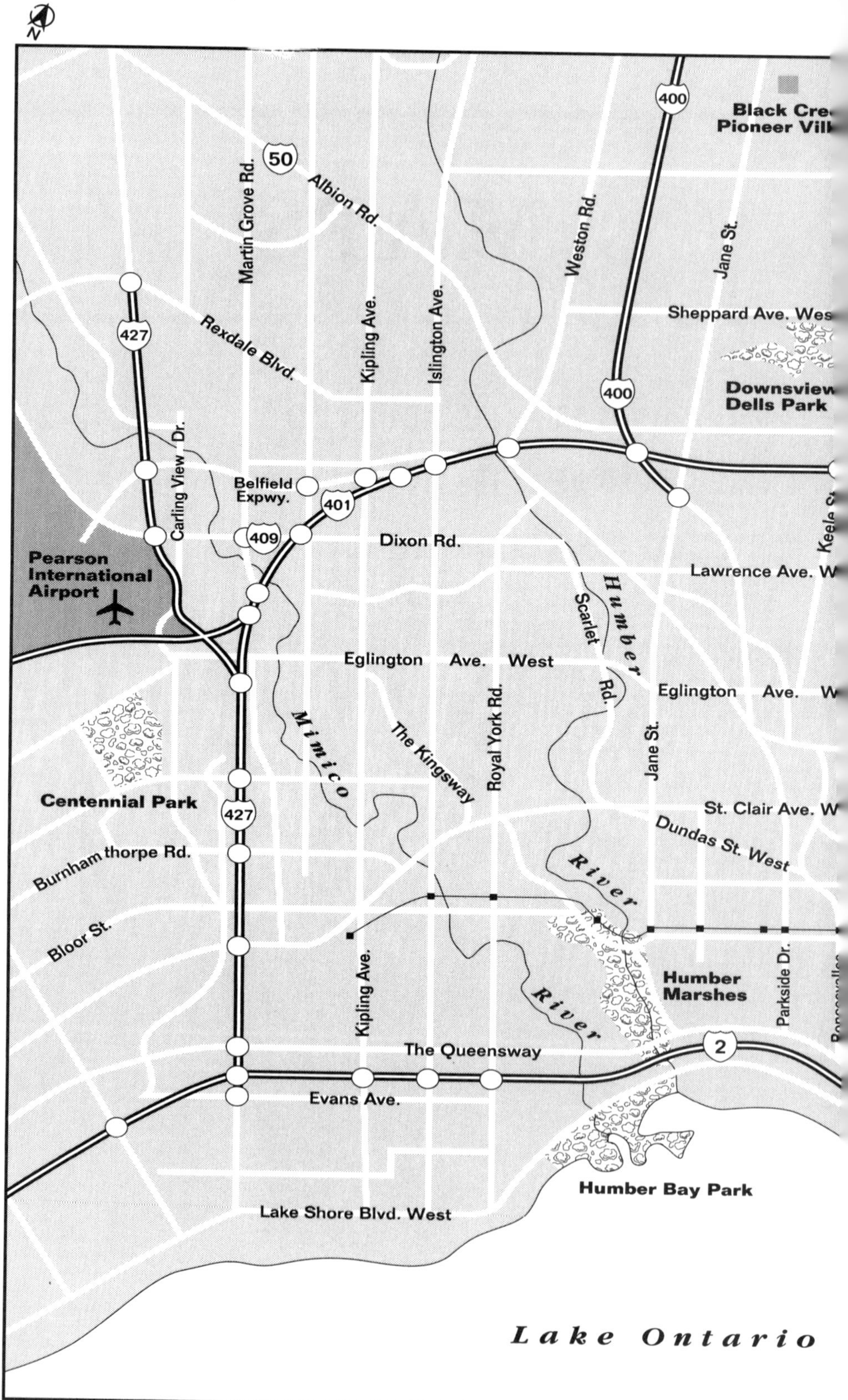

N
400
Black Cre
Pioneer Vill
50
Albion Rd.
Martin Grove Rd.
Weston Rd.
Jane St.
Rexdale Blvd.
Kipling Ave.
Islington Ave.
427
Sheppard Ave. Wes
Downsview
Dells Park
400
Carling View Dr.
Belfield
Expwy.
401
409
Dixon Rd.
Keele St
Pearson
International
Airport
Lawrence Ave. W
Humber
Scarlet Rd.
Eglington Ave. West
Eglington Ave. W
Mimico
The Kingsway
Royal York Rd.
Jane St.
Centennial Park
427
St. Clair Ave. W
Dundas St. West
Burnhamthorpe Rd.
River
Bloor St.
Kipling Ave.
River
Humber
Marshes
Parkside Dr.
The Queensway
2
Evans Ave.
Humber Bay Park
Lake Shore Blvd. West
Lake Ontario

METROPOLITAN TORONTO

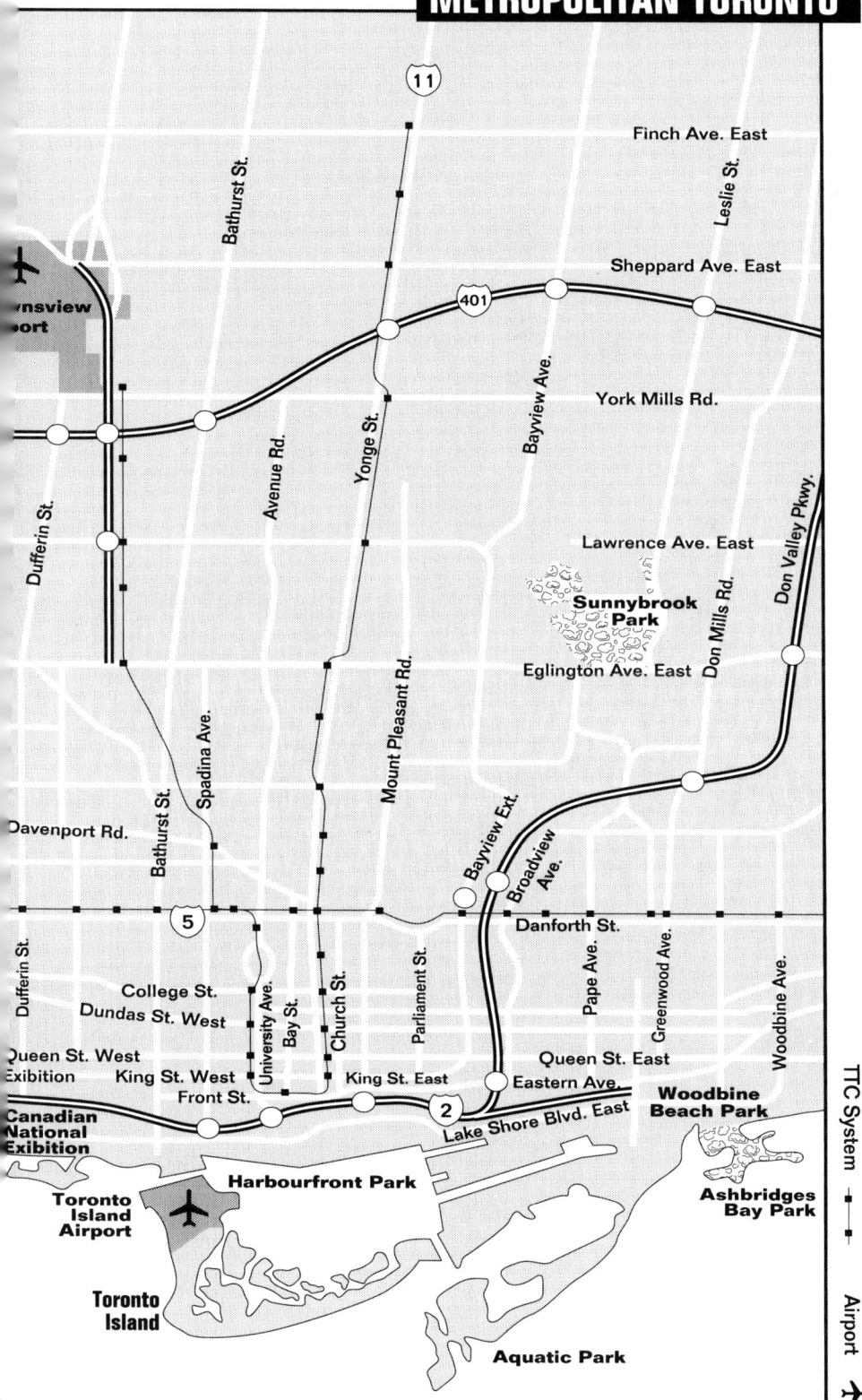

TORONTO
Downtown Toronto

- Allan Gardens ❷
- Art Gallery of Toronto ❹
- Bus Station ❸
- Campbell House ❻
- City Hall ❼
- CN Tower ⑰
- Convention Centre ⑱
- Toronto Dominion Centre ⑫
- Eaton Centre ❾
- The Grange ❺
- Harbourfront Antiques Market ⑳
- Maple Leaf Gardens ❶
- O'Keefe Centre ⑭
- Old City Hall ❽
- Royal Alexandra Theatre ⑩
- Royal Bank Plaza ⑬
- Roy Thomson Hall ⑪
- St. Lawrence Market ⑮
- SkyDome ⑲
- Union Station ⑯

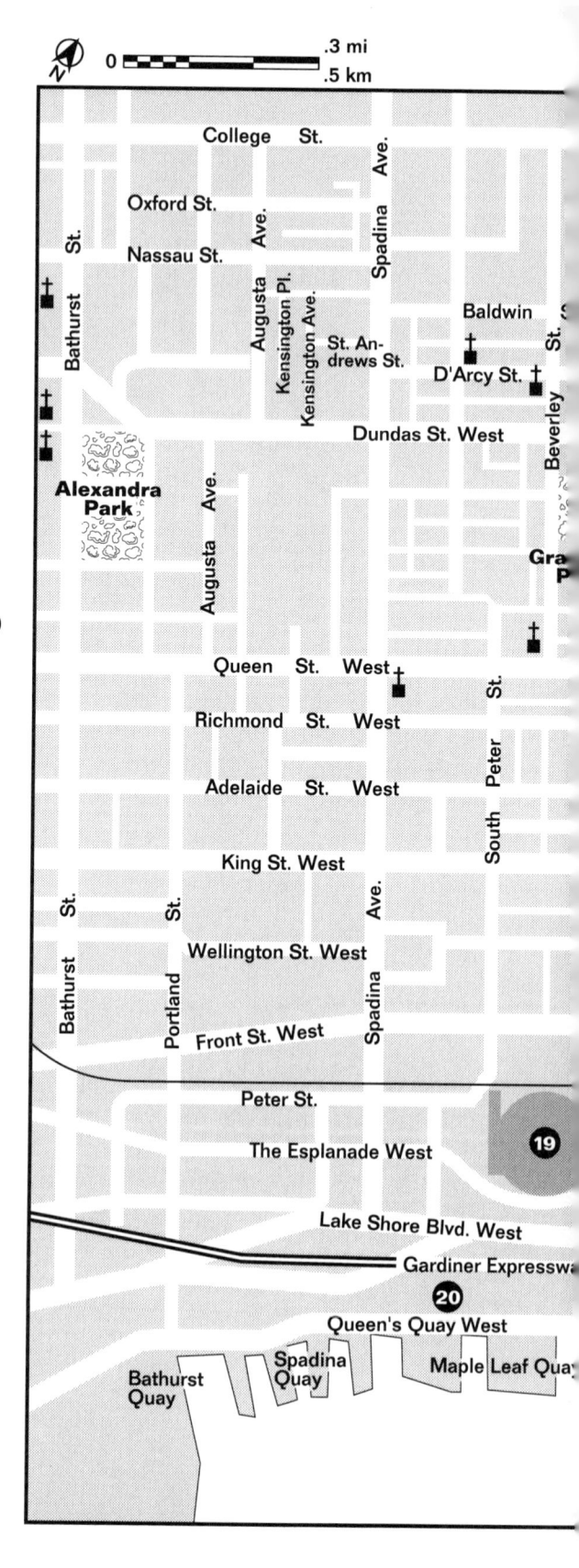

.3 mi
.5 km

College St.
Oxford St.
Nassau St.
Bathurst St.
Augusta Ave.
Kensington Pl.
Kensington Ave.
Spadina Ave.
Baldwin St.
St. Andrews St.
D'Arcy St.
Beverley St.
Alexandra Park
Dundas St. West
Augusta Ave.
Queen St. West
Richmond St. West
Adelaide St. West
Peter St.
King St. West
South Ave.
Bathurst St.
Portland St.
Wellington St. West
Spadina Ave.
Front St. West
Peter St.
The Esplanade West ⑲
Lake Shore Blvd. West
Gardiner Expressway
⑳
Queen's Quay West
Bathurst Quay
Spadina Quay
Maple Leaf Quay

DOWNTOWN TORONTO

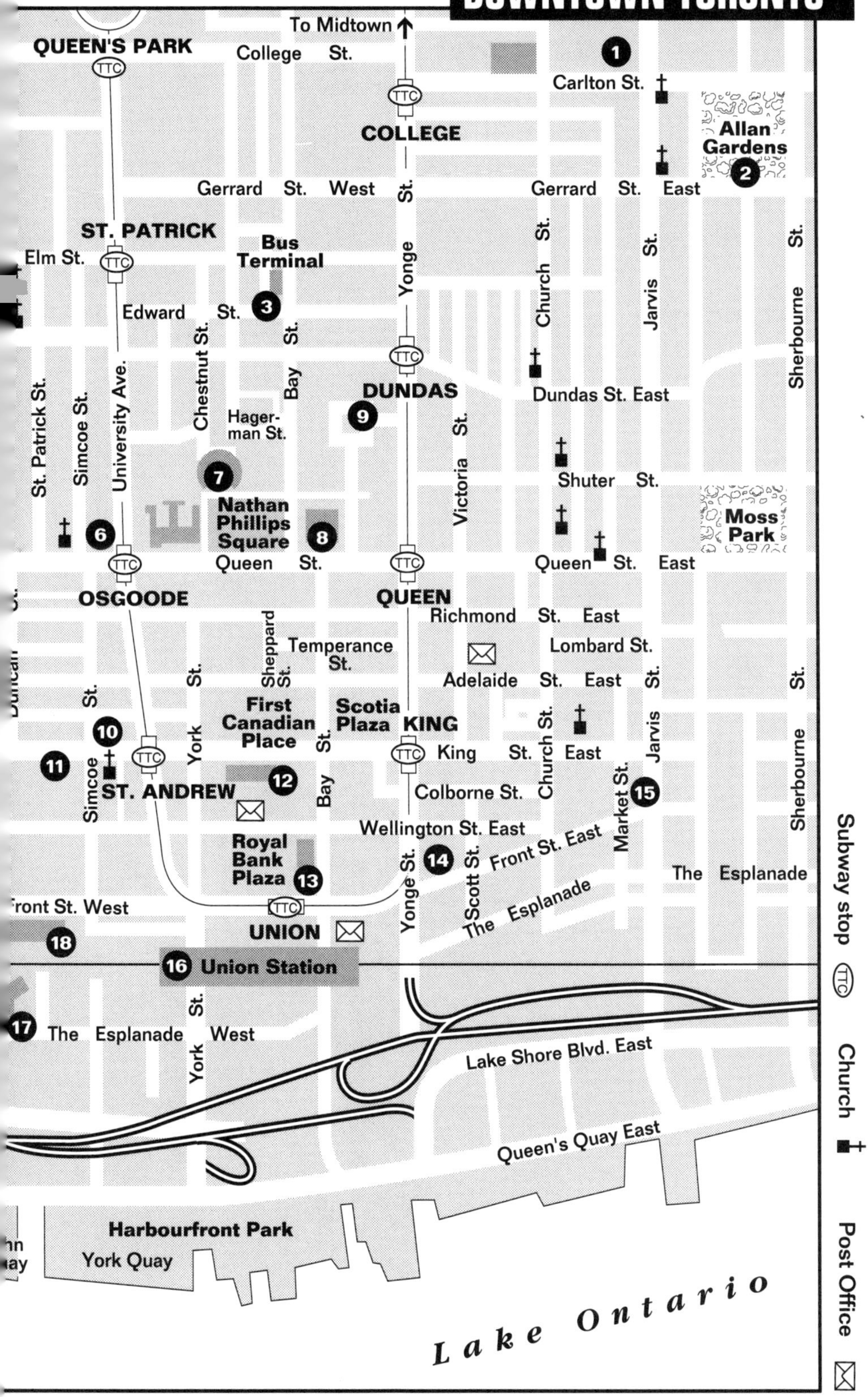

THE TTC SYSTEM

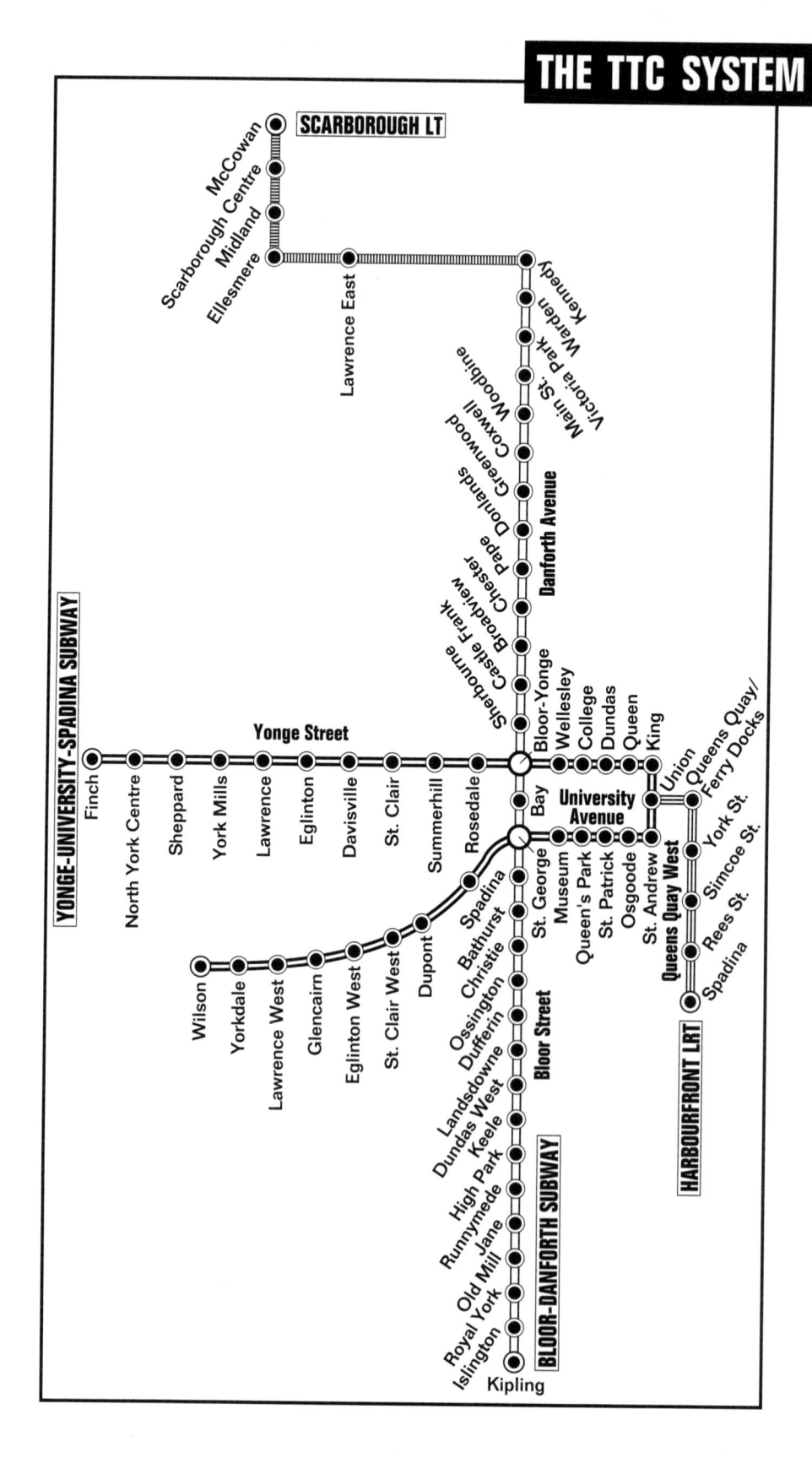

SCARBOROUGH LT
McCowan — Scarborough Centre — Midland — Ellesmere — Lawrence East — Kennedy

YONGE-UNIVERSITY-SPADINA SUBWAY

Yonge Street: Finch — North York Centre — Sheppard — York Mills — Lawrence — Eglinton — Davisville — St. Clair — Summerhill — Rosedale — Bloor-Yonge — Wellesley — College — Dundas — Queen — King — Union

University Avenue: Bay — St. George — Museum — Queen's Park — St. Patrick — Osgoode — St. Andrew — Union

Danforth Avenue: Bloor-Yonge — Sherbourne — Castle Frank — Broadview — Chester — Pape — Donlands — Greenwood — Coxwell — Woodbine — Main St. — Victoria Park — Warden — Kennedy

BLOOR-DANFORTH SUBWAY
Kipling — Islington — Royal York — Old Mill — Jane — Runnymede — High Park — Keele — Dundas West — Lansdowne — Dufferin — Ossington — Christie — Bathurst — Spadina — St. George — Bay — Bloor-Yonge

Bloor Street: Spadina — Dupont — St. Clair West — Eglinton West — Glencairn — Lawrence West — Yorkdale — Wilson

HARBOURFRONT LRT
Union — Queens Quay/Ferry Docks — York St. — Simcoe St. — Rees St. — Spadina (Queens Quay West)

TORONTO ORIENTATION

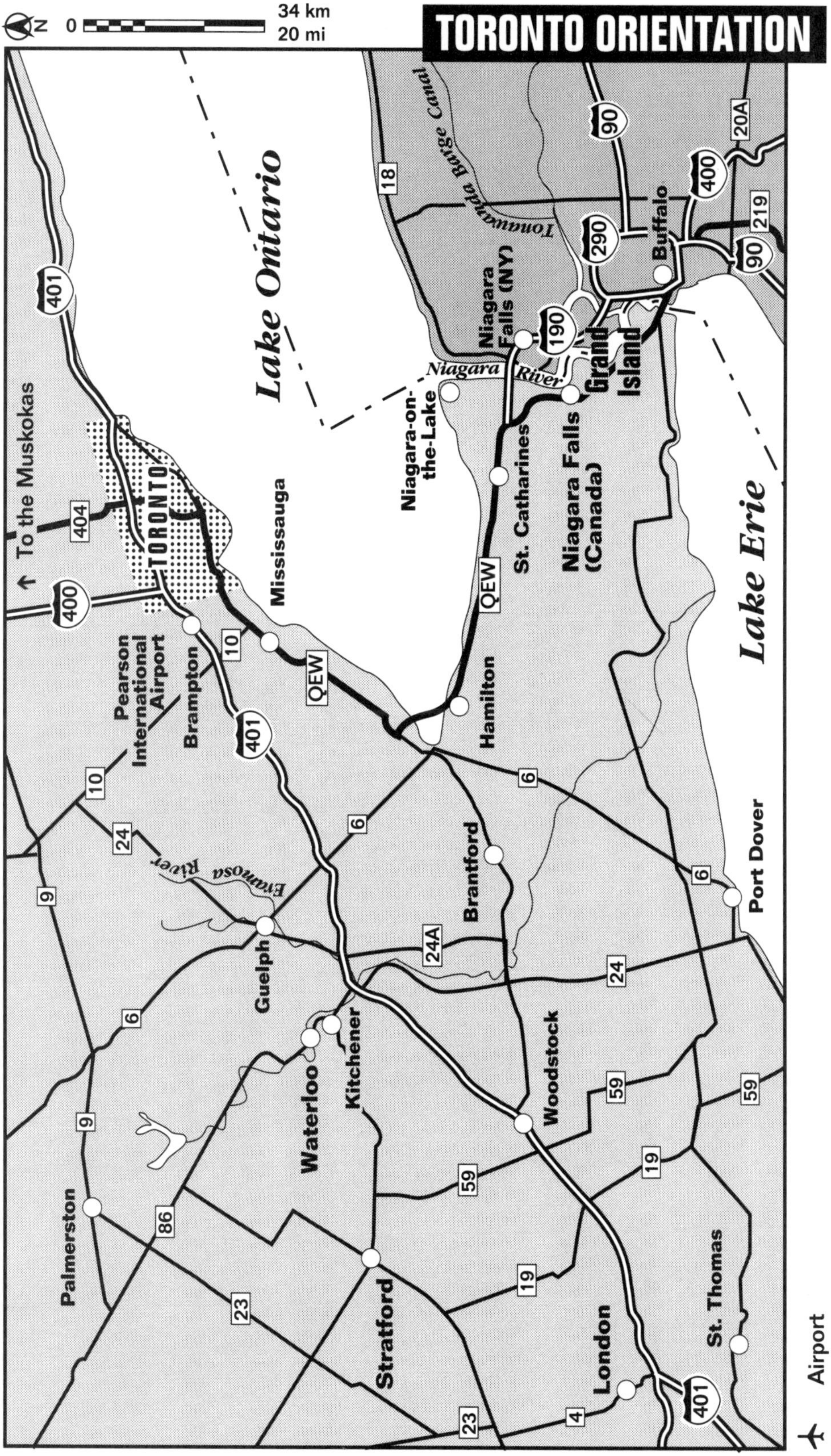

INDEX

A

A Space 192
Abbey Bookshop.........................153
Abelard Books.............................153
Abundance Restaurant 93
Accessity 155
Aerofleet 235
African Lion Safari 179
Air Flight Services 235
Alan Goouch...............................158
Albert Britnell Book Shop 150
Albert's Hall 141
Algonquin Provincial Park.........221
Allan Gardens 178
Alumnae Theatre Company 197
Amsterdam Brasserie &
Brewpub................................93, 130
AMUSEMENTS.........................174
An Evening at La Cage 136
The Angel Inn Restaurant 210
Angie Strauss Gallery 210
The Annex 184
ANTIQUES 148
Aquarius 51 Lounge 143
Arax Armenian Restaurant 14
Art Gallery of Ontario 191
Ashbridge's Bay Park 176
ASIAN FAST FOOD 92
At My Table 168
Atelier Art and Antiques.............148
Athenian Garden Restaurant 15
Auberge du Pommier....................16
Auberge Gavroche/
L' Entrecôte 15
AUTO SERVICE 233
Avocado Club 17

B

Bakka Science
Fiction Book Shoppe 151
Ballenford Architectural Books...151
Bally..165
Bally(children) 153
Balmy Beach 177
The Bamboo Club 18, 144
Bangkok Garden 18
Bank of America Canada 233
Barolo Ristorante 19
The Barn 133
BARS 130
BASEBALL 186
The Bay 166
Beach Hotline 176
BEACHES & PARKS.................176
The Beaches................................184
BEAUTY 149

Bemelmans....................20, 234
Beni Sung 156
Benson and Hedges Fireworks ...239
Bentley's Bar and Restaurant 227
Bentley's Inn........................228
Berkeley Café 20
Best Western–Primrose Hotel 109
The Big Bop 139
Bigliardi's Steak, Veal and
Seafood Restaurant................21
BILLIARDS..........................233
Bindi Ristorante 22
Le Bistingo 22
Bistro Bernard 23
Bistro 990 23
Black Creek Pioneer
Village..........................182, 213
Bloor Street Diner..................24
Blue Mountain Inn 218
Blue Mountain Slide Rides 222
Blue Night Service 236
Bluffer's Park 177
The Body Shop 149
Bodywear.............................160
Bond Place Hotel..................109
BOOKS & NEWSSTANDS......150
The Book Cellar...................150
Boomer................................158
Boulevard Café......................25
BOWLING LANES...............233
Bradgate Arms 122
Bretton's........................149, 161
The Bristol Place Hotel 126
Browne's Bistro.....................25
The Brownstone Hotel 118
Buckingham Livery Service........237
Buddies in Bad Times Theatre.....199
Budget Car Rentals 236
Bus Terminal........................235
The Buttery Theatre
Restaurant...........................208

C

CABARETS 136
Cabbagetown........................184
Cabbagetown Festival 240
Café des Copains..................141
CAFES 93
Café La Gaffe 26
Café Victoria 27
Cake Master Ltd. 94
California Sandwiches 98
Cambridge...........................216
The Cameron Public House 144
Canada's Wonderland 174, 238
Canada's Wonderland/
Kingswood Music Theatre........215

Canadian Helicopters 187
Canadian National
Exhibition 239
Canadian Opera
Company 195, 237
Canadian Spring Boat and
Cottage Show 238
Canadian Stage
Company 197, 237
Canadiana Shoppe 168
Cap's 130
Capezio 165
Cappuccino Greek &
Italian Food.............................102
Le Caprice de Marie-Claude......169
Caribana 239
CAR TRAVEL 236
CAR WASH 233
Carlton Inn 110
Carmen Lamanna Gallery 192
Carman's 27
Cartier......................................157
Casa Loma 181
Centre Island...........................177
Celestino's 28
Centre Street Deli.....................97
Centro Grill and Wine Bar........29
C'est What 30
Chanel 161
Chaps 133
Charmers 30
Cherry Street Beach................177
Chestnut Park Hotel 110
Chez Cappuccino 94, 233
CHILDREN'S SHOPS.............153
Chiaro's 31
Children's Bookstore 151
China Blues 31
Chinatown 184
Chris & Frog Emporium 169
Church and Wellesley 185
The Church Restaurant 226
Cibo 32
Citipark....................................236
City Express 235
City of Toronto Archives...........194
Clevelands House Resort 219
Clinton's Tavern......................145
CLOTHES & JEWELRY 155
Club Colby's 134
Club Monaco 158
CN Tower................................181
Co-Op Taxi 236
Cobble-Stone Galleries 211
COMEDY & MAGIC..............137
Consort Bar.............................131
The Cookbook Store 151
The Copa 139

249

INDEX

COPY CENTER.......................233
Cottage Country....................217
Cotton Basics.......................153
Court of Miracles.................240
Craft Studio at Harbourfront...192
Croissant House 94
Cuisine of India 33
CURRENCY EXCHANGE.......233

D

Daily Planet 33
Dancemakers....................190
DANCE.............................190
DANCE CLUBS 139
DanceWorks 190
The Danforth 185
Danny Grossman Dance Co....190
David's................................165
Deerhurst Resort....................219
Del Bello Gallery......................192
DELIS 97
Delta Chelsea Inn 111
DEPARTMENT STORES &
SHOPPING CENTERS..........166
Desrossiers Dance Theatre 190
Diamond Taxi......................236
Discount Car and Truck
Rental.............................236
The Doctor's House and
Livery..............................213
Domain of Killien 219
Donna Elena 161
Dr. Denton 154
The Dream in High Park 239
DRUGSTORE 233
Druxy's................................97
DuMaurier
Downtown Jazz Festival..........239
Du Verre............................169
Dufflet Pastries...................168

E

Eaton Centre 166, 181
Eaton's 166
Eddie Bauer 155
Edward's Books & Art 151
Edwards Gardens 178
18 Karat.............................157
Elgin and Winter
Garden Theatre Centre 182
EMERGENCY PHONE
NUMBERS 232
Emily Zarb............................161
Emporio Armani..............159, 161
L'Entrecôte..........................15
Epicure Café 34
Equity Showcase Theatre 199
Essex Park Hotel 111
Estate Collection 148
European Jewelry 157
EXCURSIONS 179

F

Fab 162
Fabrice 157
Factory Theatre....................197
Factory Theatre Studio Café....199
Falafel Falafel 101
Farmer's Market....................179

La Fenice 34
Ferragamo...................162, 165
Festival Inn 228
Festival of Canadian Fashion 238
Festival of Festivals 240
Filet of Sole 35
Flowers for My Daughter 214
Foodworks 35
FOOD SHOPS 168
FOOTBALL 186
Fort George National
Historic Site 211
Fort York............................182
Four Seasons Hotel 118
Four Seasons Inn on the Park...124
Fran's Restaurant 36, 234
French Fry Freddie's 99
Future Bakery 36

G

GALLERIES.........................191
Gallery Moos 192
The Gallery Stratford 229
Gate House Hotel 210
The General Store 156
Geomania..........................169
Georg Jensen 169
George R. Gardiner
Museum of Ceramic Art.....193
George's Spaghetti House......142
Georges Rech.....................162
GIFTS & HOUSEWARES 168
Giorgio..............................162
Glen Abbey Golf 187
GO Transit 235, 237
GOLF 187
Grano 37
Gray Coach Bus 235
Gray Line Boat
Tours 188
Gray Line Bus Tours 188
Greenwood Race Track 187
La Grenouille 37
GROCERY STORES..............234
Grossman's Tavern 131
Gulliver's Travel Bookshop 152
Gypsy Hungarian Restaurant....99

H

H. Rooneem's.......................95
H₂0....................................150
Halfway House Dining
Room..............................214
HAMBURGERS &
SANDWICHES 98
Hanlon's Point......................177
Harbourfront 185
Harbourfront Antique
Market............................148
Hard Rock Café 38
Harper's Restaurant and
Dinner Theatre 137
Harry Rosen.......................159
Harvey's..............................99
Hazelton Lanes 167
Hermès 156
Hertz 236
High Park...........................178
HIGH TEA 100
Hilton Toronto 112

His Majesty's Feast...............136
Hoax............................159, 162
HOCKEY............................187
Hockey Hall of
Fame and Museum............194
Holiday Inn Downtown 112
Holt Renfrew.......................167
Holt Renfrew Café 39
HORSE RACING 187
The Horseshoe Tavern 145
L'Hôtel...............................112
Hotel Admiral 106
Hotel Ibis...........................113
Hotel Inter-Continental 119
Hotel Selby 120
Hotel Victoria 114
Houseboat Vacations 222
Hsin Kuang 39
Hughie's..............................40
Hungarian
Goulash Party Tavern 95

I

Iguana.................................41
The Imperial Room...............143
Indian Rice Factory 41
The Inn and Tennis Club
at Manitou......................220
The Inn at Horseshoe 220
Inniskillin Winery 212
International Festival of
Authors 240
International News 152
Irish Design 210
Irish Shop 170

J

Jade Garden 42
James Gardens....................178
Japanese Restaurant Ematei....42
JAZZ & BLUES 141
Jennie's..............................43
Josaly................................163
Joso's.................................44
Journey's End 120
Journey's End Antiques 148
Judith Teller........................171
Just Desserts............123, 234

K

Kahee Restaurant 44
Karir.................................156
Kensington 73 Café................95
Kensington Kitchen...............101
Kensington Market........168, 185
Kensington Silver Studio 170
Kew Beach 177
Kidstuff..............................154
Kimina................................159
The King Edward..................114
Kleinburg............................212
Komrads.............................134
Kortright Centre for
Conservation.....................179
KSP Jewellery......................157
Kwangtung Dim Sum
Restaurant 92

INDEX

L

LANDMARKS 181
Langdon Hall 216
Lanzi of Italy 171
Last Temptation 45
LATE-NIGHT EATERIES,
SHOPS & SERVICES 233
LAUNDROMAT 234
Laura Ashley 154
LEATHER & LUGGAGE 171
Lee Garden Restaurant 46
Lee's Palace 145
The Legendary Club Bluenote ... 146
Lester B. Pearson
International Airport 235
Let Them Eat Cake Dessert
Café, Bakery & Take Out 228
Liberty Café 46
Lichtman's 150
Lick's 100
Limelight Dinner Theatre 137
Little Italy 185
The Lizard Lounge 140
Lobster Trap 47
Lotus 48
Louis Vuitton 171
Louis Wine 148
LOUNGES 143
Lumière 158

M

Mabel's Fables 152
Mad Apples Restaurant 49
Madison Avenue Pub 131
Madras Express Café 49
Maid of the Mist 205
Maple Leaf Gardens 181
Maple Sands Resort 220
Marci Lipman 154
Mari Boutique 159
Marie Curtis Park 178
Mariko Japanese Restaurant 50
Marine Museum of Upper
Canada 193
Marineland 206
Market Gallery (City of
Toronto Archives) 194
Marky's Fine Dining 95
Martin Goodman
Fitness Trail 186
Massey Hall 183
Massimo Rosticceria 51
Massimo's 102
Max Mara 163
McLaughlin Planetarium 174
McMichael Canadian Art
Collection 180, 215
Mercer Union Gallery 192
Metro Home Show 237
Metro International Caravan 239
Metro Licensing Commission 236
Metropolis 52
Metro Taxi 236
Metro Toronto Zoo 174
MEXICAN FAST FOOD 101
La Mexicana 101
Michel Taschereau 148
MIDDLE EASTERN FAST
FOOD 101

Mira Goddard Gallery 192
Mira Linder 150
Mr. Video 234
Mobay Caribbean Cuisine 53
Molson Indy 239
Mövenpick 53
Moving Forward 154
MUSEUMS 193
Museum + Design 170
Museum for Textiles 194
Museum of the History of
Medicine 195
MUSIC 195
MUSIC CLUBS 144
My Cahn 54

N

Nami Japanese Restaurant 54
Natalie's House 55
National Ballet of
Canada 191, 237
National Home Show 238
Native Earth Performing Arts ... 199
NEIGHBORHOODS 184
New Year's Eve Party 240
Niagara Apothecary Museum 212
Niagara Falls 202
Niagara Falls Museum 206
Niagara Helicopters 206
Niagara Spanish Aero Car 206
Niagara-on-the-Lake 180, 207
N44° 56
Novotel Toronto Centre 106
The Nutcracker 240

O

The Oban Inn Restaurant 209
OBoy 96
Old City Hall 183
The Old Prune 226
Old Towne Antiques 211
One of a Kind Canadian Craft
Show 238
Ontario Parliament Buildings ... 183
Ontario Place 175
Ontario Science Centre 175
Open Air Books & Maps 152
The Original Vietnam 92
Orso 57
Ouzeri 58

P

Pam Chorley Fashion Crimes 163
Pantages Theatre 183
Parade 163
Le Paradis 59
Park Plaza Hotel 121
The Parking Authority of
Toronto 236
Pat & Mario's Restaurant 102
Pearl Court Restaurant 59
Peppinello 60
Peter Pan 61
Peter's Chung King
Restaurant 61
Le Petit Gaston 62
The Pickle Barrel Restaurant
and Deli 97

The Pillar and Post Inn
Restaurant 209
Pimblett's 63
Pink House 164
PIZZA & PASTA 102
Pizza Gigi 234
Polo/Ralph Lauren 159
Il Posto 64
The Power Plant 191
Prego della Piazza 64
Premiere Dance Theatre 237
Price Roman 164
Prince Hotel Toronto 124
The Prince of Wales
Hotel Restaurant 209
Pronto Ristorante 65
PUBLIC
TRANSPORTATION 236
The Puppet Centre 199

Q

Queen Street West 185
The Queen's Head Pub 132
Queen's Inn at Stratford 229
Queen's Inn at Stratford
Dining Room 226
Queen Mother Café 66
Queen of Sheba 66
Queen's Plate 239

R

Ramada Renaissance Hotel 121
The Real Jerk 67
Redpath Sugar Museum 195
Remy's 132
RESTAURANTS
   About the Reviews 7
   By Cuisine 11
   Reviews 14
   Toque Tally 9
Richardson's Tartan Shop 170
Riverdale Farm 175
Rivoli Café & Club 68, 132
Roberto's 68
Rodney's Oyster House 69
Roehampton Hotel 123
Roncesvalles 185
The Roof Restaurant, Park
Plaza 70
The Rose Café 135
Rosedale 186
The Rosedale Diner 70
Rosedale Livery Limited 237
Royal Alexandra Theatre 183
Royal Agricultural Winter Fair ... 240
Royal Ontario Museum 194
Royal York Hotel 115
RPM 140
Rundles 227

S

Sainte-Marie Among the
Hurons 223
Sai Woo 71
Santa Claus Parade 240
Samovar Barmalay Restaurant ... 71
Sam the Chinese Food Man
Tavern 92

INDEX

Sanssouci 72
Santa Fe 73
Satay Satay 92
Savunth Restaurant 74
Scaramouche Restaurant/
Pasta Bar and Grill 74
Schola Cantorum Concerts 196
Science City, Jr. 155
The Second City 138
Segwun Steamship Cruises 223
Le Sélect Bistro 75, 133
Senator Diner 76
Senator Steak House 76
Shaw Festival 197, 212, 238
The Sheraton Centre 116
The Sheraton Toronto East 125
Sherwood Inn 220
Shopsy's 77
Simcoe North 77
Simply Delicious 96
Simpson's 167
Sir Sam's Inn 221
Sisi Trattoria 78
SkyDome 182
SkyDome Hotel 107
Skylon Tower 204, 206
Southern Accent 78
Sparkles Nightclub 143
Specchio 165
Spectrum Restaurant and
Disco 141
Sportables 164
SPORTS 186
St. Lawrence Market 149, 184
Staccato 158
Stage West Hotel and Theatre
Restaurant 137
Stanley Wagman Antiques and
Gifts 149
Storkland 154
Stratford 224
Stratford Festival 198, 229, 238
Stratford's Olde English
Parlour 228
Strathcona Hotel 116
Studio 267 160
Sunnyside Beach 178
Sutton Place Hotel Kempinski ...117
Switzer's 97

T

Table Rock Restaurant 205
Table Rock Scenic Tunnels 207
Tall Poppies 79
Tapas Bar 80
Tarragon Theatre 198
TAXIS 236

Tea Masters International Café 96
TELEPHONE NUMBERS 232
Ten Ren Tea 168
Thai Magic 81
Thai Shan Inn 81
THEATER 197
Théatre Français de Toronto 200
Theatre Passe Muraille 198
Theatresports 138
This Ain't the Rosedale Library ..152
Thomas Cook Foreign
Exchange 233
Tilden 236
Tipplers Restaurant 82
Toby's Goodeats 100
Top of the Senator 142
TOQUE TALLY 9
The Toronto Airport Marriott
Hotel 126
Toronto Antiquarian Book
Fair 238
Toronto Argonaut
Football 186, 239
Toronto Arts Week 240
Toronto Blue Jays
Baseball 186, 238
Toronto Boys' Choir 196
Toronto Currency Exchange 233
Toronto Dance Theatre 191
Toronto International Auto
Show 238
Toronto Islands 179
Toronto Island Airport 235
Toronto Maple Leafs
Hockey 187, 240
Toronto Mendelssohn Choir......196
Toronto Pops Orchestra 196, 237
Toronto Sculpture Garden 193
Toronto Sportsmen's Show 238
Toronto Symphony
Orchestra 196, 237
Toronto Transit Commission 236
Toronto Truck Theatre 198
Toronto's First Post Office 195
Tortilla Flats 83
Tour of the Universe 176
TOURS 187
The Toy Shop 155
TRAIN TRAVEL 237
Trapper's Restaurant 83
Trata Psaro Taverna 84
Trattoria Giancarlo 85
Trax Toronto 135
Truffles 86
Tutti Frutti 98
24-HOUR EATERIES,
SHOPS & SERVICES 233
290 Ion 164

U

Ulysses 152
Underground City 182
United Bakers Dairy
Restaurant 87

V

Vanipha Fine Cuisine 87
Venture Inn 122
Via Rail 237
Victoria Park Cafeteria 205
The Victorian Inn 229
VIDEO RENTAL 234
Vietnam Village 88
Vintage Streetcar Tour 188
Vivian Shyu 164

W

Ward's Island 178
Wasaga Landing 223
Wasaga Waterworld 223
The Waterlot Restaurant 227
Westin Harbour Castle 108
Whitewater Water Park 207
Wigamog Inn 221
William Ashley 170
Windsor Arms Hotel Fireside
Lounge 100
Women Players Ltd.
International Tennis 239
Woodbine Race Track 187
Woody's 135
World Poetry Festival 238

Y

Yamase 88
Yokohama Restaurant 93
Yorkville 186
The Yorkviller 156
Young People's Theatre 198, 237
Yuk Yuks 138
Yukata 160
Yushi 160, 165
YYZ Artist's Outlet 193

Z

Zydeco 89

252